STREETWISE

STREETWISE

How Taxi Drivers Establish
Their Customers' Trustworthiness

Diego Gambetta and Heather Hamill

VOLUME X IN THE RUSSELL SAGE FOUNDATION SERIES ON TRUST

Russell Sage Foundation · New York

The Russell Sage Foundation

The Russell Sage Foundation, one of the oldest of America's general purpose foundations, was established in 1907 by Mrs. Margaret Olivia Sage for "the improvement of social and living conditions in the United States." The Foundation seeks to fulfill this mandate by fostering the development and dissemination of knowledge about the country's political, social, and economic problems. While the Foundation endeavors to assure the accuracy and objectivity of each book it publishes, the conclusions and interpretations in Russell Sage Foundation publications are those of the authors and not of the Foundation, its Trustees, or its staff. Publication by Russell Sage, therefore, does not imply Foundation endorsement.

Library of Congress Cataloging-in-Publication Data

Gambetta, Diego, 1952-
  Streetwise : how taxi drivers establish their customers' trustworthiness / Diego Gambetta and Heather Hamill.
    p. cm. — (The Russell Sage Foundation series on trust ; v. 10)
    Includes bibliographical references and index.
    ISBN 0-87154-308-7 (cloth)   ISBN 0-87154-309-5 (paper)
    1. Taxicab drivers—Psychology. 2. Consumer behavior—Psychological aspects. 3. Trust. 4. Interpersonal communication. 5. Decision making. 6. Taxicab drivers—New York—New York—Case studies. 7. Taxicab drivers—Northern Ireland—Belfast—Case studies. I. Title: Taxi drivers establish their customers' trustworthiness. II. Hamill, Heather, 1971- III. Title. IV. Series.
    HD8039.T16G36 2005
    388.4′13214′019—dc22

                                                                    2004061494

Text design by Suzanne Nichols.

RUSSELL SAGE FOUNDATION
112 East 64th Street, New York, New York 10021
10 9 8 7 6 5 4 3 2 1

In memory of Michael Bacharach
1936–2002

The Russell Sage Foundation Series on Trust

THE RUSSELL Sage Foundation Series on Trust examines the conceptual structure and the empirical basis of claims concerning the role of trust and trustworthiness in establishing and maintaining cooperative behavior in a wide variety of social, economic, and political contexts. The focus is on concepts, methods, and findings that will enrich social science and inform public policy.

The books in the series raise questions about how trust can be distinguished from other means of promoting cooperation and explore those analytic and empirical issues that advance our comprehension of the roles and limits of trust in social, political, and economic life. Because trust is at the core of understandings of social order from varied disciplinary perspectives, the series offers the best work of scholars from diverse backgrounds and, through the edited volumes, encourages engagement across disciplines and orientations. The goal of the series is to improve the current state of trust research by providing a clear theoretical account of the causal role of trust within given institutional, organizational, and interpersonal situations, developing sound measures of trust to test theoretical claims within relevant settings, and establishing some common ground among concerned scholars and policymakers.

Karen S. Cook
Russell Hardin
Margaret Levi

SERIES EDITORS

Previous Volumes in the Series

Contents

About the Authors

Diego Gambetta is official fellow of Nuffield College and professor of sociology at the University of Oxford.

Heather Hamill is university lecturer in sociology at the University of Oxford and fellow of St. Cross College, Oxford.

Acknowledgments

THIS PROJECT began with four investigators but ends with two. Rod Kramer, whose infectious enthusiasm propelled us to launch it in the first place, became overcommitted and could not keep up with its demands, and tragically, Michael Bacharach died suddenly and unexpectedly on August 12, 2002. His demise has affected us deeply, both personally and professionally. This book could not benefit from his sharpness and clarity of mind, which would have significantly improved it. As a small gesture of our affection, we dedicate it to his memory.

The project was inspired by an article in the *New York Times*, "For a Cabby, a Night of Calculating Risks" (May 1, 2000) by Sarah Kershaw, who described in detail a night in the life of a New York taxi driver. Diego Gambetta had picked the example of taxi drivers for a conference presentation in which he hoped to convey as simply as possible some new theoretical ideas on trust and its abuse by mimics that he had been developing with Michael Bacharach.[1] Encouraged by the positive reception of his paper at the conference, he began to realize the potential of testing those ideas by studying taxi drivers' decisions.

We would like to express our thanks to all those who helped us with the fieldwork and data collection. In Belfast, Deborah Ballentine collected the newspaper archive, and Mark Jordan assisted with the interviews. Arthur Magill, Jimmy Quinn, Tommy Poland, Peter Morris, Angela Morris, and Gary Symington enthusiastically helped us contact drivers and the charity People's Alternative to Drugs and Narcotics (PANDA) kindly supplied us with a room from which to operate. We are also indebted to Donna Winter, who transcribed the Belfast interviews.

In New York, Chris Fisher collected the newspaper archive. Derek Steele, Rob Ford, and Charles Walls helped with the interviews and transcription, and Yesenia Piscis and Laura Picquardo were our translators. We would like to express our deepest gratitude to the staff at the New York State Federation of Taxi Drivers, and in particular to vice president Hector Santana, whose assistance in contacting drivers was invaluable. Our thanks also to Will Coley and Rachael Reilly for their general assistance and support throughout our stay in New York.

The University of Oxford Department of Sociology administered the grant, and we are especially grateful to the ever-helpful Bhee Bellew. The Political Science Department at Columbia University provided important support during our stay in New York; in particular we are grateful to Aida Llabaly and Kay Achar. Our particular thanks go to Jon Elster, who not only generously shared his office during our fieldwork in New York but gave us many extremely useful comments on the manuscript. Gerardo Guerra, Marek Kaminski, Avinash Dixit, and Margaret Levi helped us to improve the manuscript with their generous comments and suggestions.

We would like to acknowledge with gratitude the support of the British Academy for granting Diego Gambetta a two-year research readership, which allowed him to take time out from his normal academic commitments and without which his contribution would not have been possible. Heather Hamill also used some of her time as a British Academy postdoctoral research fellow to complete this manuscript. Above all, we are very grateful to the Russell Sage Foundation, which generously provided the grant that enabled us to carry out this research. In particular, Nancy Weinberg, who kept in touch with us throughout the project, was always very prompt and helpful in answering all our queries.

Finally, it would have been impossible to undertake research of this kind without the cooperation of the taxi drivers themselves. Our greatest debt is therefore to the individuals who participated in this research. Their stories, sometimes moving and inspiring, were of fundamental importance to our understanding of the research issues.

Introduction

ALL YOU need to know to be a taxi driver is how to drive a car and find your way around the city, and sometimes not even that much. You pick up customers, drive them to where they want to go, get your due, and cruise off to collect yet another caller or to hunt for yet another hailer. Sometimes you negotiate the traffic, paying no attention to the passengers. Sometimes you vent your spleen on punishing taxation or corrupt local politicians to your captive audience. Occasionally you meet interesting or eccentric people, and sometimes you even act as a passenger's impromptu counselor. Then, when you have had enough after usually a long and tiring shift, you go home."At the end of the day," as drivers might put it, the job is quite simply boring and does not take much out of you. Or does it?

In this study, we investigate how taxi drivers assess the trustworthiness of prospective passengers in two cities—Belfast, Northern Ireland, and New York—that differ in all respects except one: in both cities there are villains, such as terrorists and robbers, who pose as passengers in order to harm drivers. To appreciate just how costly mistakes in assessing prospective passengers' trustworthiness can be, consider that taxi drivers are the victims of the highest homicide rate of any occupation in the United States.[1] According to the National Institute for Occupational Safety and Health (1996), in the United States a taxi driver is sixty times more likely to be murdered on the job than the average worker. Taxi drivers are also victim to more violent assaults (184 per 1,000 workers) than any other occupation with the exception of police (306 per 1,000) and security guards (218 per 1,000) (U.S. Department of Labor 1999).[2] In New York City at least 250 livery cab drivers were murdered between 1990 and May 2002.

Theory and Hypotheses

Taxiing in dangerous cities dramatically intensifies the pressure on drivers' cognitive skills. Taxi drivers who work in high-crime urban areas

1

confront, every day and night, a series of hard trust-decision problems. Their profits depend on taking in as many passengers as possible. But typically, most passengers are unknown to them. In New York City, where the chances of carrying the same passenger more than once is low, a driver could meet as many as twenty to twenty-five new individuals on average every working day, which could add up to well over seven thousand new encounters a year.

Driving a taxi involves more than just a high number of transactions with strangers. Unlike sellers of train tickets or doughnuts on the streets, who also have many transactions with strangers, drivers are in an exposed position once they accept a passenger. They are on their own and unarmed, with one or more individuals sitting in close proximity, cruising sometimes unfriendly neighborhoods where there are few witnesses or helping hands. A study of 280 homicides of taxi drivers in the United States and Canada between 1980 and 1994 found that 75 percent of the victims were attacked by passengers inside the car (Rathbone 1994/2002).

Taxi drivers are thus under severe pressure to decide quickly, on the basis of only a little information acquired from either direct observation or the dispatcher, whether or not to accept certain passengers. Few other occupations are under a similar strain.[3] Only police officers on the streets have perhaps a more demanding occupation in terms of the risks they face and the consequent importance of deciding how dangerous the individuals they meet really are. Yet law enforcers can hardly grumble since this is part of their job. Ready to face danger, they are trained to defend themselves, often armed, and able to rely on colleagues for backup. Not so the taxi drivers in hazardous cities. Ordinary men and women for whom the dangers are a nasty side effect of doing an ordinary job, they are interesting because they are more like us.

But is their ability to avoid dangerous situations purely a matter of trust? Given the fleeting nature of taxi drivers' encounters with strangers with whom they can exchange little information, one might expect taxi drivers to treat their problem as one of risk management rather than one of trust. Rather than ask, *Is this particular passenger trustworthy?* they could simply take general precautions to avoid or deter attackers, and they could think of remedies for limiting the damage in case of a bad surprise. They do take such precautions, as we shall see, but as a complement to treating their problem as one of trust rather than as an alternative to it. We devote a sizable part of our study to describing these strategies and discussing the extent to which they are adopted to limit the problem of trust.

An essential feature of our study is that we treat drivers' trust decisions in conjunction with the "sign-management" strategies of the other two protagonists of the game, the bona-fide passengers and the villains who mimic being passengers. We explore the dynamic relationships between drivers and their fares as they learn from their own experience and that of other agents and adjust their behavior accordingly. In dangerous cities, passengers must communicate that they have the capacity to pay and that they are not dangerous. For example, savvy drivers pick up passengers only at well-lit corners, not in dark alleys, and savvy passengers go to such safe places if they want to be picked up. Mimics learn and then also adopt such behavior in order to deceive drivers into picking them up. Our study explores how the three sides of this social transaction—drivers, customers, and mimics of customers—confront the challenges they face. They represent a near-perfect microcosm in which to research decisions about trust that arise in natural settings.[4] The interactions of these players are at once simple enough to make them relatively easy to research and rich enough to contain the basic components of trust decisions.

The Basic Trust Game

The trust situation we consider is best conveyed by an example. Suppose a person extends a loan to another because she expects him to do his best to repay it, though it is clear that she would do better to refuse to make the loan if he will make no effort to repay it and it is also clear that his selfish interest is to make no effort. Then, we would say, she *trusts him to repay the loan*. The notion of trust that we adopt in this book is related to specific tasks and payoffs: the trust we have for someone in one context does not necessarily extend to other contexts (Bacharach and Gambetta 2001, 150; Hardin 2002, 9). In general, we say that a person trusts someone to do X if she acts on the expectation that he will do X when both know that two conditions obtain: if he fails to do X, she would have done better to act otherwise, and her acting in the way she does gives him a selfish reason not to do X.[5]

In any trust situation, there are no less than two players—the truster and the trustee. For the problem of trust to be a problem at all, however, the truster must be thinking about at least two possible *types* of trustee. One type of trustee is a person driven by "raw" self-interested impulses that lead him not to do X when given the opportunity. The other type is a person who has trustworthy-making qualities that motivate him to resist the pull of his raw self-interest and instead to do X (Dasgupta 1987, 53; Bacharach and Gambetta 2001, 148–52).

It is not enough to predict, say, that people will behave in a trustworthy manner if doing so is in their self-interest. This removes the problem of trust altogether by removing the tension between the two types of trustees, which is essential for being able to perceive a decision as one of trust. For if in a given situation the good trustee behaves in his self-interest, what would make the bad trustee misbehave in the same situation? Untrustworthiness would not be imaginable, and the problem of trust would disappear.[6] Even if we assumed that people are trustworthy when the trustworthy act is in their self-interest, in order to have a problem of trust at all we still need at least two notions of self-interest: one that is, say, short-term or "raw," untamed by any other consideration, and another that is long-term and "encapsulates" the truster's interests as well (Hardin 2002), so that the truster is uncertain about which type of self-interest motivates the trustee in a particular situation.

The truster's *primary trust dilemma* is thus her uncertainty over which type the trustee really is, the bad or the good type. On the one hand, to perceive that trust is a problem at all the truster must have in mind the possibility that the trustee is motivated by raw self-interest. At the same time, the truster can avoid being paralyzed by distrust only by admitting to the possibility that the truster has other qualities capable of overcoming his temptation not to do X.

The primary trust dilemmas can be applied to the driver-passenger case. Sometimes it is passengers who wonder whether the taxi driver is of the honest sort (we discuss this case later), but in this study we have looked only at the interactions in which the driver is the *truster*. It is thus the driver's problem to decide which trustee-customer he is observing— the trustworthy one who will pay his fare and not harm him, or the untrustworthy one who only looks like a customer but is bent on harming him in some way ranging from not paying the fare to robbery or even murder.

We can make the interaction more precise by describing it as a simple game, which we refer to as the *basic trust game* (for a full discussion of the basic trust game, see Bacharach and Gambetta 2001). The payoffs of the three types of players in a basic trust game are presented in figures I.1 and I.2; the numbers are purely illustrative. In risky areas, the driver may meet a hailer of a bad type whose payoffs are expressed in figure I.1. Such a hailer wants to be picked up only to take advantage of the driver, since for him "exploiting" is better than "behaving"—that is, 4 is better than 1. In this case, the truster-driver is facing a bad customer, and "refusing" is better than "picking up" for him— that is, a payoff 0 is better than –3. By contrast, if the truster-driver is facing a good customer (figure I.2) for whom "behaving" is better than "exploiting" (that is, 2 is better than –4), for him the best choice is to "pick up" rather than "refuse," since 3 is better than 0.

Figure I.1   Driver's Payoffs and Bad Customer's Payoffs

		Customer	
		Behave	Exploit
Driver	Pick up	3, 1	–3, 4
	Refuse	0, 0	0, 0

Source: Authors' compilation.

The primary trust problem for the truster-driver lies in identifying which type the hailer or caller is—a genuine customer or a villain. This dilemma epitomizes countless situations in which we find ourselves in the position of either the truster or the trustee. However, there is nothing in the game as such that suggests a solution; the game simply describes a situation of uncertainty about the true nature of a trustee with whom it is to the truster's advantage to deal only if the trustee is of a good sort. The dilemma lies in the uncertainty over the real payoffs of the trustee-customers. Once the truster knows the type of trustee he is facing, the solution of the game is trivial. But how does the truster find out, and can the trustee do anything to inform him, truthfully or otherwise, about his type?

Trust and Signs

Michael Bacharach and Diego Gambetta (2001; see also Gambetta 2005) have articulated a new theoretical framework that can answer that question, and this study was inspired by, and aims to test, some of the ideas they developed.

The theory's crucial step is to establish a link between the trust dilemma and signaling theory, a branch of rational choice theory. How-

Figure I.2   Driver's Payoffs and Good Customer's Payoffs

		Customer	
		Behave	Exploit
Driver	Pick up	–3, –2	–3, –4
	Refuse	0, 0	0, 0

Source: Authors' compilation.

ever, the particular assumptions about people's motivations that are characteristic of the rational choice approach to trust play no role in the theory we develop here.

> It is not essential to our theory that trust is the product of some system of rewards and penalties which act as incentives to the trustee in repeated interactions. . . . We treat trust as the product of underlying trustworthy-making character features—one of which can be, of course, the degree of susceptibility to rewards and punishments. (Bacharach and Gambetta 2001, 149)

Our approach, which we believe to be more realistic than the rational choice approach, accommodates a wide variety of sources of trustworthiness, which include not only one's self-interest but also moral principles, social norms, and even specific dispositions that, in a given game, can make one trustworthy. The source of trustworthiness depends on which trustworthy act we expect of others in a given situation.

The first step of our theory is to hypothesize that trusters acquire, in various ways, an idea of which trust-warranting properties a trustee needs in order to be trustworthy in a given game (as well as of the obverse properties that make a trustee untrustworthy). Some of these properties—such as honesty, benevolence, a long-term horizon, a pro-social upbringing—can make a person trustworthy in many trust games, while other properties have a limited range and suffice to make someone trustworthy only in doing something in particular, as, for instance, love of children, sect membership, or, in our case, simply being busy enough or wealthy enough not to bother causing trouble to a taxi driver.[7] The notion of trustworthiness that we use refers to properties of persons that are not necessarily applicable to all situations but can be related to specific actions. We trust someone when we trust him to do one thing we have in mind, but we may or may not trust him to do something else. People who happen to be honest can be trusted in many different instances, but in our daily interactions we often trust people to do certain things for us even if they are not honest in all respects. Tony "The Ant" Spilotro's son Vincent could trust his father, a Mafia hard man, to come home and cook him breakfast every day even after Tony separated from his wife (Pileggi 1996, 157). Someone may be trustworthy as a husband and yet an opportunist with his colleagues or the Internal Revenue Service. Trustworthiness, in this narrow sense, can be sustained not only by virtues but also by nonvirtues. Laziness, fearfulness, or a physical handicap can lead us to believe that a person will not attack or cheat us if what is required for him to be untrustworthy in a given game is energy, courage, or dexterity.

However, the presence of trustworthy-making properties is not sufficient to induce trust. Trust has two enemies, not just one: bad character and poor information. The incidence of trustworthy-making qualities that sustain good character sets an upper bound on the amount of well-placed trust in a community. Actual trust, however, may fall below that threshold because of the difficulties of communicating the presence of these qualities. As we shall see, many passengers fail to communicate their trustworthiness to drivers and to be picked up. The trouble, in particular, is that the trustee's trust-warranting properties cannot be discovered from observation. One cannot see "self-interest," "honesty," or even "identity" as such.

> One may say, "I could see at once that he was an honest fellow." But it is in *signs* that one *sees* it. One observes, for instance, physiognomic features—the set of the eyes, a firm chin—and behavioral features—a steady look, relaxed shoulders—and treats them as evidence of an internal disposition. . . . Trust-warranting properties may come variably close to being observable. But, except in limiting cases, they are unobservable and signs mediate the knowledge of them. (Bacharach and Gambetta 2001, 155)

Our second step is thus to assume that a person's trustworthiness can be assessed by *evaluating observable signs of him* that the truster believes to be correlated with the unobservable trust-warranting properties.

We suppose, realistically, that the vast majority of basic trust games include some observation by trusters of features of their trustees. Any piece of observable, or otherwise perceivable, behavior, including a message, an accent, or an item of clothing, counts as a feature. It follows then that every trust-involving interaction initiated by a trustee contains an episode of the kind described here:

> A truster may observe the tweed jacket and shooting stick of a woman in a departure lounge, and may infer that she is to be trusted to look after the truster's bag while he posts a last-minute letter. Or, a truster may recognize her trustee, by her face, or signature, as someone who has always repaid loans in the past, and may infer that she has now, as then, those properties of character and liquidity which make her creditworthy. Or, finally, a truster, having heard of the trust-warranting properties of a person of a certain description, may try to match that description with the person in front of her: "Is this the person picked out by the signs of identification I heard of?" (Bacharach and Gambetta 2001, 155)

Mimicry

The use of signs to solve the primary problem of trust brings up a new dilemma for trusters. "The observable features (the tweeds, the signature, the name, the accent, the club membership) are sometimes good enough signs. Sometimes, however, it is not certain that signs of trust-warranting properties are to be trusted" (156). One reason for this is that the correlation with the trust-warranting property may be weak or nonexistent—one may simply be wrong about the link between signs and properties, as in the case of prejudices. Another, more interesting reason is that there may be untrustworthy trustees who endeavor to display fraudulently the signs that can convince the truster of their trustworthiness.

Suppose there is a sign m, such as looking people in the eye, that people take to be evidence of honesty. Deliberately displaying m is then a way of signaling that you are honest. The problem, however, is that both honest and dishonest people may have a motive for signaling m.

> Rich people sometimes wear expensive clothes to show that they are rich; poor people sometimes wear expensive clothes to seem to be rich. Benevolent uncles smile to show they are benevolently disposed; wicked uncles smile to seem to be benevolently disposed. The deceptive instances of the strategy we call "mimicking." More precisely, a mimic of a property [k] is a person who does not have the property and deliberately displays m in order to be taken to have k by another. (Bacharach and Gambetta 2001, 157)

This framework is applicable also to *negative mimicry*—that is, "camouflage."

> There are often signs of a trustee which are likely to be interpreted by the truster, rightly or wrongly, as indicating the lack of a trust-making quality, and so untrustworthiness. Both a trustworthy signaler who expects to be unjustly perceived if he displays such a sign s, or an untrustworthy one who is afraid of being detected if he does, have a reason to camouflage. That is, they can be expected to take steps *not* to show s. For our purposes we can therefore consider deceptive camouflaging as a special case of mimicking. The strategy of camouflaging the signs of untrustworthiness by suppressing s is just that of mimicking trustworthiness through displaying the notional sign "no s." (Bacharach and Gambetta 2001, 155n13)

We regard mimicry, both positive and negative, as a crucial component of most trust episodes in which trust is misplaced. In basic trust games, the truster reasons, as we argue he does, that there is a motive for an opportunistic trustee to mimic—that is, to emit signs of trustworthy qualities when he lacks them. Almost invariably when trust is abused, the trustee will have engaged in some act of deception aimed at making the truster think that he is the good type when this is not true. The trustee is a strategic player, not inert matter passively waiting to be appraised by the truster.

Although signs can solve the primary trust dilemma, they can also complicate the problem for the truster, who must judge whether apparent signs of trust-warranting properties are themselves to be trusted. The primary problem of trust (is this passenger a good or bad type?) is transformed into the *secondary trust dilemma:* is the sign a genuine sign of a certain trust-warranting property, or is it a mimicked sign?

Notice that the secondary trust dilemma applies also to repeated encounters in which we deal again with someone with whom we have dealt successfully in the past. In this case, the trustee enjoys a good reputation with us. Having been trustworthy in the past is his trust-warranting property in a repeated trust game. The problem is that his past trustworthiness is not directly observable; we infer it by reidentifying the person as the same person we dealt with in the past. But even the identity is not a directly observable property. We establish it through signs that uniquely belong to that person. Some of these signs, such as the face, may be resistant to mimicry, but mimics can imitate other properties, such as the voice or the signature. And this possibility gives rise to the secondary trust dilemma.

James Coleman (1990, ch. 5), who was among the first scholars to offer a sophisticated conceptualization of the notion of trust, discusses an episode taken from *The Merchant Bankers* by Joseph Wechsberg (1966) that is useful in conveying this point. The Norwegian manager of the merchant banker Hambros in London receives a call for help from a prominent ship owner in Norway who says he needs 200,000 pounds within the next half-hour or else one of his ships that was recently repaired in Amsterdam will not be released and he will lose a sizable profit. While holding the ship owner on the phone, the unfazed Hambros manager sends a telex message instructing the Amsterdam branch to pay the sum to the ship owner and have his ship released at once. A young German trainee banker who witnesses the exchange is amazed at the speed and smoothness of this transaction and asks the manager some pertinent questions: "How can you be sure that you really talked to that ship owner in Norway? It's easy to imitate a voice over the phone. How do you know he's good for two hundred thousands pounds?" (Coleman 1990, 91–93).

Coleman reports this key question—how does the manager know that he is speaking with the real ship owner rather than someone who is mimicking him?—but does not follow it up. Moreover, its importance is overlooked not only by Coleman but by most trust research, and thus the manner in which it is solved in real life has not been investigated. In the list of key features of a trust decision, Coleman includes whether or not to trust the ship owner, which is our first trust dilemma, but does not include the further essential question of whether he is *really* the ship owner. The two trust dilemmas need to be disentangled. The Hambros manager knows he can trust the ship owner to be trustworthy because he knows him personally and knows that the ship owner has long-term interests and wants to behave well so as not to spoil his relations with the bank. In addition, the ship owner must have a special way of identifying himself to the manager, which reassures the manager of his identity. Similarly, our taxi drivers know that they can trust a *real* passenger to behave. But how do they know that a certain hailer *is* a real passenger rather than a mimicking villain?

Signaling Theory and Hypotheses

Our approach marks a departure from current theories of trust. The answers to that question in the literature vary. For some authors, trusters manage to appraise trustees' trustworthiness by a rather ineffable process. By contrast, our central hypothesis is that taxi drivers' decisions are supported by cogent reasoning. When asked, drivers often say their assessment of customers' trustworthiness is driven by "gut feelings" or a "sixth sense." Our expectation is that a logic underlies these feelings and that it consists of several cognitive steps, including an intuitive application of signaling theory. We expect that the subtlety and richness of the judgments a truster makes are due only to the complexity of the game that he is playing. The apparently ineffable nature of these judgments is an illusion that we hope to dispel by describing in detail drivers' cognitive processes.

For other, indeed for most, authors, trustworthiness is assessed by obtaining information about the real interests, constraints, and dispositions of the trustees and working out how we would behave in their position (Dasgupta 1988; Gambetta 1988, 217–24). Although this description reflects what we rationally do, it does not take into account the secondary dilemma—that is, whether and how we can trust the information we use for that reasoning. There is nothing in current approaches to say that trusters pay attention to signs; this implies, of course, that they are silent on which signs they disregard and which signs they heed.[8] Our expectation is that drivers look for properties that are trust- or distrust-warranting ones in the game they are playing. More precisely, *they look for signs that manifest these properties.* Above all, we expect drivers to look for *reliable* signs of these properties.

The framework we use to conceptualize trust interactions has the advantage of allowing the application of signaling theory, which defines clearly what we mean by "reliable." This framework is a well-developed part of game theory, and it provides the general principles to which the information we collect about the trustees must adhere to enable us to solve the secondary trust dilemma.

A signaling game is said to have a "sorting" or "separating" equilibrium if, in equilibrium, a good type emits one kind of signal and a bad type emits a different kind. No mimicry is possible in this case. The conditions for a signaling game to have a sorting equilibrium are well known. A genuine customer always emits a signal s, and a nongenuine one never emits s, if two conditions hold:

1. The benefit to a genuine customer of being treated as a genuine customer exceeds the cost for him of emitting s.

2. The benefit to a nongenuine customer of being treated as a genuine customer is less than the cost for him of emitting s.

We call these the "can" and "cannot" conditions. If the truster can see or hear the trustee, as in most basic trust games naturally occurring, the "can" condition is easily met since the trustee can communicate almost costlessly with the truster. Sorting therefore depends essentially on the "cannot" condition—on whether among these signals are some that nongenuine customers cannot afford to use. No poisoner seeks to demonstrate his honesty by drinking from the poisoned chalice. The best situation from a taxi driver's perspective is when a genuine customer can afford to emit s and a nongenuine customer cannot.

Our general prediction is therefore that *drivers screen passengers looking for reliable signs of trust- or distrust-warranting properties,* in the sense that they look for signs that are too costly for a mimic to fake but affordable for the genuine article, given the benefit that each can expect in the situation. In other words, drivers will not be either erratic in the signs they watch for or easily satisfied by cheaply mimickable ones.

Some customers display signs that are not just unaffordable to the mimic but outright impossible to fake. In the economics jargon, they have an infinite cost. In ordinary parlance, they are quite simply constraints on mimics' options. These signs, such as the face or DNA, are uniquely attached to the bearer and impossible for the mimic to reproduce, regardless of payoffs. Constraints are perfectly separating. In many real-world cases, however, we are not so lucky and find that most signals at our disposal are not perfectly separating. There are many signs that to some degree are more costly for a mimic (because of, say, penalties for their abuse) but are still emitted by a small number of mimics. Most of the time someone who looks like a Hasidic Jew will be a Hasidic Jew, but occasionally he may be a Palestinian suicide bomber. When the signal is only partly contaminated, it remains credible enough for a minority of mimics to gain from using it and for the majority of honest signalers to keep using it. In such an equilibrium, called "semi-sorting," at least some truth can be transmitted. The prospects for even a semi-sorting signal are worse, however, in dangerous areas. The higher the base-rate probability of encountering a villain, the more credible, or separating, a signal needs to be to be effective. Sometimes, we further predict, no single sign suffices and *drivers look for clusters of signs* that, if pointing in the same direction, may together come close to discriminating the good from the bad passengers. The cost of mimicry grows as the number of signs to be manipulated in order to persuade also grows.

In most practical circumstances, good customers display, as a matter of course, signs that are correlated with being a good customer. If one is middle-aged, white, and female, in face-to-face encounters one automatically reveals those features, and at no cost. If drivers know that there is a negligible probability that a woman will turn out to be a robber, they will look for signs of gender that the hailer displays. If persuaded that the hailer is a woman, they will decide to pick her up. These "cues" are "there anyway," and the genuine possessor of the right properties need take no action to manifest them. Indeed, she need hardly be aware of the cues' effect. Moreover, a feature of cues is that while costless for true possessors, they are very costly to produce and display for those who are not true possessors of the property, so they amply meet both the "can" and "cannot" conditions. If the properties to which cues refer are thought to make their owner trustworthy, the taxi business can proceed unimpeded, and trust is not perceived as much of a problem.

The trust game that taxi drivers play, however, is not always so smoothly resolved. It becomes more challenging, and thus potentially more revealing of agents' reasoning, under two conditions. The first condition is either an absence of cues or uninformative cues. For instance, in Northern Ireland religious affiliation often cannot be established just by looking at people. Most young males look alike, whether Catholic or Protestant. This is problematic for Catholic drivers, who fear becoming the target of a sectarian attack by picking up a Protestant man. In these cases, we hypothesize, *drivers "probe" further or customers volunteer additional information of a kind that a mimic would find hard to fake.* Because these information-enhancing activities are costly, the driver and the customer are more strategically aware.

Under the second condition, customers are genuine but cannot avoid displaying the "wrong" cues. For instance, young black males in New York or groups of young men in Belfast who are bona-fide customers face higher costs of signaling to drivers that they are bona fide, since their manifest features are associated with negative properties. To be picked up, we hypothesize, *they need either to display further reassuring signals or to invite probing* if they are to offset the effect of these negative cues. For example, they may stress their reassuring features: if the driver is Catholic, a passenger may choose to display or stress his own "Catholic" features. Or an African American passenger can send a white friend to hail a cab, as black English soccer players have had to do in London at night (Thorpe 1994).[9] They may even equip themselves in advance of hailing a taxi with reassuring objects to display. For instance, the black academic Lawrence Otis Graham buys and waves the *Wall Street Journal* to make drivers stop (Graham 1995).[10] We expect, however, that it will not always be possible for customers to find signals of this kind that meet the "can" condition as well as the "cannot" condition, and even if they are genuine, they may end up having to walk home.

At the same time, we expect to observe drivers *behaving rationally and not being persuaded by easy-to-mimic positive signs.* We expect that drivers discount signs such as a smile or a necklace with a cross or a T-shirt inscribed with "Make Love Not War" and that they watch instead for signs that are cheap to observe but relatively hard to mimic. These could include a physical disability, a familiar face, or the "goodness" of the establishment from which the customer is emerging.

Notice, however, that there are some persuasive signals an honest customer can transmit only if the driver decides to stop and probe and not if he drives away. We therefore also expect that honest customers engage in signaling actions that are insufficient to reassure a rational driver fully—for a mimic too would find these actions cheap—but are nonetheless sufficient to make him stop. For example, a customer could remove or veil all the signs that are easy to remove or veil, such as holding his leather jacket on his arm to display the absence of concealed weapons or covering up a tattoo by wearing long sleeves. We also expect to find that bona-fide passengers with negative cues will induce drivers to stop not only by hiding their indicators of untrustworthiness but also, if that is not enough, by displaying some of the same "fraudulent" signs used by mimics. They will deceive, of course, but only in order to tell the truth: once the driver stops, they are then in a better position to convey the "separating" signals necessary to reassure him fully as to their true type.

By testing these hypotheses, we should be able to establish the validity of our general claims—namely, that drivers and customers conform to the signaling theory of trust by means of a wealth of detailed instances of suitable behavior that could hardly be cogently explained by other theories of trust.

So far we have mentioned signs and signals interchangeably without drawing a distinction between them, but there is one, and an important one at that. Signals are any observable features of an agent that are *intentionally* displayed by a signaler for the purpose of raising the probability that the receiver assigns to a certain state of affairs. A sign, by contrast, can be anything pertaining to a person that is perceptible and can modify our beliefs about that person while not being displayed with the intention of achieving that result. Signs, however, are dormant potential signals. They are the raw material of signals to which signalers who are aware of playing a strategic game can choose to resort. The basic form of a sign-signal transformation is a signaler taking steps to display a preexisting sign. One trigger of this transformation is the bearer's realization of the meaning of certain signs in the eyes of an observer. An individual may be unaware that his accent is informing others of a quality of his until an observer acts in a way that makes him aware.

The interactions between mimics, taxi drivers, and passengers tread the fine line between signs and signals. The mimics with villainous intentions are always aware that they are signaling, albeit fraudulently. They veil or hide their bad signs and forge and imitate the signs that a normal passenger would show. Sometimes an act of deceitful mimicry consists precisely of making a deceitful signal look like an innocent sign that a nonvillainous customer would carry without thinking. Taxi drivers can be taken in, but, as we hypothesize, they are generally on guard, screening first and then probing, if not persuaded, by encouraging passengers to display more convincing signals. By contrast, prospective passengers who are good types and carry no negative cues automatically persuade drivers of their goodness and are unaware that any signaling is going on. They become aware of their signs only when they expect to be or are refused by drivers. They may then try to discern what it is that puts taxi drivers off before resorting to conscious signaling that either masks their negative signs or displays new ones that offset the others.

Despite the difference, the reliability of signs and signals is governed by the same condition of signaling theory: signs, just like signals, transmit discriminating information to drivers to the extent to which they conform to the "cannot" condition.

The Acquisition of Background Knowledge

Signaling theory is an abstract tool, but some strong assumptions about the players' background knowledge are crucial to the solutions it offers. Players need to know the size of both the benefits and the costs—for both possessors and nonpossessors of the trust-warranting properties—of emitting a given signal, and the truster needs to know the base-rate probability that a signaler has them. Players must also know a range of signs, their association with the relevant properties, and how others interpret them. If religiosity is known to make a person trustworthy, the players need to know which signs express it. They must know, for instance, that skullcaps are donned by male orthodox Jews, roughly how difficult it is for someone else to find and wear one convincingly, and that by convention women do not wear them. So although we hypothesize that players use strategies with the same abstract properties wherever they are, *the actual parameters of their strategies are very particular to their situation.* Like the devil, the knowledge required to play a trust game lies in the details.

Much background knowledge is learned simply as a by-product of living and observing life in a certain area, either by direct experience or through information sources that one trusts. A focused effort may be needed, however, to learn this knowledge, or to teach others like themselves, when the area of operation is complex, the agents are new to it, or new situations and new kinds of informative episodes have arisen. This should be true, for instance, in cities in which many drivers are immigrants or in which passengers include not only residents but also transient people of diverse kinds. Even an experienced taxi driver from Bogotá has much to learn before he can feel comfortable in New York City. Mimics too have an interest in observing the behavior of both drivers and the genuine passengers on whom they plan to model their actions.

Although we do not make any specific hypotheses about knowledge acquisition and diffusion, our research pays descriptive attention to how real-world players acquire and update the knowledge needed for playing the trust game. Taxi drivers may receive formal training and be socialized by their organizations. They talk to other drivers, engage in queries with dispatchers, compare notes, and warn each other; older, more experienced drivers socialize younger, more naive drivers into the rules of the game and what to look for when deciding whether to pick up a passenger. Similarly, both mimics and customers experience success and failure and adjust their behavior accordingly. They read the news about incidents involving taxi drivers and learn whom to fear and how not to look. Mimics try to look tame and have to learn the salient features of "tameness"; so too do genuine passengers who have learned that something about them displays the wrong kind of sign and makes drivers avoid them.

Whereas signaling theory assumes that players have rational beliefs, we do not rule out the possibility that a certain amount of inaccurate or stereotypical knowledge permeates drivers' "street-level epistemology," as Russell Hardin (1993) puts it. A distinctive feature of our research is that we investigate empirically the actual judgment and decision-making processes that taxi drivers, passengers, and mimics use in such situations. In other words, rather than presume full rationality, our study explicates the actual content of the "street-level epistemologies" of the respective players about such decisions and works out the extent to which nonrational reasoning affects judgment and choice. For instance, in Northern Ireland there is a widespread and inaccurate belief that one can identify Catholics by the fact that their eyes are set closer to each other. In the United States some drivers may make decisions driven by crude racism. Or subtler dynamics involving, for instance, availability biases may be at work. For example, in the aftermath of an incident drivers may for some time become excessively prudent.

Thus, our approach does not rule out the possibility that the beliefs that enter into drivers' applications of signaling theory may sometime be wrong. On the one hand, we seek to verify a series of signal-theoretic predictions for drivers' and customers' behavior. On the other hand, we do not exclude the influence on the decisionmakers' judgments of "extrarational" factors, such as their preexisting stereotypes. In particular, we expect drivers to be more rational in assessing positive signs than they are in assessing negative ones. Because of the well-known asymmetry between trust and distrust, false negative beliefs about the import of signs are likely to be more durable than false positive ones. Drivers do not pick up people displaying the former, so they do not get counterevidence directly, and if all drivers hold the wrong beliefs, they do not even get it indirectly by communicating with each other.

In conclusion, our understanding of the steps that one needs to take to establish a trustee's trustworthiness can be summarized in terms of three ways in which one can err and make the wrong judgment. These mistakes are hierarchically ordered in that if one commits the first mistake, the second will be irrelevant, and so on.

The first mistake is to look for the wrong trust- or distrust-warranting property—that is, a property unrelated to trustworthiness. This is the case when one entertains *unfounded beliefs.* One may think that Latino women are more dangerous than white ones, or one may infer from the property of one member of a group that all members of that group have that property, but neither belief is true. Or one may have the wrong causal theory. For example, one may believe that voting Democratic or being a Scorpio makes one more dangerous.

The second mistake is also due to wrong beliefs, in this case about the signs involved. One variety of this mistake is wrongly picking a sign of a trust-warranting property that is not in fact a sign of the property. A driver may be interested, for instance, in whether a fare is Catholic and may further believe that he can identify Catholics by their narrow-set eyes, which is an *unfounded stereotype.* Or he may misinterpret a sign that has multiple causes by picking the wrong cause: reading illness-related hand tremors, for instance, as the result of nervousness brought on by bad intentions, or interpreting dark glasses as an attempt to avoid eye contact because of nasty intentions rather than an attempt to hide grief.

The third kind of mistake—and the crucial one in terms of our theory—is to be persuaded of a passenger's trustworthiness by a signal that, if the signaler is honest, is truly connected with the trust-warranting property the driver is looking for but that can be easily mimicked by a dishonest signaler. Assuming that the qualities drivers look for are truly associated with trustworthiness or untrustworthiness and that the signs they observe are truly signs of those qualities, there is still the question of how reliable the signs are.

When the Passenger Is the Truster

We should also briefly mention the trust game that is the reverse of the one we consider in this study: when the passenger is the truster and worries about the type and intentions of the driver-trustee. This is a serious problem in many cities of the world where passengers are cheated, robbed, or raped by "taxi drivers." For example, the London Metropolitan Police report that in 2001, 233 women were sexually assaulted by mimic-rapists who passed themselves off as minicab drivers (the London equivalent of Belfast private-hire taxis and New York livery cabs). That amounted to 24 percent of all rapes and serious sexual assaults in London in that year.[11] Mimicking can be of two kinds: a villain may mimic being a taxi driver when he is not by using a plausible car and showing up in the rich pickup points at the right time of day or night. Razaq Assadullah was jailed for eight years for raping a twenty-eight-year-old secretary on her way home after a night out with friends. The victim thought she was safe because rather than pick one of the drivers touting for business—the riskiest way of getting a ride—she had gone to the minicab office to get a car. But her rapist was working with a false ID, a fake driving license, and no insurance. The victim was also with a friend, but after Assadullah dropped off her friend, he drove her to a deserted street, climbed into the back of the car, and raped her (Weale 2003). Alternatively, genuine taxi drivers may switch to rapist mode. In this case, they mimic not being a taxi driver generally but being one on *that* occasion. The latter case is not so infrequent; the *Observer* reported on November 17, 2002, that "one police operation revealed that half the mini cab drivers [in London] stopped at roadside checks had criminal records, including convictions for serious sex and assault offenses."

Originally we thought of investigating this side of the problem too, since it obviously needs to be studied, but decided against it. We needed to limit the size and scope of our fieldwork, and we could not have used the same sources to study both games. Also, drivers meet the problem of trustworthiness far more frequently than passengers do. One reason is the mere numerical property of this market: a passenger will get far fewer rides than a driver will supply, so the risk of any one passenger meeting a bad driver is, a priori at least, lower than the risk of any one driver meeting a bad customer.

A second, and more important, reason is that in cities where the taxi industry is regulated—such as both of the cities in this study—the problem of mimicking taxi drivers is limited. In particular this is so because the industry has developed standardized insignias that make it easier for passengers not just to identify a taxi in the traffic and distinguish it from other cars but also to distinguish a real taxi from a mimic taxi. In addition, personalized identifiers displayed in cars make it easy to catch a driver if he misbehaves. An aspiring mimic cannot easily pretend to be a genuine yellow cab, for instance. He would have to steal one, but once other drivers know the number of the medallion, the thief would not be able to go far in the city before he would be very quickly spotted.

His face would not match that of the driver in the photo card displayed in the cab, and passengers would quickly become suspicious. And one cannot easily set up a phony phone line pretending to be a livery car company just for the sake of taking advantage of passengers. One can put up a sign to pretend to be a livery cab or a minicab belonging to a nonexistent firm, but the chances of success will be lower. People will be familiar with the name and emblems of genuine companies and thus less inclined to trust taxis displaying unknown identifiers. The risk of encountering mimic-taxis goes up in cities in which most cars are unmarked and anyone can act as a taxi driver. The actual number of incidents may, however, be lower in the latter case, for passengers, anticipating the higher risk, may more often choose other means of transport or screen drivers' identities more carefully.

That is the case in Derry, the second largest city in Northern Ireland, which we briefly investigated. Over two-thirds of the 1,500 taxis that operate there are now illegal, according to Eamon O'Donnell, development worker for North West Taxi Proprietors Ltd. (NWTP), which aims to represent and regulate the taxi industry in Derry (personal communication, June 21, 2001). NWTP has proposed a "code of practice" that sets out obligations to be placed on all members of the taxi industry in the city, including depot owners as well as drivers, and a "bill of rights" for taxicab passengers entitling them to, among other things, a safe and secure journey. The NWTP proposal, which has not been accepted yet, includes the introduction of a unique logo to be shared by all firms. Within the logo, they plan to insert two numbers, one to identify the firm and the other the driver. The logo would then be either painted on the side of the car or posted on the windshield. Their suggestion would be that passengers only enter cars displaying this logo.

We found that one of the two main reasons to regulate the industry in that way is precisely that of reassuring customers who, according to our interviewee, use taxis less than they would for fear of being attacked by phony drivers. (The other reason is to limit the competition.) This proposal indicates an awareness of the importance of introducing hard-to-fake and easy-to-observe signs to limit villains' ability to mimic a taxi or a taxi driver, and it shows the importance of standardization as a means to achieve that.

Sources and Method

The core data for this study are of an ethnographic kind. The data were collected in both New York City and Belfast using partially structured interviews and participant observation with drivers, dispatchers, and passengers. The interviews were taped and transcribed; in analyzing the transcriptions, we focused on respondents' accounts of the signs they look for or display and on the reasoning behind their actions. Additional data were collected from newspaper reports, taxi industry reports, statistical sources, and the academic literature.[12] We should stress that the two cities we selected, Belfast and New York, are both notorious for the risks they pose for drivers but differ with respect to the kinds of such risks. We expect that the strategies brought to bear on trust games will differ in interesting ways as well. The choice of cities was intended to provide us with a vivid contrast in the extent to which trust games depend on particular local conditions and the knowledge derived from them and, at the same time, to enable us to make a preliminary test of whether the principles underlying agents' "street-level epistemologies" (Hardin 1993) are, as we anticipate, the same everywhere.

We have no special attachment to the research method we chose. Its main drawback is, of course, that it does not allow a proper scientific test of our hypotheses, for we cannot control and measure the variables relevant to trust decisions. However, given the complexity of the cognitive steps involved in trust decisions, there are serious obstacles in designing controlled studies and employing subjects like taxi drivers. The designs ought to maintain a sufficiently strong incentive-compatibility and avoid narrowing or trivializing the stimuli so as to make the results relevant for real-world decisions.

We considered two alternative designs to test whether taxi drivers conform, in their acceptance decisions, to the predictions of signaling theory, notably that, where would-be fares may be dangerous, the cheaper it is to fake a sign of being a safe fare, the lower the acceptance rate. The two designs were:

1. Presenting drivers with photographs or "vignettes" of would-be fares and asking whether they would accept such a fare

2. Presenting drivers with a conventionally designed isomorph of the real-life trust game—for example, a game with money payoffs having the same strategic structure as the real-life encounter

In the end we decided against both designs. The first design suffers from two drawbacks: it is not "incentive-compatible," and more importantly, the display gives only partial information about the situation and is therefore bound to prompt questions about other, contextual factors that form part of the standard decision process for real drivers. For example, drivers might ask, "Where do I see this person? What time is it? Is there a football match in town?" These questions cover many dimensions, so if we supplied the information, we would then lack statistical power to disentangle their effects. If, conversely, we left them unspecified, we would have no control over what is really going on in the minds of the subjects. We were no longer convinced that we could get clear confirming evidence of appropriate sensitivity to the costs of mimicry—not because drivers do not have this sensitivity, but because of the inevitable noisiness of the data that we would get from directing subjects' attention to real-world scenarios.

The second design, by contrast, lacks ecological validity and fails to tap into the specialized knowledge and "gut feelings" of taxi drivers for their real environment. Yet our central interest is in determining how adept taxi drivers are at making these decisions. Offering money payments would give incentives but change the frame (partly because the strategic situation is presented neutrally). These well-known difficulties about this experimental methodology, which is standard in experimental economics, apply here with special force because of our interest in whether signaling theory works in a particular form of real-life interactions.

Thus, the design of future research ought to tap into the decision-making know-how of taxi drivers on the ground while at the same time not stimulating the full complexity of their real-life heuristics; this complexity is too great for effective hypothesis-testing. Since we have not as yet clearly devised how to steer a middle course between this Scylla and Charybdis, we decided to limit ourselves to the ethnographic study. The fieldwork had the advantage of allowing us to observe the agents under their natural and often stringent constraint; in the lab no one is going to come after you if you get the wrong answer. It also allowed us to collect a wealth of vivid details on the "semiotics" of trust that no experimental or narrowly focused research could have yielded. We hope that our fieldwork, whose features we now describe, will inspire and guide further experimental and survey research.

Belfast

Much of the research work in Belfast went as planned; it took twenty weeks, from mid-April 2001 to the end of August 2001. First, we carried out an extensive search of five Northern Ireland newspapers over the past thirty years, looking for accounts of incidents in which taxi drivers had been involved as either victims or perpetrators of attacks since the so-called political "Troubles" began. We found forty-nine such reported incidents.

Next we interviewed forty-five taxi drivers in Belfast, including four who also worked as dispatchers and one person who worked only as a dispatcher. The bulk of the interviews were done with drivers from twelve private-hire firms from across the city. We also interviewed drivers who drove public-hire taxis based at Belfast City Airport and the City Center. In total in Belfast, we interviewed nineteen Catholic and twenty-six Protestant drivers.[13]

We contacted the drivers in a variety of ways. First of all, Heather Hamill reestablished contacts with three former taxi drivers she had met during previous fieldwork research in West Belfast. Our interviews with the former drivers proved to be a valuable pilot for this study by helping us to formulate our interview questions. These drivers also introduced us to a number of their colleagues, some of whom agreed to participate in the study.

To broaden the sample and contact drivers who worked in other areas, we put up posters and left flyers in taxi depots, but we did not get even one driver from advertising in this way. So we simply phoned for taxis. In a sense, we too mimicked an ordinary customer. We chose safe pickup and drop-off locations within each geographical area, such as a library or college. During the journey we explained who we really were and what we were doing and asked the driver if we could interview him, either there and then or at a later date. This strategy bore varying results. The first time we tried it, the driver's opening question, after asking Heather her destination, was, "So what do you do then?" To which she replied, "Well, it's funny that you should ask. . . ." He subsequently introduced us to his two brothers-in-law, who were also taxi drivers.

The novelty of our study impressed a number of our friends in Belfast, who, as they took taxis in the course of their daily business, took it upon themselves to advertise our work to the perhaps unlucky drivers who picked them up. Our sample thus snowballed outward as our interviewees passed us on to their friends and colleagues.

Other encounters were less positive. Some cabbies paranoically thought that we had targeted them specifically and were undercover police or government employees (for the Department of Health and Social Security, DHSS) checking on whether they were working while claiming unemployment benefits. Others thought we were from the Child Support Agency and had been sent by their ex-wife. Mark Jordan, our straight research assistant, had the additional problem of having his invitation to participate taken for a gay pickup line.

Because of Belfast's sectarian divisions (see table I.1), we needed a neutral location where we could carry out prearranged interviews. Fortunately, a local charity offered us a room in its offices located in a religiously neutral area near the City Center of Belfast. On other occasions, we went to taxi depots and interviewed the drivers as we sat beside them in their parked cars. The cars offered the drivers both privacy and the comfort of being in their own environment, and thus we were often seen jumping out of one taxi and into another as the next interviewee pulled up alongside.

We sat in the dispatch office of five different taxi companies and observed the dispatcher and the interaction between the drivers; we also drove around with five drivers while they were working. Heather Hamill's presence in the taxi prompted ironic comments from cus-

Table I.1   Belfast Interviewee Codes

Characteristics of Interviewees	Codes
Job or role	
Driver	—
Customer	Cust
Dispatcher	D
Bouncer	B
Religion	
Catholic	C
Protestant	P
Type of taxi driven	
Public hire	PH
Private hire	—
Area in which driver, dispatcher, or bouncer worked	
City Center	CC
West Belfast	WB
East Belfast	EB
North Belfast	NB
Gender	
Male	—
Female	F

Source: Authors' compilation.

tomers, particularly from late-night customers, many of whom thought she was the driver's untrusting wife or girlfriend. We were not sure whether this assumption was due to Belfast taxi drivers' reputations in matters of money or matrimony, or perhaps both.

We then interviewed customers and mimics: forty ordinary customers, ten "bad-looking" customers, and ten runners and three robbers who posed as good customers.[14] We also arranged a group discussion with eight of the "bad-looking" customers. Finally, we took a large number of taxi rides posing as customers in a variety of locations and times of day and night.

The Belfast drivers' fondness for, and skill in, storytelling provided us with very rich data. Acting on information from one of our interviewees, we learned that staff from the Department of Environment (DOE) enforcement department, which polices the taxi industry, were posing as passengers in order to catch unlicensed "pirate" drivers and private-hire drivers illegally picking up fares off the street. We met with the head of the DOE's enforcement team to learn more about the strategies of these unexpected mimics.

We also interviewed the coordinator of North West Taxi Proprietors Ltd., who drove a taxi in Derry; five members of the Department of Vehicle Licensing Northern Ireland (DVLNI), the local government department that regulates the taxi industry; and four bouncers, or doormen, an occupation that faces screening problems similar to those faced by drivers.

New York

By contrast, not much went as planned in the New York City fieldwork. We worked harder and longer but gained less information of the type and quality we wanted.[15] We focused on livery cab drivers rather than yellow cabs because the former, as we make clear in chapter 7, take much greater risks.

Despite our impeccable academic credentials—in addition to the University of Oxford and the Russell Sage Foundation, Heather Hamill also obtained a very useful attachment to Columbia University—we met with uncooperative and suspicious responses from all quarters. We cannot really say how much this response was intensified by the gloom that the terrorist attacks had caused, or whether perhaps this response was compounded by the anthrax scare that occurred during the first few months of our fieldwork.

In addition, the fieldwork suffered from specific shortcomings. First, we did not have informal contacts in New York, as we had among taxi drivers in Belfast. The people we knew were not the type to have personal contacts with taxi drivers—the total population and the social segregation in New York are much greater than they are in Belfast. We also encountered language barriers in the predominantly Spanish-speaking world of livery drivers. We found it difficult to make ourselves understood by the drivers we encountered when we phoned up a base and requested a taxi in the hope of recruiting a driver for an interview, as we had done in Belfast.

After a false start, we decided to go through more formal channels, starting with the Taxi and Limousine Commission (TLC), the regulating body of the taxi industry in New York. That agency, however, was not at all cooperative and showed little interest in the study. We were unable to interview any TLC employees and thus could get neither their views nor as much background data as was desirable. We made tactful, if relentless, requests for interviews until the last week of the fieldwork, to no avail. We were referred from person to person, promises went unfulfilled, and phone calls were not returned.

We turned to the New York State Federation of Taxi Drivers (NYSFTD), the largest union representing livery drivers. Although it took some time to make contact with this group, the strategy proved to be a good one, and their help was invaluable. We interviewed forty-five livery drivers at NYSFTD offices in the Bronx, Queens, and Brooklyn. The bulk of the interviews were done with drivers from livery companies. We also interviewed two dispatchers and five drivers who drove yellow taxis based in Manhattan.

If Belfast drivers tended toward logorrhoea, the New Yorkers veered toward aphasia; they were less articulate and prone to provide monosyllabic answers. The deficiency of their responses was compounded by the language problem. Although we requested English-speaking drivers, a proportion did not speak English well enough to understand our questions or answer them fully, and our Spanish was rudimentary. The NYSFTD kindly provided us with a translator, who helped immensely, but the involvement of a translator prevented the free-flowing conversational style that elicited many of the rich details we obtained in Belfast, and many of the finer points were lost in translation. (We used the translator for seventeen of the interviews with drivers.) Furthermore, even with the help of NYSFTD staff, some of the drivers did not really understand our interests and were nervous and suspicious. Some doubted our intentions, wondering if we worked for the government or a newspaper and were keen to confirm that they had legal status in the United States. Although we interviewed forty-five Hispanic drivers, only thirty-two of the interviews were of sufficient quality to be usefully analyzed.[16]

We then turned our attention to drivers who worked in northern Manhattan. These drivers, who were mostly West African or African American, did not belong to the NYSFTD or any other union, so we had no official channels by which we could gain access to them. Instead, we decamped to the Metro North station at 125th Street and Lexington Avenue in Harlem, where we approached drivers waiting for passengers leaving the station. Although we had a varied reception, we were able to interview eighteen drivers using this strategy.

In addition to interviewing sixty-three drivers, we interviewed ten ordinary customers, twenty "bad-looking" customers, and six NYSFTD employees. We also took a large number of taxi rides posing as customers in a variety of locations and times of day and night.

The one aspect of our research in New York that did go better than in Belfast was the collection of material from newspaper archives. We did an extensive search of the *New York Times* and the *New York Post* since 1990, looking for accounts of incidents in which taxi drivers (both livery and yellow cab) had been involved as either victims or perpetrators of attacks and also looking for accounts of changes in policy and legislation that had affected the taxi industry. This yielded a great deal more information, both in quantity and quality, than our newspaper search in Belfast. We collected 128 cases of drivers murdered or violently attacked and 59 cases of individuals accused of attacking a taxi driver. We also supplemented our data by subscribing to an Internet newsgroup to which taxi drivers contribute from the United States, the United Kingdom, and Australia.

Ideally, we would have liked to interview mimics of the worst sort—namely, those who were or had been arrested for attacking drivers, with either sectarian (Belfast) or robbery (New York) motives. In the time scale and with the resources available to us, we were unable to track these people down. Most of the information we have on mimics is derived from other sources, either the drivers themselves or the accounts of various incidents that we collected through our newspaper search.[17]

Anonymity

In return for the opportunity to tape-record the interviews, we promised the drivers that we would not reveal their identity. We removed any reference to specific taxi firms in Belfast or taxi bases in New York, and we gave each driver a code. In Belfast (see table I.1), the code provides information about the drivers' religion, the type of taxis they drove, the areas they drove in, and their gender. The private-hire drivers are coded first by religion, followed by area in which they worked, their gender (if female), and then an identifying number. "C-WBF3" tells us that the driver was Catholic, worked in West Belfast, was female, and was interview number 3. Public-hire drivers are coded by religion and a number. "P-PH5" describes a Protestant driver who drove a public-hire taxi and was interview number 5.

Customers are coded by religion, identified as a customer, gender-coded if female, and assigned a number. "P-Cust2" tells us that the respondent was Protestant, a customer, and a male and that his interview number was 2.

Dispatchers are coded by religion, identified as a dispatcher, coded by the area in which they work and their gender (if female), and given a number. "C-WBDF2" tells us that the respondent was a female Catholic who worked as a dispatcher in West Belfast and that her interview number was 2.

Bouncers are coded by religion, identified as a bouncer, coded by gender (if female), and given a number. "P-BF6" refers to a female Protestant bouncer whose interview number was 6.

In New York (see table I.2), drivers are coded by area in which they worked, gender (if female), and type of taxi they drove, and they are given a number. "BX7" is the code for a male driver who worked in the Bronx and was given the interview number 7. Customers are coded by skin color, identified as a customer, coded by gender (if female), and given a number. "BCustF1" refers to a black, female customer who was

Table I.2   New York Interviewee Codes

Characteristics of Interviewees	Codes
Job or role	
Driver	—
Customer	Cust
Dispatcher	D
Skin color	
Black	B
White	W
Hispanic	S
Type of taxi driven	
Yellow cab	YC
Livery cab	—
Area in which driver or dispatcher worked	
Bronx	BX
Brooklyn	BR
Queens	Q
North Manhattan	NM
Gender	
Male	—
Female	F

Source: Authors' compilation.

interview number 1. Dispatchers are coded by area in which they worked, identified as a dispatcher, coded by gender (if female), and given a number. "BRD2" is the code for a male dispatcher who worked in Brooklyn and was interview number 2.

Outline of the Book

The book is divided into two parts, one for each city, beginning with Belfast. Within each part we follow the same sequence of chapters. In the first chapter of each part, we describe the city and the toll that taxiing has taken on drivers. We give an account of the origins and motivations of the drivers and of the general dangers they face when driving in their city. Finally, we describe how they become knowledgeable about the city in which they work and how they exchange information about the dangers they face. In the next chapters (chapters 2 and 7), we give an account of the various types of mimics who pose as bona-fide passengers in order to harm the drivers in some way and describe the strategies that mimics use to persuade drivers to pick them up. In chapters 3 and 8, we describe the vast array of general precautions, deterrents, and remedial actions that drivers take to protect their safety. In chapters 4 and 9, we discuss the various ways in which drivers screen passengers, the signs they consider, how they reason about signs, and the choices they make. In chapters 5 and 10, we look at how drivers further probe passengers, either before picking them up or after they are in the car. We also look at the problem of probing from the point of view of bona-fide customers who display negative cues and want to persuade drivers to pick them up. In the conclusion, we discuss our findings from the research, both expected and unexpected.

PART I

BELFAST

Chapter 1

Belfast and Its Taxi Drivers

SINCE 1969, Belfast has been at the epicenter of a political and civil conflict in Northern Ireland that has exacted a heavy toll on the population.[1] According to the Police Service for Northern Ireland (PSNI), between 1969 and September 2001 there were 3,321 deaths and over 40,000 injuries as a result of the conflict; of this number, over half were civilians. Most of those killed (91 percent) were male, and the majority of deaths (53 percent) were among people under thirty years of age. Forty-three percent of those killed were Catholic, compared with 30 percent who were Protestant. Most of the fatalities (59 percent) were inflicted by Republican (Catholic) paramilitaries; 28 percent were killed by Loyalist (Protestant) paramilitaries, and 11 percent by the security forces.[2] Just over one-third of all those who died lived in five postal districts located in North and West Belfast (Fay, Morrissey, and Smyth 1999).

The "Troubles" and Their Toll on Taxi Drivers

Taxi drivers in Belfast are a particularly vulnerable group of civilians. As driver C-WB6 told us: "During the 'Troubles,' drivers have been hijacked, bombs put in their cars, threatened and shot." Since 1972, seventeen drivers have been killed, most of them Catholic, and many more have suffered attempts on their lives. Since 1992, there have been four attacks in which Loyalist paramilitaries walked into taxi depots and fired at whoever was there at that moment. In 1993, in two separate incidents, the Ulster Freedom Fighters (UFF) indiscriminately fired at two taxi ranks in Catholic areas. This threat to drivers was recognized in 1997 when Gerry Adams, president of Sinn Féin, the Irish Republican political party, unveiled a memorial to members of the West Belfast Taxi Association who had been murdered in the previous twenty years. The plaque bore seven names with the epitaph: "Murdered in the service of their community" (Fay, Morrissey, and Smyth 1999).

The political "peace process" and the Republican and Loyalist paramilitary ceasefires, which began in 1994, have reduced the threat of major violent attacks against commercial targets or the security forces. Despite the ceasefire, however, the threat of sectarian violence against civilians remains high, and the dangers for drivers have not necessarily diminished. According to driver P-CC2, "I have driven through Belfast during the worst of the 'Troubles,' and I would honestly say that because of the fact that the security forces are off the street, now it is more dangerous." Driver P-CC2 was not being paranoid. In 1998 the Loyalist Volunteer Force (LVF) issued a death threat against Catholic taxi firms. The persistent seriousness of drivers' exposure to this danger is starkly brought home by the fact that driver C-WB4 got a letter from the police the same day we interviewed him, warning him that his name had been found on a Loyalist death squad hit list: "You know a lot of taxi drivers will get them," he said. The plight of taxi drivers was again recognized in May 2001, during our fieldwork, when Gerry Adams unveiled another mural on the Falls Road commemorating Catholic taxi drivers killed during the Troubles.

The perils of the sectarian conflict have also involved Protestant drivers caught up in Loyalist feuds between the Ulster Volunteer Force (UVF) and the Ulster Defence Association (UDA). For example, armed and masked men fired at Jackie Mahood, hitting him three times in the head and neck, as he operated the dispatch desk in his North Belfast taxi depot on November 27, 1997. Trevor Kell was shot dead on December 5, 2000, when he was lured by a bogus call. Between June and September 2000, a bitter revival of the feud between the UVF and the UDA placed Protestant black taxi drivers in the firing line; in an unprecedented move, they sought safety in a Catholic Nationalist area.[3]

Types of Taxis

There are two types of taxis in Belfast: private-hire and public-hire. The private-hire taxis are saloon cars that pick up prearranged fares through a depot. It is illegal for them to pick up hailing passengers off the street, but many do, especially on weekends. The Department of Vehicle Licensing Northern Ireland (DVLNI), the government body that regulates the taxi industry in Northern Ireland, was unable to provide us with the exact number of firms or taxis operating in Belfast, but did tell us that the department issued 3,003 new taxi licenses in Northern Ireland between 1999 and 2000. We consulted the yellow pages and found ninety-one taxi firms listed in Belfast: forty-two in Catholic areas, forty-four in Protestant areas, and five in neutral areas. This is an exceptionally large number of firms. In Oxford, England, for instance, where the population is half that of Belfast, the number of private-hire taxi firms is only about one-tenth of that in Belfast. This is probably one of the reasons why taxis in Belfast are much less expensive than elsewhere in the United Kingdom.

The public-hire vehicles are all London hackney-style taxis with meters, and they are allowed to pick up hailing customers off the street within a five-mile radius of Belfast's City Center. These drivers are self-employed and own their vehicles. There are approximately 220 public-hire taxis in Belfast. Included in this group are thirteen public-hire taxi drivers who operate from Belfast City Airport.[4] Both Catholics and Protestants drive these taxis (see table 1.1). Although these taxi drivers only pick up customers off the street and would seem to be a better group to study, they are more protected from potential attackers because there is a dividing screen between the front and back seats in their cars. The partition is not bullet-proof, but it provides the drivers with some protection, making them less vulnerable than the private-hire drivers. Nevertheless, we did interview six drivers who drove public-hire taxis based at Belfast City Airport and the City Center.

A third group of public-hire taxis operate a shuttle system: they travel up and down set routes and pick up and drop off passengers at any point, charging a set fare for the journey. This service operates in North and West Belfast, where it is divided into taxis that work in Catholic areas under the West Belfast Taxi Association (approximately 250 taxis) and taxis that work in Protestant areas under the Shankill Taxi Association (approximately 80 taxis).[5] We chose not to interview this group of taxi drivers because of the special nature of their service, which is closer to an unscheduled bus service. They have little choice in terms of the routes

Table 1.1   Religion, Type of Firm, Job, and Gender of Belfast Taxi Employees Interviewed

Type of Firm or Job	Catholic	Protestant	Male	Female	Total
Private-hire					
Drivers	14	20	31	3	33
Drivers and dispatchers	2	2	3	1	4
Dispatcher	1	—	—	1	1
Public-hire					
Airport or City Center	2	3	5	—	5
City Center (only)	—	1	1	—	1
West Belfast taxis	1	—	1	—	1
Derry taxis	1	—	1	—	1
Bouncers	2	2	3	1	4

Source: Authors' compilation.

they can take and the passengers they can pick up; given that they normally carry several passengers unrelated to each other at any one time, they are also less vulnerable than the other drivers to being attacked.

There are frequent conflicts between public- and private-hire taxis because the former object to the latter illegally picking up hailing customers. Public-hire drivers are also unhappy about the police and the DOE, which they feel are not doing enough to deter the practice, as driver P-PH4, the most militant public-hire driver we interviewed, makes clear: "I have reported loads of [cases of private-hire taxis picking up off the street], and they say, 'Yes, we will do something' . . . you get to the stage where you're banging your head off a brick wall. There have been a lot of court cases lately, but the guys are getting fined twenty and thirty pounds and walking out of court laughing."

One reason the police are reluctant to enforce the law against private-hire taxis picking up off the street is that on weekends their primary goal is to clear the streets of rowdy, drunken crowds that may otherwise cause trouble. The police want people to be picked up at the fastest possible rate, and thus they turn a blind eye to unlicensed "pirate" drivers who pick up off the street: "Yeah, well, apparently one of the big shots [senior policemen] down there was quoted as saying he didn't care who was picking who up off the streets as long as his men were stood down by three o'clock in the morning on a Friday and Saturday night" (driver P-CC4).

Taxi Regulations

In 1996 changes brought about by two pieces of legislation had a dramatic effect on the industry. First, the introduction and enforcement of stricter drunk-driving laws increased the population's dependence on taxis, and second, the taxi industry was deregulated. The requirement that all taxi drivers pass a test was removed. As a result, the demand for taxi licenses increased.

To get a taxi license a driver must now pass a medical examination (and be reexamined every five years), not have a criminal conviction within the previous five years, and be "of good repute." The last two requirements are subject to a degree of interpretation. For example, despite being convicted of indecent exposure in a public place, one applicant was granted a taxi license because of the specific details of his case. The police had arrested him for urinating against a wall, and the DVLNI deemed it unfortunate that he was charged with such a serious offense for what the department considered to be a minor misdemeanor.[6]

Licensed taxi drivers are obliged to display a TAXI sign on their car, and by way of identification drivers are obliged to display a badge with their photograph. It is not required that the taxi firm's name or telephone numbers be displayed on the car, and the driver's badge displays only an identification number but does not display the driver's name or address. Because of the religious and residential segregation in Belfast, these pieces of information would identify the driver's religion, making him vulnerable to sectarian attack.

The Demand for Taxis

In Belfast the demand for taxis is high not only during the weekend but also on a daily basis. The political conflict has placed the public transport system in Northern Ireland under severe pressure, especially in West and North Belfast—areas that have experienced the worst effects of the Troubles. Buses are withdrawn on a regular basis when street violence flares and vehicles are used to erect barricades; train service is often disrupted by the threat of bombs on the line. Such disruption causes severe hardship to the many people who have to walk long distances to work, and everyday activities, like shopping, become dangerous ordeals. The only source of transport for many people is a taxi.

Further, the 1991 census revealed that in the poorer areas of Belfast 63 percent of households did not own a car. To travel any distance people living in poorer areas, which are also those most affected by the sectarian violence, have to find other means of transport. In Northern Ireland the bus and train companies are publicly owned, and their schedules have been limited owing to "inadequate capital investment and paltry operating subsidies" (General Consumer Council for Northern Ireland 2001). In addition, public financial support per head for bus and rail service in Northern Ireland has been less than half of that provided to the predominantly private-sector operators in Great Britain (General Consumer Council for Northern Ireland 2000).

The dearth of public transport has increased the everyday reliance on taxis of people living in poorer areas. Jim Neeson, head of the West Belfast Taxi Association, described the service offered by drivers as a "lifeline":

> Throughout the Troubles, the black taxis kept this community going. No matter what was happening on the Falls Road, you could rely on the black taxis to get you to work. Our drivers kept this service on the road through thick and thin, often at great personal risk to themselves. West Belfast has the highest unemployment rates in the North [of Ireland] and the lowest level of car ownership, so many people in this community still rely on us as their only means of transport. (*Andersonstown News* 2001)

Four out of ten people in Northern Ireland regularly take taxis for social and leisure outings, but a substantial minority also take taxis for shopping trips and to go to work or school (General Consumer Council for Northern Ireland 1997). The relatively low cost of taxis makes this an accessible form of transport for poorer people. One consequence is that a sizable proportion of customers are less well dressed and look "rough."

Drivers

Taxi drivers are very diverse in terms of their origins and connections, and the majority of them are not involved with the paramilitaries. There are, however, historical links between the industry and paramilitarism that are etched in the public consciousness. In Catholic West Belfast, the black taxis are run by the West Belfast Taxi Association, which was established in the 1970s to provide employment for Republican activists after they were released from prison. A similar scheme was established in Protestant areas of Belfast for Loyalist prisoners. Throughout the Troubles, the black taxis have had a high profile. For example, in 1988, during the funeral of IRA man Kevin Brady, two plainclothes British soldiers drove into the path of the funeral cortege by mistake. Mourners claimed that they believed they were under attack from Loyalists, and as the soldiers tried to turn around and get away, black taxis blocked their path (*Times of London* 1988). The soldiers were taken away and shot dead by two gunmen. The attack was captured by television crews and photographers covering the funeral and by the camera on an army observation helicopter as it circled overhead. For some customers, the image of the taxis involved in this incident remains powerful and frightening: "There's something about the black taxis. I know there's all the different dynamics to them, black taxis do this, black taxis do that, and I don't understand it, and they terrify me, black taxis really frighten me. I think it's seeing those soldiers being killed by them on the TV. So I just won't get one" (customer P-CustF1). However, as driver C-WB4 told us, "See, those black taxis on the Falls Road . . . are classed as Republican and the ones on the Shankill are classed as Loyalist, even though 75 percent of those people driving them black taxis have never been nothing, or involved in nothing, in their lives."

The taxi associations remain committed to their political roots, but "only" 10 percent of the current West Belfast black taxi drivers are ex-prisoners:

> It used to be that you had to have been in jail in order to get on them [black taxis], or if there was a big waiting list of maybe two or three hundred people, but if you were a Republican and just out of jail, you were automatically moved up to the top of the list. If there was, say, two places and there were two Republicans waiting, they got them no matter how long the list. Whereas now it has turned more into a sort of community thing—it's first man in. The days of special privileges are over. (driver C-WB4)

This reputation for paramilitary involvement extends to the private-hire drivers, and many firms outside the City Center are thought to have strong ties with either Republican or Loyalist paramilitaries. In 1986 the UFF issued death threats to taxi firms that, it claimed, paid protection money to the IRA. Driver C-WB4 pointed out to us a number of firms that he said were associated with the paramilitaries: "That firm, they used to be called————. It was well known that the UVF owned————. Don't get me wrong—the IRA also owned taxi depots in their day."

Some firms have a reputation for employing ex-prisoners: "The taxi depot I work for," driver C-WB4 noted, "would probably be the biggest in West Belfast, probably be the biggest amount of drivers. I think you've got about eight out of about seventy-five drivers who have done time in jail, about eight or nine. You'll find that they'll be the most safety-conscious."

Although we did not intentionally set out to interview drivers who had paramilitary involvement, seven of those contacted at random and interviewed had been imprisoned for either Republican or Loyalist paramilitary-related incidents, and five out of twelve of the taxi companies from which our interviewees were drawn had a reputation for supporting paramilitary organizations from one community or the other.

Whatever their background, all taxi drivers are motivated to do their job by a number of factors, including a lack of alternatives, the flexibility of the job, and the opportunity to be their own boss:

> You know, I'm a spark [electrician] by trade, so I could even go back to being a spark. I would probably get more money sparking, but if I took on a job, I would have to be there in the morning fucking until it's finished. You know, I've no commitments. I'm not married. If I want to go away, I go away. I just do what I want to do. Nobody's there to tell me you can't or you can or yaps [nags] at me. That's the way I like life. I like life easy. I would only work one of the nights at the weekend. I wouldn't work both. (driver C-WB4)

> I work to suit myself. I come in, in the morning, work whatever, and if I want to go away for two hours, I go away for two hours. And if I want to work all day, I work all day. I'm not tied down, there's no real boss. I come and go as I please. If I need extra money, I'll go and work the hours and get the extra money, and if I'm going on holiday or I'm going away for two days, I just go away. So I can't see me settling down to another type of job. (driver C-WB6)

Some like the adrenaline rush:

> I don't know, I just sort of drifted into it, and when I got into it, I really enjoyed it. There was always the adrenaline from not knowing what was going to come next. In my opinion, it is a very exciting thing, because one

minute you could be driving an old person going to the hospital, or maybe someone has just had a bereavement or something. The next minute you could be out in the middle of big trouble. It is actually like a drug, to be honest, just like a drug. There is an adrenaline kick, and it is a terrible thing to say, but sometimes the more dangerous it is, the more of adrenaline there is. The more the kick there is—for me anyhow. I come out in the morning, and I actually get enjoyment out of the fact that I don't know what is round the corner. You know, I have had some bad experiences, but at the same time it is the thrill of not knowing what you are coming out to. I actually worked for contractors, which was a very safe job, and left it to come back to the taxiing because I missed it so much. (driver P-CC2)

Some do it because the job satisfies their curiosity about people and their affairs:

Taxi drivers are counselors, if you get the right one, because they have a vast amount of experience, and that is to me what makes my job worthwhile. I get something back. [Passengers] tell you things. A boyfriend and girlfriend have split up. Husband and wife split up. Husband caught doing a line with someone else. Fella tried to touch for a girl all night, nothing happens, and he is grumpy in the car.

I remember one incident. I picked up these two women—Lily would have been about forty-eight to fifty—and we just started talking, and she asked me, "What do you do at the weekends, what do you do to go out?" I said, "I don't drink, so there is no sense in me going out to pubs." So then she started to ask me, "Do you never drink?" "Yes, I did. Drank too much, ended up in hospital." She went on then to tell me she had a drink problem. I then asked her what caused it. Well, you don't start drinking for nothing, there is always something there—should it be small, big, there is always something that triggers it off. She said, "No," and I said, "There is always a reason." It turned out she had had a child twenty-five years earlier outside of marriage, which her family made her give up, and she had punished herself ever since. My heart went out to her—she wants to find her son—and I said, "What are you going to do? Show that his mother is a drunk? What will that do to him then? You had to leave him twenty-five years ago, you had to let him lead a different life, and then come back twenty-five years later a drunk and make him feel worse than he did when you initially gave him up?" I said, "That would be a wrong move, love." She told me then she had a daughter, also at home, who constantly tries to commit suicide, and she thought it would be good for the daughter to find out she had a brother. I said, "Not only are you going to turn up as a drunk, but you are bringing a psychopath with you." I said, "No, Lily, get off the drink. Find AA [Alcoholics Anonymous], go down and talk to them, try and get off the bottle." I think I sat talking to {the two women} for easily over an hour and a half, and when we left she told me she would go to the AA, and I saw her about three months later coming out of a club in town, so she never did. I feel I did my bit—the rest was up to her. She needed someone to tell her, wake up and smell the coffee. We are not trained for this, it is just an ability that we pick up. There are some taxi drivers that go through spells like that where you feel you can do something. But there is the other majority which would tell them to "piss off, get out, and give me the money." (driver P-CC7)

Some drivers taxied when other jobs were not so readily available: "I worked on building sites, and then, with the winter coming in, work started to slack off, and I started taxi driving—November through to March—and then stopped it again for the summer, and then back on it again for five or six months in the winter" (driver C-WB7). Others have lost a job: "I was laid off at my last job, and basically I haven't got a trade, so it seemed the easiest way to make a living. This firm was advertising in the local paper—*East Belfast News.* I knew three fellas that worked for him. So I came in that way" (driver P-EB7).

Being laid off was a blessing in disguise for driver P-PH1:

I love the shipyard, but I was made redundant, and I was taxiing intermittently all through that, but this is a kind [of] job now where you are so independent, it is very difficult for me to go to anything else. At times I would love to. There is times you just get pissed off, you just get fed up with it. You maybe had a bad month, and something goes wrong with the taxi, and you are looking this and you are looking that. It can be difficult at times, and you would say, I would love a [different] job, but when you get it back on the road again, *you are captain of your own wee ship.* It is good to be like that, if you are that way inclined. I like to start when I want, finish when I want, and when I need more money, I will go out and work, and that is a big, big asset to me.

Dangers of Taxiing in Belfast

One result of the ongoing civil and political conflict in Northern Ireland is the high level of residential segregation in Belfast, a fact that is well illustrated by the map showing the religious distribution within the city (see figure 1.1). Protestant and Catholic communities are clearly defined geographically and separated by "peacelines" (Doherty and Poole 1995). West Belfast is predominantly Catholic, and East Belfast is overwhelmingly Protestant. North Belfast contains pockets of Catholic and Protestant communities, which are often separated by just one street. The City Center is neutral territory with mixed bars and clubs.

North, West, and East Belfast can be very hazardous for drivers, especially at night. "Interface areas," where Catholics and Protestants live separately but in close proximity, are flashpoints for sectarian violence as youths throw stones and petrol bombs at each other. Compelled to travel through the "opposing" neighborhood, both Catholic and Protestant taxis

Figure 1.1   Proportion of Catholic Residents in Belfast Electoral Wards, 1991

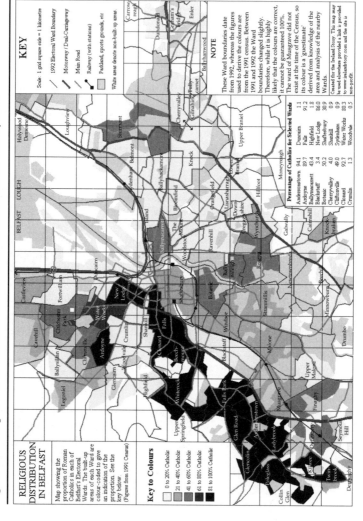

Source: The Ireland Story website (www.irelandstory.com). "Maps of Ireland." Available at: www.wesleyjohnston.com/users/Ireland/maps/towns/belfast_religion.gif (accessed April 25, 2005).

frequently come under attack. The following is an account by a Catholic driver:

> [In West Belfast] Blacks Road is . . . a wee pocket of Protestants, only about 150 houses, and they're surrounded by thousands and thousands of Catholics. But to be honest, they can be annoying because they are stoning the taxis. If you have a TAXI sign on, they will throw stones at it. A black taxi going up Andytown [Andersonstown] is a Catholic— there's no way a black taxi from the Shankill [Protestant area] goes to Andytown, [the driver's] a Catholic. So breaking his windows or doing what they're doing, they get away with it, they actually do get away with it, and you'll see the peelers [police] sitting there, and they'll do nothing about it. (driver C-WB4)

While driving around with this same driver, we experienced these dangers firsthand when we had to speed through red lights at a busy junction to avoid the hail of stones and bricks being thrown at us. Protestant drivers are also subject to this type of attack (*Irish News* 2000a).

In West and North Belfast, taxi drivers face another danger: "joyriders" who recklessly drive stolen cars and often target taxi drivers and ram them at high speed.[7] Driver C-WB4 is all too familiar with these young people:

> Well, if they hit you like, and they're going the speed they're going at, it mightn't be so bad if they hit you frontal, but if they hit you side on, you know there's nothing there for protection. And if you notice, I don't wear a seat belt. I never wear a seat belt, even when I'm on my own. Now, if you drive a taxi, you have to have an airbag—and whether it fucking works or not, I don't know.

Joyriders also try to engage taxis in dangerous high-speed races:

> See this car, this car here? People would say it's a flashy car. I don't know; it looks to be a fast motor, [but] it's not. It's just that I look after it, but joyriders seem to have the tendency of trying to race me, and I've no intentions of trying to race them. You don't want to know, you just don't want to fucking have anything to do with them. But I've seen them on a Saturday night going up the Monagh Bypass, and they're behind me, and they're flashing, and they're beeping, and they're trying to get you to go that wee bit faster and race. (driver C-WB4)

Belfast City Center becomes hazardous on weekends when thousands of people pour onto the streets between midnight and two o'clock in the morning. The streets become very crowded with drunk and disorderly people, and many of them are trying to get a taxi home. The danger comes from customers using aggressive tactics, such as running out in front of a traveling taxi to get it to stop or trying to get into the car without permission from the driver. "You see the likes of that [on] Bradbury Place and Wellington Park, they are trying to jump into your motor, and you are over for somebody [else]. You have to stick the central locking on and only put the window down a bit. You get some people jumping on your bonnet waving ten-pound notes, 'Take me home.' . . . I feel very threatened" (driver P-EB7).

The environment in which taxi drivers work is not just generally dangerous. In chapter 2, we review the specific threats that drivers face from various villains who pose as bona-fide customers. First, however, we describe the essential background knowledge that taxi drivers need to do their job and how they acquire it.

Information Diffusion and Background Knowledge

Among Belfast taxi drivers, there is no organized information exchange—they have no dedicated radio station or website—but we did observe numerous informal communications between drivers and their depots. Furthermore, once drivers begin work and become acquainted with their colleagues, they become part of an information-sharing network and cope with the perils of their occupation by frequently exchanging information as daily and nightly events unfold. Eighty-eight percent of the Belfast drivers we interviewed said that drivers share information and offer each other support. According to driver C-WB4, "Taxi men will stick together," but driver P-PH5 was not so sure: "They'd cut your throat for a fiver. Half the taxi drivers in Belfast wouldn't speak to the other half. They fell out maybe twenty-five years ago, and if you asked them what they fell out over, they'd just say, 'Ahh, I don't talk to him,' and if you said, 'Why?' they'd say, 'I can't remember.' "

Specific details—such as addresses, features of problematic passengers, accidents, roadblocks, traffic buildup, or the presence of joyriders, stone-throwers, or undercover DOE agents (see chapter 2)—are updated daily and disseminated through the dispatcher or between drivers using their cell phones. "For instance, if there is a riot somewhere, the driver on the scene would call into the office. They then will put it out to all drivers. . . . Even if there has been an accident, they would get back to the depot, and the depot would put out a message, for they don't want their cars heading towards a [traffic] block. So the information would come out fairly quickly" (driver P-CC2).

If a driver is unsure of an address, he can ask friends and colleagues for help: "The fellas just normally kept you right of where to go" (driver

P-CC4). Dispatcher C-WBDF1 was given some guidance when she started but learned primarily from the experience of doing the job:

> You are shown the ropes, you're shown what to do, who to pick up, who not to pick up, and there's times when I did start I had to ask the drivers, "So is this address okay, is that address okay?" and they'd have given me their opinion on it: "Aye, that's dead on," or, "No, that's a dodgy one, don't be sending a taxi to there." So you learn as you along. You . . . get to know the regulars but . . . it was mostly local people from the area who used them anyway. But then I went to that other [depot] in Twinbrook. I hadn't a clue up there, because I didn't know anybody, because I wasn't from there, and that was very dodgy, because I didn't know the estate, [and] you were very close to the other side [Protestants] and you weren't sure what the score was going to be, whether this is a bomber or this is a safe one. I just took the calls down and again asked the drivers what sort of job it was and was it okay.

Being stopped by the police is of particular concern to the pirate drivers who don't have a license or insurance. They need to know how to avoid prosecution by waiving the fare if the passenger tells the police that they are simply getting a lift from the driver, who is their friend or relative (see chapter 2). They inform each other if they see "Driver 13" on the road. (In Catholic areas they refer to the police as "Driver 13" because superstition keeps any genuine taxi driver from ever being given the number thirteen.) "Taxi men will stop for each other. They will guard themselves, or you'll see them flashing the lights at each other, and that means the peelers [police] is stopped up the street, and if you're using red diesel or you're not legit or . . . that'll let you know" (driver C-WB4).

Sometimes the gathering and exchange of information combines the interests of drivers with the interests of the various paramilitary groups. All drivers associated with a paramilitary group pass on their "intelligence" as a matter of course. Taxi drivers who work in a small area become very familiar with the local inhabitants and the patterns of daily life and notice any irregularities:

> We know all their taxis, and [the Loyalists] know our taxis, and even driving up and down the road over the years, they know the cars. There could be a guy drive up behind you, he'd look in [the depot] and he'd know every one of these cars because he's been taxiing for years. . . . I'm the same. . . . As I drive into the village [a Protestant area], there's a taxi company down there now with about ten motors, and I know every one of them—the Sierras, the Fords, I know every one of them. And if I see one of them on the road [in West Belfast], I would know them. (driver C-WB6)

Drivers also need a large amount of background knowledge to cope with the demands of their profession. With one exception, all the drivers we interviewed originated in Northern Ireland, and most were from Belfast.[8] Therefore, most of them had acquired much of the relevant knowledge of the city and the characteristics associated with being Catholic or Protestant before they started taxi driving. Much of their background knowledge was learned simply as a by-product of living and observing life in the city, and we did not observe them making a very focused effort to learn more or to teach others. The rest of what they needed to know they had learned from each other or from direct experience; none of the depots offered formal training. Drivers are given only limited technical information—how to use the radio equipment, for instance, and, in some firms, the computerized data head. Fewer than half of the drivers (44 percent) had received any advice from more experienced cabbies when they started working. Driver P-EBF1, one of the five female drivers we interviewed, felt that most were "thrown in at the deep end." She herself "wasn't set up for . . . what the work was going to be like, what I actually had to do." Driver P-CC7 agreed: "You basically learn most of it by yourself." As driver P-CC12 pointed out, however, "Belfast isn't really that big, so knowledge-wise you can pick it up pretty quickly."

Drivers gain a detailed mapping of Belfast's physical and political geography. Given that the greatest threat to drivers is sectarian attack ("There is areas in Belfast where you could run into trouble, but it's tribal trouble," said driver P-CC2), they must know which areas are Catholic and which are Protestant not only so that they can get their passengers to their destinations but also because, as driver P-CC12 explained, "people will suspect that you are a different religion because you don't know the area" (see chapters 3 and 4). Driver P-CC4 concurred: "You don't want to stop and say to them, 'Where's such and such?' because they'd automatically say, 'He's of the other kind [religion],' and the next minute you're getting bricked."

In addition, drivers learn which social venues are Protestant and which are Catholic: "If you're taxiing, well, you kinda have to know where all the pubs or clubs are, so as you know where you're going or where you're picking up," said driver C-WB6. He added: "You know all your own clubs, you know all the clubs. And if I was picking up in the town and someone said, 'Take me to Bailey's,' you have to know where it is, [and] you know right away [whether] this fella's a Catholic or this fella's a Protestant."

There are also dangers associated with specific clubs: "Where they're hard to get to—maybe somewhere where there's only one way in and out of it—. . . I generally wouldn't go in there" (driver P-CC4). Having such detailed knowledge of the different areas of Belfast, as we see in chapters 4 and 5, also enables drivers to screen customers who they suspect are "mimics" and probe them for knowledge that only a good customer is likely to have. They are also able to give advice to customers: "You need to know where clubs and pubs in the City Center are because some people . . . would ask your advice on . . . where to go and [ask,] 'What is a good spot tonight?' . . . 'What time are they open to tonight?'—basically things like that" (driver P-PEB7).

To minimize the dangers, drivers learn the safest route to their destination and stay away from certain areas during particular times of the year when the likelihood of street violence increases the risk of being attacked: "Well, you're not going to go up the Shankill Road on the twelfth of July basically. You might not come back again. I mean, you might, but the car won't. It's happened to a couple of guys who've had their cars taken, hijacked, set on fire" (driver C-CC1).

In addition to the threat of sectarian violence, drivers are aware of the dangers of joyriders and thieves in high-crime areas: "Going up the Monagh Bypass [in Catholic West Belfast] late at night, it is just scary, because you have guys stealing cars and driving about. I have actually taken people into Twinbrook about two in the morning and have cars just whiz past me and nearly put me off the road. It is not a nice feeling" (driver P-CC7).

By talking to drivers who had only recently started driving taxis, we observed that they quickly become more realistic and less stereotypical in their judgments. Driver P-EBF9, who started six weeks before our interview, said:

> I have been really surprised [by] people who have got [into the car], and I have thought, what is this coming? [And it's] turned out they aren't what they appear to be at all. They might get in, and they might look like trouble, but they aren't. People who appear more likely to cause trouble—just to look at them—they can be gentle. . . . I mean, you do try to weigh people up and put them in their slots, but it doesn't always work that way.

In conclusion, the safe navigation of Belfast's complex sectarian topography depends on the accretion of a large amount of detailed knowledge and information, some of which drivers have already and some of which they learn from each other and from experience. How drivers put this knowledge to work in order to screen and probe customers forms the object of chapters 4 and 5.

Chapter 2

Mimics in Belfast

S OME OF the work-related risks to which drivers are exposed in Belfast—such as having one's car pelted with projectiles by thugs while driving through rough areas or being confronted by armed men for whatever reason—are not part of a trust game and do not involve mimicry. Seven Catholic black taxi drivers were murdered in the past twenty years not by paramilitaries posing as customers but by attackers directly shooting them. These murderers did not pretend to be anybody other than who they were.

Other dangers may involve trust in some respect but not mimicry. When approached by a drunken customer who is patently intoxicated and unable to hide his state, a driver still has to exercise some generic sense of trust to take such a passenger on board. The driver must rely on this person to have the money to pay for the ride, to be fit enough to pay, to be coherent enough to give the driver the right address, and to be controlled enough not to foul the car.

Our research focuses on the more insidious perils that involve both a basic trust game between driver-trusters and their customer-trustees and the potential for mimicry. The cases that concern us are those in which a prospective customer engages in some signaling act to make the driver believe that he is a genuine customer. Sometimes this is also the case with a drunken customer, who may try to veil his state or who may send a sober friend to find a taxi for him. However, the serious perils that Belfast drivers face involve three types of mimics: "runners," who get a ride and run off without paying the fare; robbers, who want their money; and paramilitaries, who want to hijack their cars or subject them to a sectarian attack. Furthermore, the drivers who break the law, either by taxiing without a license or, as almost all private-hire drivers do, by illegally picking up street-hailers, also fear the Department of Environment, whose undercover agents try to entrap them. There are very few women among taxi drivers; according to driver C-CC1, in his firm only five out of three hundred drivers are female. The four women we interviewed said that they also fear sexual assaults to a limited extent, and one of them had been the victim of harassment by a well-known local politician. All drivers are aware of the dangers, and even though five of the drivers we interviewed said they had never experienced any trouble, most of our interviewees had been involved in several incidents.

Runners

Runners are the most common and least harmful group of mimics. Driver P-PH5 explained runners in terms of a generalized reluctance to pay drivers:

> Nobody wants to pay for a taxi for some reason. We find the same at the airport. People come out in their sandals and they're freezing:
>
> "Where were you?"
>
> "Miami. How much is it to the bus station?"
>
> They've spent three thousand pounds on the flight, and they're going to go home on the bus when another twenty pounds would get them home. Nobody wants to pay for a taxi—nobody. . . . Do you like paying for taxis?

Driver P-CC2, who claims runners are not that common, has had about ten in his twenty-year career. Driver P-CC12 had three in twelve years. There is, however, a certain reluctance among drivers to report runners for fear of being seen as gullible. According to driver P-PH5: "There's a lot of drivers that would say they never had runners, and they're telling lies." Driver C-WB6 said he had "loads of them. Jesus, if I had the money for all the ones that done runners, I'd have a few quid." In total, 73 percent of our drivers admitted that they had suffered from runners.

Runners seem to be mostly young men and women. Teenagers duped 91 percent of those drivers who had experienced at least one runner:

> I'll tell you one I had—now there was one girl. . . . She went into a block of flats to get the money and never came back. I wouldn't go into a block of flats, because you don't know where she went. There was a taxi driver at the City Airport who got caught very nicely one Sunday night at an estate in Bangor, which is a bit rough, off the Rathgael Road. She came out with a baby and a small bag—"Take me to the Drumsilly Estate." So he stopped at the house and she says, "I'll go and get you the money." She went down the path, opened the door with the key and went in, switched the hall light on, and that was all—the door closed. So the driver waited a couple of minutes and went down, and the house was empty but the back door was lying open. So he ran around the back and she was gone. Now this was very professionally done. So the woman next door heard the noise, and she came

out: "What's wrong, driver?" He says, "I brought a young girl here, and she went in the front door and has disappeared. She owes me twelve pounds." She says, "She used to live here, she must have held on to the key." Now that's worse because that's planned. (driver P-PH5)

The kind and amount of signaling work that a mimic has to do to induce a driver to trust him varies depending on, among other things, what the mimic wants to achieve and how risk-prone the driver is. The mimicking acts can also take place at different stages of the transactions. Somebody planning to do a runner may look just like an ordinary customer at first sight and even when talking to the driver. So she may have little extra work to do in order to be picked up. Her trick will come at the end of the ride, and it is designed to make the driver continue to believe that she is a safe fare: "One runner sat with *a cash card in his hand* and asked to be dropped off at a cash point where he could pick up some money. The name of the bank coincided with the name on the card [First Trust], so the driver never had any suspicion and even applauded when he run off" (driver P-CC7).

Other common strategies—according to customer P-CF1, herself a runner—include waiting until the taxi pulls up at a set of traffic lights close to the desired destination and running from the car. Another customer versed in the practice told us that she and three or four of her friends would continue to let the driver believe he was going to be paid right up to the last minute. They would all leave the taxi except one, who would walk around to the driver's window pretending to be about to pay the fare, but then run off.

Runners' creativity can reach vertiginous heights, as in the case reported by driver P-CC12:

The worst thing that ever happened to me, the most embarrassing thing, was the nicest girl you will ever meet, and I picked her up from a phone box in the Cregagh Estate. She said, "Look, I'm going to the Shankill Road, and do you mind if I brought a snake in the car?" I said, "I do, to tell you the truth," and she said, "It's in a glass case, it won't get out, I'm just back from holiday, and I live with my granny, and I couldn't expect her to look after the snake, but it's in a reptile shop being looked after for me for a fortnight." "Well, okay, as long as you sit beside me and if it escapes you get it." So the reptile shop was in Ballybeen. She got me to drop her off at the corner of Ballybeen, and I never seen her again. It was the most elaborate runner I have ever had—it was such an incredible story, I never thought it was a lie. I sat for forty minutes and I thought, this is getting more embarrassing by the minute, and it was so difficult to get parked, and I couldn't leave the car to look in case she had been held up, and maybe the snake, there was something wrong with it. I sat for a full hour before I drove off totally embarrassed.

Most drivers say they do not give chase because they think it is not worth the risk of getting into a fight:

I know one guy who drives a black taxi, got this boy and took him into East Belfast, and the guy wouldn't pay him, and when Gary got out to chase after him, Gary actually tripped on the curb and fell. The guy was drunk and was running away, but when he [saw] he had tripped and fell, he came back and beat the crap out of him, and he still tells that story today. "I never forget," he says. "I was going to give him such a beating, but I tripped on the curb, and he came back and danced all over me, so not only did I get the crap beat out of me, I still didn't get paid." (driver P-CC7)

When I was younger, I'd've got out and chased them, but what can you do when you catch them? Fisticuffs? It's no good. You end up digging him, or him digging you, or whatever. But most of the time I do just sit and laugh at them because there's nothing [I can do]. (driver C-WB6)

Or they risk getting their car damaged:

My attitude, for a fare of four or five pound, when I have a pretty decent car, is if they want to run away, let them run, because if they turn around and kick your door or kick your mudguard or kick your lights, it's one hundred pounds to get it painted or fifty pounds to get a light, or worse thing, they could give you a kicking, so you're better to let them go for a fiver, because the next person will maybe give you a two-pound tip, so you're better letting them go. (driver P-PH5)

Or drivers risk losing their car altogether: "Joyriders now have started going out to get taxis and then do a runner. Then, when you get out to run after them, when you come back to get your car . . . they're away with your car" (driver P-CC4). The joyriders engage in a double mimicry act: they first pretend to be good passengers, and then they pretend to be runners to lure the driver away from his car and steal it.

Some drivers are reluctant to admit to having experienced runners, but others realize that, if unpunished, they will continue to victimize other drivers: "If a driver came back and said, 'I got a fare there to 21, University Street, and he didn't pay me,' it would put the rest of us on guard for the house. But a lot of boys come back and say, 'Ahh, I never had one, I never had one,' and then once a guy gets away without paying, it's like a boy who steals—if he gets away once, he'll do it, and do it, and do it" (driver P-PH5).

Five of the drivers said they would report an incident with a runner to the police, especially if they had an address where they had picked up or dropped off the cheaters.

Robbers

Drivers are much more worried, of course, about robbers than about runners, but robbery appears to occur less frequently in Belfast than in other parts of the United Kingdom or in New York (see table 2.1). Only two (4 percent) of our interviewees had been robbed: "There's very few taxi drivers robbed. In all the time that I've been here, I've never been robbed, and I can't really say there's any drivers that I know—and I know some drivers over the years, like, thousands—I've never known a taxi driver to be robbed" (driver C-WB6).

Driver P-CC7 said:

> There is only about 3 percent of your working day that you would ever be in that position, and the majority of that would be at night—if you were working at night. Very seldom during the day would you be in a predicament like that, but certainly at night, especially at weekends. There is one guy in our place who I think was stabbed twenty-seven times. Another one had a knife stuck through the back of his seat. It just goes on. There are different cases, but it wouldn't be a consistent thing—it wouldn't happen all the time. Personally, no, I have never been in a position [of danger].

Driver P-CC2 stressed that it is very hard to see a robbery coming: "You just don't know, there is no guarantee." Maybe this was his own problem in particular given that he had been robbed several times:

> They are as skilled as what you are. They get into the car, and they can be quite nice to you until they get you into the area they want you . . . or they can be silent till they reach the destination where they want you. If they are silent, there is not much you can tell about them.

> Those you can tell are the useless ones, [whereas] the ones that you are looking for, the robbers—the violent ones—are very, very hard to tell. These people are walking about year after year never going to prison, and

Table 2.1   Drivers' Bad Encounters in Belfast and New York

Bad Encounters	Belfast (N = 45)	New York (N = 50)
Had runners	73% (33)	100% (50)
Was threatened	69 (31)	100 (50)
Was attacked	29 (13)	50 (25)
Was robbed	4 (2)	18 (9)
Was hijacked	16 (7)	N/A

Source: Authors' compilation.
Note: N/A = not applicable.

the reason for it is they know what they are doing, so no driver will tell one of these people walking to his car—no driver will. The ones that they are talking about, that they can tell coming towards their car, are people who are useless people, who are easy, because the angry arrogant [men], they are not usually criminals. Criminals are never angry. They are calculating, they know exactly what they want, and they are very cool and calculated. These are people that can go into prison and can talk to psychiatrists, and they can bluff them and can make people think that they have changed their ways. That is the people that is going to rob you, and that is the people that is going to be violent to you, not the ordinary lad from the street who goes on about having a bad time—they are easy because you can talk them down. The other fella is not going on the spur of the moment, he is coming in calculating, knowing before, and he is not going to give it away by his walk over to your car, by the one-second conversation while the door is open, or by anything—he will not give his strategy away. He knows where he is going, and he knows what he wants. If he wants your money, he wants your car, and he knows that, so he will get in, and he will give very little away about himself. He will give nothing away about himself.

Driver C-WB5, who also used to be a robber, corroborated these observations from the mimic's point of view: "I was successful because I hadn't got that look of a criminal, and I didn't sound like a criminal—but I was a criminal."

Undercover Agents

During the fieldwork we learned that the Department of Environment's driver and vehicle licensing branch had been trying to catch drivers who were illegally picking up hailing passengers off the street. Driver C-CC1, who had two colleagues who had been caught and charged by the DOE, described this unexpected brand of mimics: "There's a hippie-looking guy knocking about and some girl with blond hair knocking about. They hang out around the City Hall—hotels and things. If you pick them up off the street it's illegal." "The DOE agents," he added, "are just ordinary punters as far as we're concerned, or that's what they're trying to be, but they haven't got me yet anyway."

Acting on this information, we interviewed the head of enforcement at the DOE. Most of the department's work is aimed at preventing people from driving taxis without a taxi license or insurance and ensuring that private-hire taxis do not act as public-hire taxis and pick up people off the street, which is against the law. Initially, with police assistance, they carried out high-profile enforcement campaigns by setting up roadblocks to carry out vehicle inspections. They stayed in one place for only fifteen or twenty minutes to minimize security risks to the police (who fear a paramilitary attack if they stay in any location for too long) and to ensure that drivers did not detour around them, because once one driver was caught he would warn other drivers to avoid the roadblock. Furthermore, if stopped, an illegal driver would ask his passengers to pretend that he was merely a friend giving them a lift, in return for a free ride. The high-profile operations were not very effective, in this respondent's view.

The DOE has since resorted to undercover agents posing as ordinary customers. To convict a driver, the DOE needs evidence: either the driver admitting to driving illegally or the passengers providing a statement that they are paying a fare. Before setting up the undercover "sting," the DOE profiles the driver, and if he is thought to be well connected with paramilitary groups and therefore too dangerous, they do not attempt to catch him. Enforcement officers believe that it is not worthwhile to go after such a driver, since, unlike the police, they have no protection.

The sting operation usually begins with a period of surveillance for five or six weeks. Officers order taxis from a particular firm over this period to check whether they are operating illegally and to become familiar with their pickup and drop-off locations. They make wide use of the company's services, taking lots of rides so that they can detect all the illegal cars on one night, and they listen in to the depot's radio communications. They do not reveal themselves as agents yet. Then they set up a sting. The busier the night, the more illegal taxis there are likely to be, so Thursday, Friday, and Saturday nights are the best times for these operations.

To pose convincingly as customers, undercover DOE agents take a number of steps. They go out in groups of two or three, dressed casually and appearing relaxed. If it is early in the evening, they try to appear jolly, as if going out to have a good time and anticipating the night ahead. They often assume other names when talking among themselves and have a prepared story about their jobs and the places they are going to, or have been to, that evening. To hail a taxi they go to venues where there are lots of people (a cinema, for example, or busy pubs and clubs), and they actually enter the venue so that they can be seen coming out of it. They must know that drivers take this as a good sign. If the team decides to use the airport or ferry ports as a pickup point, they emerge at busy times in the flight and ferry schedules in order to make their presence seem credible. All DOE officers are males, and most are in their thirties; the oldest is forty-nine. To deceive drivers further, the teams use different combinations of officers and are accompanied by female administrative staff.

Most of the DOE's operations take place around the City Center; they are much more careful in Republican and Loyalist areas, where depots have well-known customers and strangers stand out. In these areas, unfamiliarity breeds suspicion. The DOE agents were unwilling to talk about their strategies in those areas.

Mimicking good customers has proved to be very effective. In two and a half years of carrying out this policy, the DOE gained over one hundred convictions in Belfast alone. For example, they knew that eleven out of thirteen cars at one company were operating illegally, and they caught nine. The knowledge of this type of operation has also had a deterrent effect on drivers in other cities of Northern Ireland. In Derry applications for taxi licenses increased by 20 percent as drivers chose to become legal. On only one occasion did the DOE mimics arouse the taxi drivers' suspicions to the extent that he charged them no fare. Our DOE interviewee suggested that the driver sensed that something was wrong because the enforcement officer sitting in the passenger seat did not appear natural enough, his language was too formal, and his body language was too stiff.

Although their operations have been successful, the DOE face the problem of relying on a small team of enforcement officers, and there is a real danger of their identities being widely exposed among taxi drivers. It is no longer safe for the officers to socialize in some parts of Belfast, lest they be recognized and attacked by aggrieved drivers.

In view of what some drivers told us, however, the actual rate of failure of the DOE undercover operations may be higher than the department appreciates: drivers who know who the DOE mimics are may simply fail to pick them up, thus pretending to behave lawfully when the potential passenger is a known agent. This decision would not be perceived by the DOE as a failure but as an instance of good behavior.

Car Hijackers

Drivers could confront the perils described thus far in any large city in the world. In this regard, Belfast seems relatively less dangerous than, for example, Bogotá or Johannesburg. However, the dangers specific to Belfast—most of them connected to the city's protracted sectarian conflict—are serious and trouble drivers very much. One such danger is car hijacking. Drivers reported a number of car hijackings perpetrated by joyriders; driver C-WB5, the robber-turned-taxi-driver, told us that he himself had hijacked taxis in order to use the cars in robberies.

The greatest threat of car hijacking, however, comes from paramilitaries on both sides of the political divide. They need cars to carry out their actions, and though of course they can steal cars, they have often chosen to "borrow" them from taxi drivers, often drivers from their own religious side. Seven (16 percent) of our interviewees had had their cars hijacked by paramilitaries, who used a number of methods: directly attacking the taxi, a method that did not require mimicry; telling a driver to go off and have a drink for a few hours, leaving them with his car; and posing as customers before taking the car. Driver C-WB6 told us:

> If you're . . . driving your car and a guy behind you puts a gun to your head, and he says, "Right," and you're saying to yourself, I hope he's going to hijack me here because at least . . . you know you're not going to be killed. And . . . he says, . . . "We're the [Irish] Republican Army and we're taking your car." And you say, "Jesus, it's all right, no problem." They just take your car and away you go. But when they stick a gun to your head and say, keep driving, turn by here, that's when you worry, you know.

Driver P-CC2 thought he was going to pick up a female fare in an estate in West Belfast but instead was greeted by a group of men:

> What happened to me was, I got a job in Ballymurphy. So whenever I went up to the house, there were guys actually round the gable of the house which I didn't see, so I was out of my car [and] couldn't drive away. So the guys came, and they took me. As it turned out, it was the IRA. They took me into a house, and they questioned me, and stuff like that there. They then put the hood on me, and then they decided they were having a bit of fun, so they decided that they were going to shoot me. They asked me, did I want to pray, did I want to say a prayer? or anything like this, and it was all about building up the tension. I said, no, I didn't want to pray, because I was an atheist, so they put the gun in my mouth, and I remember whenever the gun went into my mouth I kept saying to myself, I wonder if this is going to be sore, because I am a coward, and I said to myself, God, I can't go to the dentist, what is this going to be like? So that was all that was going through my head. I wondered, was it going to be sore? Was it going to hurt much? And the guy pulled the trigger, and there was no bullet in it, so to be honest I wet myself. They all laughed, and they kept me for about three hours, sitting with a hood on my head up the stairs. Then they came and said, "Go ahead and report your car to the police that it was stolen." And whenever I went round to report my car to the police, I told them that they had taken my car, and they said it had been driven [with a bomb] straight to the Europa Hotel. That was quite a few years ago.

Often the hijackers want a car belonging to a taxi driver who has had no involvement with paramilitarism on either side. This choice is made partly to avoid direct retaliation and partly to ensure that the car does not arouse the suspicions of the security forces. Several of the drivers have had frightening experiences at the hands of hijackers:

> I have a friend who got held up at Easter. Now, as it turned out, they only wanted his car, but they wanted him to walk into an alleyway. He said, "No, I am not doing it." They said, "Look, it's like this. We don't want you,

we want your car, but we need a couple of hours here, and you are not going to step in the way. You are a liability," was the exact terms they used on him. He says, "Look, you can deal with me whatever way you want to—take the car, take the money—but I am not going up that entry." So they tied him up, and they struggled with him, and he said, "Look, mate, I will walk away. I will not contact the police for three hours if you want, but I am not going up that entry." They had a gun out, pointing it in his face—"We are going to do you," et cetera, "If you don't do what you are told"—so they tied him up, but not very well, and eventually he broke himself loose. But he won't work at night at all now. (driver P-CC2)

The mimics may call from what drivers regard as a safe location and mention another safe place as a destination: "They knew by saying the International Airport was the destination that what they were doing was immediately putting everybody off their guard, including our radio operators, [and] the job was from the City Hall, which was a respectable place. And then on the way up they say, 'Turn in here just for a minute' " (driver P-CC2).

When driver P-CC2 realized that his passengers wanted him to go via the Shankill—a Loyalist area—he drove faster in order to prevent an attack on the car ("they would wreck us all") and then stopped a police car to get help to remove the passengers. Although the passengers did not actually threaten him, lying about their destination was enough evidence for this driver to feel very vulnerable:

It happened to a friend of mine who was sent to a place called Dermot Hill [in Catholic West Belfast]. The house had doorways, and the old trick in those days was, see a derelict house, ring from a phone box, run over and stand in the hallway, and when the taxi pulls up you walk out of the hallway so the driver does not suspect anything. So he got them, and they were going down to the hospital, and he looked in the mirror and one of them was pulling a hood on, and he thought, well, this isn't good, but the guy had seen him seeing him, so he grabbed the driver by the hair and pulled his head back, and the driver said to him, "Look, I am not going to do anything here, just let go of my hair, I can't see." The guy said, "We are from this organization, we are going to take the car when we get down here, and we want you to stand at the corner. There will be somebody watching you." What they used to do was take the driver's taxi license or his driver's license. "We have identification of where you live, so if you do anything, like tell the police, we will come to your house."

When they got down, the guy told him to get out of the car, and he asked, could he take his money, and he said, "Yeah, we are going to use the car, we don't want your money." So he got out of the car, and the guy said, "Stand at that corner," and he said his brain was telling his legs not to move, and his legs took off—he just lost total control of himself, started running. They got into his car and chased him and told him if he moved another time they would shoot him. So they let him go again, and he ran again. He said everything sensible was saying to stand still until they got out of sight, [but] he couldn't do it.

Driver C-PH3, a Catholic, suffered a form of car hijacking combined with a special kind of mimicry at the hands of a Republican paramilitary group:

> I was sitting outside the depot, and this boy came round and he jumped in, and the next minute he announces what organization he is from. He said, "You are ordered to take your car around the corner, and if you don't you will be dealt with." Because living where you live you have to—it is not a case of saying, right, get out—and then you go home to your house. . . . I drove around the corner, and my boot [trunk] was opened, and something was put in the back, and they said, "Drive that down to———," and lucky enough it wasn't a real [bomb] but it was just to disrupt the traffic, because when I drove it down [I had to tell the police,] "There is something in the boot." So for the next couple of hours the whole place was in chaos. But it could have been a real one for all I knew.

The paramilitaries in this case did not pretend they were genuine passengers; they only pretended to be putting a real bomb in driver C-PH3's car trunk.

Sectarian Attackers

Approximately one-third of the drivers had suffered some form of violent attack, almost half of which were sectarian in nature. Sectarian attacks on drivers have primarily been Loyalist paramilitary attacks on Catholic drivers (four of the Catholic drivers had suffered a serious sectarian attack), and Catholic drivers are universally worried about this kind of attack, as our interviewees made clear. But Protestant drivers, two of whom had been attacked for sectarian reasons, are also "paranoid," as driver P-CC4 illustrated:

> Well, I'm a Protestant, you know, and I wouldn't have gone into the Catholic areas around Belfast, like Poleglass and Lenadoon and all those places, for the simple fact that if you didn't know where they were, people would automatically assume, "Oh, you kick with the right foot."[1] You know, I've had a few experiences where people have said, "Oh, you're a Protestant then," just because I didn't know where it was or where they lived. It gives you an eerie feeling then, so I just didn't like it.

It was not that he felt directly threatened so much as "intimidated." He imagined that "because they knew what I was . . . maybe they'll take me up some back road and pull me out of the car, or whatever."

Sectarian attackers overwhelmingly target men. Being a woman seems to protect from these kinds of attacks. The female driver P-EBF1 said:

> The sectarian side of things for me never really felt like an issue, other than I suppose sometimes I was never really sure where I was going. Say, for example, I pick people up in the likes of Twinbrook or Poleglass. I didn't have any knowledge of that area at all, and people would have asked where I came from. I come from East Belfast, and automatically people would assume that you were a Protestant and I am so. Twinbrook and Poleglass are predominantly Nationalist, but I was usually very honest about it. I never ever said that the people were annoyed with that or took it as an issue, but again, maybe that was because of my gender.

Runners are commonly teenagers, but attackers, according to drivers, are more likely to be older—age twenty-five to forty-five: "The ones who are sixteen, seventeen, I know what they are up to, and I can handle them," said driver C-PH3. "The ones who are thirty or forty, I would be a bit more cautious. . . . I think the ones that are more mature—if something is going to happen, they will follow it through."

Ordinary Catholic drivers who are not involved with IRA activities have been targeted, according to driver C-WB4:

> How many people has it happened to who have [been involved in paramilitary activity]? You tell me—so when was the last IRA taxi man to be shot dead? Never. [It's always somebody] who's not involved. You know, if you're in the IRA or you're connected to anything that you would call dodgy in any shape or form, well, if you're shot you knew the risks. People might not like you being shot, but you [knew] [*shrugs shoulders*]. Whereas if it's a Joe Bloggs that gets shot, [people are more sympathetic].

As we reported in chapter 1, the seriousness of the exposure to this type of danger was starkly brought home when driver C-WB4's name was found on a Loyalist paramilitary death squad hit list. Furthermore, in 1999 one of our interviewees had been shot in the chest by Loyalist paramilitaries who had lain in wait for him when he went to pick up a regular fare.

In the sectarian attacks we considered, the attacker typically used mimicry in order to pass off as an ordinary, "safe" Catholic customer. Such mimics often do a lot of preparation, observing depots and drivers. Driver C-NB1 said:

> They were sussing it out, seeing how easy it is to get a taxi from the depot, how easy it is to get dropped off in an area that would be safe for them. Just sussing out the lay of the depot, and that particular depot that I was in on the Antrim Road was where basically sectarian murderers would

come over, get taxis from the depot to see if they could. [It was like] a dummy run and then [they] went on and shot drivers, tried to blow them up. I got followed right into a garage on a Sunday afternoon by a car with three well-known sectarian murderers from North Belfast. They brazed into the garage, they were checking me out, they were sussing me out. I'd no doubt that my life was in danger, and I changed my routine after that.

In nine of the forty-nine cases of sectarian attack on drivers that we reviewed from newspaper reports and the interview data, Loyalists had passed themselves off over the phone as known regular customers when they called a Catholic firm, then ambushed the driver.

A guy in our depot was seriously injured. He was shot in the chest a couple of times with a rifle, so it was an attempted murder—it wasn't just to wound this guy, they were definitely out to kill him. . . . We got a phone call to do a regular job, except it wasn't a regular job at all. . . . The job was from Belfast Castle to wherever, but that meant you were driving up through the grounds of Belfast Castle, which is very quiet, and they were lying in the bushes waiting for the first car from our depot to come up the lane. (driver C-NB1)

In four other cases, the paramilitaries took the grave risk of going to a Catholic area to hail or call a cab or even walk into a Catholic depot. For example, one of our interviewees "picked up two guys who walked into the depot in broad daylight. They were wearing jeans and leather jackets and just wanted to go to a pub a couple of minutes down the road" (driver C-WB8). The driver very quickly realized that he was in trouble when one of the passengers moved across to sit behind the driver's seat. He stopped the car and ran away.

The cost of treading on enemy turf is very high for paramilitaries. Many are known by face—through a shared prison experience, for instance—and if caught they would be dealt with severely. For example, ex-paramilitaries involved in cross-community reconciliation programs need permission from the IRA to enter West Belfast, and their movements within the area are restricted. For them, being there is not just like being anywhere else.

In at least three cases, attackers used a "honey trap": a woman either called a cab or was present in the group that hailed the cab. "Girls can set you up just as quick as a fella," noted driver C-WB4. When taxi driver John McColgan was murdered in January 1998, the Loyalists had mimicked three "safe" signs at once. Two men and a *woman* boldly hailed a taxi about *one hundred yards from Sinn Féin headquarters* in the heart of Catholic West Belfast, and they gave their destination as *a Gaelic football club*. Giving a West Belfast club as their destination implicitly conveyed knowledge that made them appear local and ensured that they did not arouse suspicions, as they might have done had the location of their stated destination been Protestant. This had been the case in other attacks in which drivers were lured out of their local areas. The mimics also concealed any Loyalist giveaway signs (such as tattoos), did not attempt to hide their faces with hoods or baseball caps, and dressed casually. They were also lucky in that the taxi they initially hailed was already busy, and when the driver called the depot to send out another car for them, McColgan was thus indirectly reassured of their legitimacy.

As we can see, drivers are vulnerable to skilled and committed mimics who are prepared to pay the cost and take the risk of emitting trust-warranting fraudulent signals. If Loyalist paramilitaries on an assassination mission in a Catholic area were to be caught, there is a high probability that they would be killed by Republican paramilitaries. What therefore do drivers do to protect themselves from this diverse fauna of predatory mimics? This is what we consider in the following chapters.

Chapter 3

Precautions in Belfast

A S WE illustrate in this chapter and the next, drivers screen their prospective customers through the signs that the customers emit. They do not, however, treat their "pick up or do not pick up" dilemma merely as a trust game. They also take many precautions to reduce the risk of bad encounters, employ a variety of deterrents, and resort to remedial actions in case they let in the wrong passengers. The actions they take depend, among other things, on which peril they are trying to avoid. Let us commence with the most fearsome one, namely, sectarian attacks.

Masking Religious Affiliation

Almost all taxi firms in Belfast are segregated along religious lines. Typically, a taxi firm situated in a Catholic area employs only Catholic drivers and operates only, or mostly, within that particular area, rarely servicing its Protestant neighbors. Protestant firms are the mirror image: they are equally reluctant to work in Catholic areas. For example, a Protestant firm in East Belfast situated across the road from a Catholic area, with the exception of one regular fare, has no Catholic customers. The only firms that employ drivers from both religions and agree to go into any area in Belfast are four large City Center firms.

It is hard to persuade a Catholic firm to take a fare to a Protestant area, as we found out when we tried to do it (see chapter 4), or a Protestant firm to take a fare into a Catholic area. Customer P-CF1 told us: "Taxis from the east won't go west. The furthest they'll go is into town and that's it. . . . If I'm going to travel with my local taxi company, they'll take me out of my area . . . but they won't take me back." Customers who want to be ferried between hostile areas have to rely on the large City Center firms. Most customers respect the drivers' reluctance to take fares into unsafe territory, though occasionally, driver P-CC12 noted, "you get an awful lot of sectarian abuse because you don't lift them. Doesn't matter if you are there for somebody or not—people come over and say, 'Take us to the Short Strand,' and you say, 'Can't, I'm booked,' and they say, 'You must be a Protestant because you are not taking us,' and you get the same from Shankill Road: [if you] can't take [the fare], some people [will say], 'You must be a Catholic. Are you?' "

Sectarian attacks, unlike other perils, are not aimed at all drivers indiscriminately. Catholic drivers have been the main targets, especially those working for identifiably Catholic firms. Since the probability of being the victim of an attack depends on being identified as a Catholic, a widespread precaution consists in camouflaging religious affiliation, making it harder for would-be attackers to identify a driver as Catholic.[1]

Driver P-PH5—as well as most of the other six public-hire drivers we interviewed—believed that he was safer driving a black public-hire taxi, not just because these taxis have partitions, but also because the cars are identical and carry no marks that would identify the driver's religious background. "All through the Troubles, the black taxis weren't too bad, it was more the private-hire. The reason being that if you rang a taxi depot on the Shankill Road, you were going to get a Protestant, and on the other side you were going to get a Catholic, whereas if you get a black taxi, you don't know what you're getting." These taxis have been targeted less often by sectarian assassins than private-hire taxis.

All of the private-hire drivers we interviewed who work for the big City Center firms prefer these firms because these are the only firms with no religious association. By looking at the taxi insignia, paramilitaries are unable to infer the driver's religion. This applies to Protestant drivers as well, because even though the IRA has never attacked them, they still worry about the possibility. Asked whether he would rather work for a large City Center company or a smaller one, driver P-CC4 replied: "A big one, because nobody knows what religion you are generally. . . . If you work for a . . . firm up the Shankill or a firm on the Falls, well, people know what you are, so you're running a bigger risk than when you go into a different area. Then they know who you are and what you are." "That is why I work in a mixed depot," said driver P-CC7.

> The way I see it, I could go to a Protestant depot on the Castlereagh Road, but if I was there to shoot a Protestant, I know I could hit any one of them, and I would know I was definitely getting a Protestant. If I wanted a Catholic, I could go to a depot where I know they are all Catholics. But to go to a big mixed depot, he [an attacker] would have to be selective; he would have to know who he was going after.

Driver P-CC7 also pointed out that even if he were followed home, a sectarian attacker would still be unable to infer his religion, for "my area doesn't tell them anything either because where I live I am one sort, my next-door neighbor is another, so they have to be selective. So I like to stay in the mixed depots." Driver P-CC8, also Protestant, would give a false address or wait until he had more information about the passenger: "If they ask me where I live, I tell them I live outside Belfast—end of story. . . . Unless someone that lives near me who would know me, and they would say, 'Do you live round the corner?' then I would say yes, because they are letting me know where they live, so I have something to go back on if anything ever happened."

Working for a mixed depot, however, may make a driver more likely to experience another peril: car hijacking. Driver P-CC2 revealed that in 1973 the IRA had hijacked his car to use in bombing a hotel precisely because they knew his company was *not* associated with any paramilitary organization and would not therefore arouse suspicion or invite reprisals (see chapter 2).

Those who work for religiously associated firms still mask cues of their religious affiliation by displaying a sign that says only TAXI without the name or telephone number of the company. Driver C-WB6 described how a taxi displaying the name of a "Catholic" taxi firm "drove through Lisburn [a Protestant area], and he got battered the whole way . . . with bricks and stones. . . . These men, they know all the Catholic depots, and they know all the names of them." Driver C-NB1 agreed that having the depot's name on the sign basically says: "I'm a driver, I'm a Catholic from the Antrim Road," and even displaying the telephone number is a giveaway because "it's easy enough to check up on this sort of thing." Drivers even go so far as to take the TAXI sign off altogether when driving through potentially hostile areas, as driver P-EB7, a Protestant, does when he traverses a Catholic area.[2]

This masking of TAXI signs intensifies in July, the month of the Loyalist marches, when the tension between the two communities increases.[3] Driver P-EB8, a Protestant, removes his sign because he fears he will get caught in the cross-fire as young people throw stones at each other across a peaceline:

> Nearly every night of the week kids are . . . throwing stones back and for-wards, you know. And the wee fellas on this side of the road were throw-ing stones back and forth. Anybody like yourself just driving past there could get a stone through the windscreen, you know what I mean. So with a sign on, that makes you more of a target too to them wee fellas, because they know you're from over this neck of the woods.

Driver P-EB8 made an interesting suggestion as he pointed out the camouflaging value of donning standardized and generic identifying insignia:

One way they could improve [safety] would be for every taxi to go to every area. I mean, if all taxi companies had only a TAXI sign rather than having [the depot names], if everybody came with one sign, nobody would know what taxi drivers were from what area, [whereas now,] if a taxi depot from East Belfast sent a car over to the Falls Road, people on the Falls Road would know he's a Protestant.

He himself realized, however, that this solution would meet with a constraint: "That wouldn't work because company————[a City Center firm] has a good reputation, a lot of cars, a lot of drivers, and they want [that reputation to be identifiable through the sign]."

Drivers also avoid displaying other signs that might identify them as belonging to one religion or the other. Revealing a lack of topographical local knowledge, for instance, makes one stand out as someone from the other side:

If it's dark, you need to be wary, especially if you're stopping to ask somebody for directions. . . . If you go up in around Poleglass, Lenadoon, the Shankill, places like that . . . [where] groups of people [are] . . . standing on the corners, you don't want to stop and say to them, "Where's such and such?" because they'd automatically say, "He's of the other kind [religion]," and the next minute you're getting bricked. (driver P-CC4)

Once inside the car, customers may observe other properties that reveal a driver's religion. Most drivers therefore keep their group-specific tattoos covered, modify how they pronounce the letter h (Catholics pronounce it haitch, while Protestants say aitch), and deflect questions about politics and football, for Catholics support Glasgow Celtic and Protestants support Glasgow Rangers. "Sometimes . . . they would say, 'What Scottish teams do you support?' and that's a giveaway right away once you say 'Celtic' or 'Rangers,' they know what you are right away. . . . I'd say, 'I don't follow football,' and then try and change the subject." (driver P-CC4).

There is two rules in taxiing: you don't talk about religion; you don't talk about football. That is it. You see, the deal is, if I go and pick someone up in Andersonstown, the minute they get into my car they feel at ease that I kick with the same foot as them. If I then drop him off and go to the Shankill, they will think the same. I have had people get in and start talking about "Rangers gave Celtic a hiding. Didn't we do well?" I would just go, "Great match"—end of story—then drive up and pick someone else up [who would say]: "What about them Rangers ones? We will get them next time." [I'd say], "You're right, mate," so they don't know [my religion]. (driver P-CC7)

There are names, especially first names, that are almost exclusively Catholic (Seamus, Eugene) or Protestant (William, Trevor). So some drivers give false names that are religiously neutral, such as Gary or Jim, or, like driver C-CC11, they hide their driver's card, which displays their name.

Still, as in the case of the same driver C-CC11, habit and affection for objects that manifest religious affiliation supersede the removal of religiously connoted signs. "I wear a cross in my ear, so a lot of people would identify with me right away as a Catholic. I have always worn it, so I have never really thought about taking it out. People said I am not wise, I should take it out, but I don't know."

Although 91 percent of the drivers masked signs of their religious affiliation, doing so does not work well for the drivers who are more at risk of a sectarian attack. Those heavily involved with their respective paramilitary groups would still be at risk, even under the disguise of mixed-depot insignia, for they would be personally known and targeted by the paramilitaries of the other side. They thus prefer to work for local firms within segregated environments to decrease the chances of bad encounters. By so doing, they avoid dangerous exposure, since they can count on having mostly familiar local customers. It would be too difficult for them to rely just on screening: "Now, if it's just a normal Joe Bloggs Protestant, and they're going to the hospital or going to the railway station, and you knew they were just genuine, you'd go and lift them. But how do you know he's genuine, how do you know? How do you tell?" (driver C-WB4). Driver C-NB1, an ex-Republican militant, told us: "The beauty about taxiing in a local depot like the one I was in is after a while you get to know your clients. You're living and you're working in that area, you just get to know who's from that area, who's not, who's local, who's not. You can spot the way people are being, whether they're trouble or not."

Driver C-WB4, a Republican ex-prisoner, works for a small West Belfast company: "I could work for better mixed depots that have a lot of Catholics working for them, but I wouldn't be safe, it's not as safe. It's not just from the ordinary punter you pick off the street. I would be worried about Loyalists." If he worked for a big company, he would be more exposed, for he would have to drive to Protestant areas or pick up less filtered customers. "Well, as I said to you, a terrible lot of taxi drivers are either ex-Republicans or ex-prisoners, and really I couldn't work in the center of town—I'm an ex-prisoner." (Interestingly, driver C-WB4 feels sufficiently relaxed to keep some giveaway signs: "I have Our Lady and Saint Patrick sitting on my dashboard, and at the end of the day, if they get in and see it, it's declaring what I am.")

Driver C-WB2, who worked in the building trade before he began driving a taxi, feared being recognized by his former workmates: "That's one reason why I wouldn't work down in one of the big City Center firms or anywhere like that, because you do go into different areas. I just couldn't take that, you know. I worked for a whole lot of different guys, and they all know you, and it would only take one of them to spot you . . . you just couldn't afford it. Too risky."

To reduce the risk of detection drivers who work for smaller local firms avoid not just areas populated by members of the other religion but also areas that are so mixed as to make it very hard to know quickly enough who is whom:

> North Belfast, where I'm originally from, now I wouldn't work in North Belfast; I wouldn't taxi in North Belfast for love nor money because it's too dodgy. Because one street, at the top end of it, would be Catholic, while if you go to the bottom end of it, it's Protestant. If you go to Halliday's Road, one side of Halliday's Road is in the New Lodge [Catholic]; the other side of Halliday's Road is in Tiger's Bay [Protestant]. Lepper Street's the same, Hillman Street's the same. So if somebody rings you up, you'd better be sure, you gotta be sure of the Catholic you're looking for. The Antrim Road, there's as many Protestants live on it. I'm not saying that they're all bad, but you gotta remember, you gotta always think [about] these things. (driver C-WB4)

The areas to avoid can be quite finely selected and come down to specific locations that have religious associations. Even hospitals are not immune:

> The City Hospital—if we bring you over, we'll collect you, but if we don't bring you over, we'll not collect you. The Royal [Victoria Hospital]—we'd go for you whether we brought you down or not, because the Royal would be sort of Catholic. You know, I'm not saying it's all Catholic, don't get me wrong, we would collect from the Royal, but the Mater [Hospital] would be a different sort. The Mater would be—we would have to bring you down plus you would have to give us the time you were coming out again, and the driver will not wait for you, he'll go straight away. (driver C-WB4)[4]

Dispatcher C-WBDF1 had worked for a Catholic firm for several years and confirmed this practice: "There was times when you'd be asked to do a lot of pickups from the Mater Hospital or the City Hospital—you know, dodgy ones. I never would have sent a driver over."

When drivers do occasionally choose to drive through areas that are unsafe for them, those who think of themselves as more exposed to sectarian attacks try at least to avoid regular patterns in their movements so as to make a potential ambush harder to execute. Driver C-WB4 told us how an elderly Catholic man uses his depot to take him from West Belfast to an estate notorious for spawning Loyalist paramilitaries:

> But if he was to come in every day at five o'clock to be brought over here [Taughmonagh Estate], we wouldn't bring him, because then it's a pattern.

But if he was to come in once a week or twice a week and he came in one day at five o'clock and the next day at a quarter to six, we might do it for him—maybe. But see, if it was every Tuesday and Thursday at a quarter to six, or even every Tuesday and Thursday between five and a quarter to six, we wouldn't do the job.

Driver C-WB6 was especially vigilant when he finished work at night:

If I finished at two in the morning, I would drive up the street and . . . I looked at every corner of the street to see if there was anybody that I didn't know, or if there was a car there I didn't know. And then, in case there was somebody I didn't see, I would go round two streets away and park my car and cut through entries and go in the back way to the house, because you couldn't really get out of your car and walk in [the front door]. You don't know who's watching what time you're coming in every day, you know. . . . I would always finish the same time, about half two, quarter to three [in the morning], and if . . . anybody was watching, [they would] see me going into the house at that same time every night.

There are also situations rather than areas in which the mixing of a large crowd makes taxiing more hazardous: At "the big [Gaelic football] matches at Casement, you have to be careful what you're lifting. Because when you get that type of crowd in West Belfast, twenty-eight, twenty-nine, thirty thousand people, they can come from anywhere, you know what I mean." (driver C-WB4)

Taking General Precautions

Drivers take several other precautions designed to decrease the chances of bad encounters of all types, not just with paramilitaries. Some drivers choose to work only from safe locations, such as driver P-PH5, who stopped working in the City Center and now operates only from the airport: "I'm too old for the boxing," he said.

Some drivers prefer to work days only, others nights, and some like to vary their shifts. The "day men" prefer to treat taxiing as more of a nine-to-five job with regular hours and time off to spend with their families and friends: "I wouldn't do nights anyway, they're just too anti-social. I want my nights to myself. I'll come in early in the morning and work through to whatever, four, five, or six in the afternoon, and then go home" (driver C-CC1). Day men like driver C-CC1 also believe it is safer to work during the day: "I know guys that have had cars stolen, guys who've had their cars hijacked, guys who have been assaulted, but all these things happen at night." Driver P-EBF1, who never works late at night, said: "Things are different at eight or nine o'clock at night than they are at one or two o'clock in the morning."

Sixteen percent of the drivers we interviewed work exclusively during the day. The rest work either nights (25 percent) or days and weekend nights (59 percent). The choice of working at night is driven by financial considerations rather than safety: "More money—that is the bottom line. There is more money at it. I was on nights, and then I came off them, and then I went back on them because basically [nights involve] less hours and more money. All right, they are more unsociable hours, but it doesn't matter, it suits me" (driver P-EB7).

"Night men" are also more impatient, citing the traffic as the most annoying daytime factor: "I don't like working days because of the traffic, so I would usually come in to work about seven o'clock" (driver C-WB4).

Driver P-CC2 denied that nights are necessarily worse. "Belfast is a great party city . . . and usually you will find at nights that people are in a happy party mood." During the day, however, he has found that "businesspeople are actually more tensed up and more aggressive . . . [because] they are under so much pressure from work. Everybody has targets to reach. People are afraid that other people are trying to get their jobs and stuff."

Other drivers said they never pick up off the street but only through the dispatcher. When asked whether he would pick up passengers off the street, driver C-CCF3 claimed:

> No, never. I would never do that. A lot of the guys in the depot, they would switch the computer off—we call it "p-u," because they think they can pick and choose their work. At the same time, you don't know who they are picking up, especially for a girl, so I wouldn't do that at all. . . . No way. Do you see, on a Saturday night you are offered all sorts of money to go to all sorts of places, but at the end of the day, you don't know who you are lifting.

Still, drivers do not apply this rule blindly but rather keep a flexible mind and pick up from the street if other signs are favorable. In this respect, drivers' precautions are conditional and taken in response to their screening of signs, which we describe in chapter 4. Drivers also take certain precautions to facilitate screening: "Generally on a Friday or Saturday night, if I'm not busy and I'm picking up off the streets . . . there's maybe three or four thousand people running about. I would normally put the lock down, and that means nobody can open [the door] from the outside, and then I just find out where they want to go by putting the window down and then let them in" (driver P-CC4). Some precautions are taken in response to unfavorable signs. For instance, when drivers stop at a passenger's house, they often sound the car-horn rather than get out of the car to ring the doorbell:

> Our guidelines say that we have to get out and knock on doors and ring bells, but you're not going to get out of the car in the middle of a dodgy

estate at four o'clock in the morning to go and ring a bell, 'cause you could look round and there'd be four boys getting into your car and driving off. Anyway, they'll hear the car coming. If they're looking out for a taxi, they'll know. If you see a house that looks pretty vacant, you're not going to get out and go ringing the bell. (driver C-CC1)

Well, we do Rathcoole, but I wouldn't worry about Rathcoole because that's the same religion [Protestant] as myself. [But] I wouldn't get out of the car in Poleglass [Catholic]. I would beep the horn, and if they don't come out . . . [*shrugs shoulders and laughs*]. Or else I'd radio through to the dispatch and they'd phone the house. (driver P-CC4)

This action (or inaction) has a double effect. It makes it more difficult for the would-be attacker to act, and easier for the driver to escape if he detects other signs of trouble.

Deterring Attacks

Drivers use deterrents that make a potential attack harder to accomplish. For example, "the majority of people would put their headrest up high so they can't get any weapons in over the top, but they can always come round" (driver P-CC7).

Another way of deterring assailants is to inform them that there may be a heavy cost for them to pay if they choose to proceed. Some drivers just do not look like the type who would take an attack lying down: "I suppose, with me, I would give out an aura of 'don't mess with me.' I don't feel as if I come across as someone who is weak and vulnerable, for someone to mess about. I don't know, it just didn't happen" (driver P-EBF1). Some drivers (36 percent) cultivate that fierce look and display it when needed. Many of driver P-CC12's colleagues are "total gentlemen, but they . . . sculpture themselves into looking rough." At nights, driver P-CC12 raises his car seat so as to look bigger and more intimidating to passengers than he actually is.

When fearing a runner, driver P-CC7 resorts to veiled threats:

[A passenger] started into me about "has anyone ever done a runner on you?" So I said, "Don't be so stupid. How could they do a runner? What you don't realize is that I have an address where I picked you up, and . . . I just go back to your house and put petrol through your letter box and just smoke your house." And he immediately turned to the guys in the back and said, "Four pounds each." So I find if someone gets in with a tough attitude, then I will put on an attitude. I will blend myself into where they are coming from, and then we do have a level of understanding.

Driver P-CC7 has a vicarious way to convey a "don't mess with me" message:

If I was to get a job up the Shankill [a Protestant area], I would automatically start a conversation about big Davy from the Shankill. So I am letting them [the passengers] know that I know him, so if you want to run, you go ahead, but I will go and see him. By the same way, if it is Poleglass [a Catholic area], I talk about big Micky. So I bluff my way through my work. They [passengers] don't know me, and I don't know them. Most people associate taxi drivers with paramilitaries—it is the standard thing—so they don't know whose car they are getting into. All they know is that this guy taxis, he works in Belfast, who is he? The only way I work it is I bluff.

Drivers take other minor steps to quell or prevent bad behavior in their car: they turn up the heating to make drunk and potentially aggressive passengers feel drowsy, and they adjust the music in the car—more upbeat at the start of the evening, slower and more relaxing at the end of the evening.

Taking Remedial Actions

Some of the drivers' precautions are designed not to reduce the chances of bad encounters or deter would-be attackers, but to limit the damage in case of an attack. For instance, 9 percent of drivers drop off their cash during their shift to prevent a substantial loss by robbery. "Yes, if I do a split [shift], I go home and leave whatever money I have, because the rest is only like a bag of change, and I just take it out with me" (driver C-CCF3). Or they hide the cash in the car: "I normally split it in two. I would always keep a float of twenty pounds in my pocket. Whatever else I have made, I put in a tub in the car" (driver P-CC7).

They also take measures to give themselves more opportunities to respond to a bad encounter. For instance, drivers do not wear a seat belt in order to be freer to run away. Driver C-CC1 was the only exception: "If I see somebody dodgy getting in, I might just take it off." Some cars are equipped with panic buttons: "There's a little button . . . everything's got a code, and there's function buttons 1 to 9, so you hit a button and a code for wherever you are, so F2 99 F5 is your panic button, and that goes straight through to the depot, and they'll put it straight through to the police" (driver C-CC1).

Other precautions we recorded include keeping the car in first gear all the time while stopped and, if picking up a fare in a cul-de-sac, always turning the car around so that it faces the exit before coming to a stop. Driver C-WB8 mentioned that if he is uncertain about the fare, "other drivers will say [to you], 'You take them and I'll follow, and if anything happens, I'll ram the back of the car.' "

With not-too-fearsome attackers, black taxi drivers use a simple mechanical bluff to get rid of undesirable passengers. By turning the ignition key a certain way, they can get the car to sound like it has broken down. Driver P-PH5 told us: "If you drove up and you didn't like the look of them and they got in before you could stop them, you would pull the thing and it would go *chug-chug* and stop. You'd say, 'Ahh, I've broke down. Will you get out and give me a push?' And they got out of your taxi, and once they were off side, you could drive off."

Modern black taxis have a central locking system such that, "whenever the driver's foot is on the brake, all the doors remain locked, so you can't get out and do a runner without paying" (driver C-CC1). Driver P-PH5 explained:

> They're usually good at it . . . they've done it before. They know where to stand, and they know where the traffic lights are. Now, I haven't had one since I've been working at the airport, but prior to that, with the older-type taxis, there was no locking system. You see, in the car I'm driving now, while I'm traveling the door's locked. If I'm stopped and I put my foot on the brake, the door's locked. But in the older taxis you stopped at a red light, and the next minute they're out the door. What we did years ago was, [in] the left-hand doors we drilled a hole right through the door post, and . . . put in a six-inch nail, so they had to get out your side, and you had a chance. But even then, they were as quick as lightning.

According to driver C-WB4:

> Most taxi drivers carry a weapon. Most taxi drivers will carry a snooker cue, and they'll cut it down, and there's a weight usually in the bottom of a snooker cue, and they'll carry that. Or you will get some of them who will actually carry a knife [as he does], and what they'll do if they get stopped [by the police], you see the wee tags on your wheel, they'll say, that's to cut them off if they get a puncture, but they're not. . . . Some taxi drivers carry wheel braces or the likes of the big locks—you'll see them lying there, by their feet.

Weapons of this kind are not displayed openly, but 36 percent of our interviewees carried some form of weapon, and we recorded several instances of drivers using their weapons. Driver C-WB6 was hit on the back of the head while driving three male customers one night. In retaliation, he "pulled out a hurley bat, opened the back door, and said, 'If you don't get out, I'm going to cut your head clean off, you hear.' "

Driver P-CC7 decided to no longer carry a weapon, believing he might inflame the situation:

> I used to have a wee stick that I called Aggie—I had it slipped up the side of my seat—but I started to realize then that it could endanger me more having a weapon. Because I could be one of these brave soldiers that think if I could just reach round and grab this, but it intimidates the guy who rocked you because the minute he sees it, he wants to do damage. So I try

to put all thoughts of defending myself to a certain degree out of my head, because a guy sat and told me once, to lose your eye, your arm, your leg, or be put in a wheelchair—is it going to be worth whatever you have in the car? You know, for the satisfaction of knowing that you had actually tried to tackle the guy for doing it? So I suppose, looking at it sensibly, you are safer handing over what you have got. It depends on who the person is. If they are on their own, if you think that you stand more than a 50 percent chance.

Even if a driver is not displaying a weapon, customers may suspect that he is carrying something and may be more cautious as a result.

In some cases, drivers respond to a threatening situation by driving to a police station or to a club with doormen. "The most aggressive customer that I ever had was talking about sticking a gun in the back of people's heads and shooting them and trying to intimidate me, and I just bounced up a curb outside the police barracks and grabbed him, and he had no choice but to comply, as we were sitting outside a cop-shop" (driver C-NB1).

Another tactic is showing greater determination than the assailant does. If threatened, driver C-WB5 might speed up, because "they're not going to shoot me if I'm doing one hundred miles per hour, are they?" He would "match their aggression with more aggression. I'd have said, 'I'll put your head through that fucking windscreen and do your pockets, wanker.' " Given driver C-WB5's past as a robber, his threats did not sound exaggerated: "I was really mad, I would have done it. Then I had totally no concept of right and wrong, I would just do it."

Driver C-WB4, however, felt that less experienced drivers would not react quickly or decisively enough: "You hear all sorts of taxi drivers saying, 'Ahh, if they do it to me, I'll drive into the wall.' Nobody knows what could happen or what they'd do. Especially a fella who's never been nothing, or involved in anything that's been related to the Loyalists." Driver C-WB6 agreed: "A lot of young fellas now, that [were] maybe electricians, plumbers, brickies . . . when things aren't going well, they all start taxiing. These guys don't have a clue."

All of the drivers interviewed agreed that it is better to avoid violent situations than to have to respond once they are in danger. By taking a range of precautions, they hope to make themselves less vulnerable to the hazards of taxiing, including the threat from determined mimics. As we shall see in the next two chapters, their precautions work in tandem with their strategies for passenger selection.

Chapter 4

Screening in Belfast

OUR EXPECTATION is that when deciding whether to trust a prospective fare, drivers pay a great deal of attention to the cues and signs displayed intentionally or otherwise by that person. Above all, we expect that they look for reliable signs in that person of being either a good or a bad customer, namely, signs that are too costly for a mimic to fake but affordable for the genuine article, given the benefit that each party can expect in the situation. Drivers are not, in other words, either erratic in the signs they watch for or easily satisfied by cheaply mimickable ones.

Drivers' Dispositions to Trust

When we examine some of the drivers' statements, that expectation may seem not to be confirmed. Most drivers appreciate very well how difficult it is to tell a good customer from a bad one. If the bad one is skilled and bent on fooling a driver, they believe that there is little a driver can do. And many drivers, having taken their more or less stringent precautions, simply take anyone on board: "You cannot tell. You could have people getting in, and they're all nice, and before they get home they're fighting each other" (driver P-PH5). Most drivers seem to have a generally trusting attitude and take the matter fatalistically, not treating their decision to trust a customer as a choice situation:

> I would think that there was part of me that was on sort of a blind trust. I trusted them until I had some evidence not to trust, rather than being really suspicious, for I don't think that I could have done the job if I had felt like that, because there were occasions where people would have been loud and brash but nothing ever happened. I think that sometimes a lot would depend on how I felt. I suppose, for me, when you are thinking about this: people you would have picked up and not picked up, that feels like *there would have been a choice in it, and it didn't really feel like that.* It felt

that this was your job from the depot, and it was up to you to pick them up unless you had a pretty good reason you were obliged to do that. So I suppose, *it never really felt like a choice for me,* unless I had some sort of reason to say they weren't there, or they were being abusive or something. . . . If [drivers] are going out and they are constantly feeling stressed and worried, I don't think that they should be [taxiing]. I don't think they would have the right sort of temperament to be doing it, and [they should] give themselves a break and look for something else. If you are living your life that way, it is not the job for you. (driver P-EBF1, emphasis added)

Driver P-CC2, like most other drivers, concurred with driver P-EBF1's view in saying that some a priori trust is indispensable:

[I am] definitely the one that trusts. I mean, the nature of the job is that you have got to trust. If somebody doesn't trust, they must be living a living hell, because they must be dreading every job that they are going to lift. I couldn't do the job that way, I would find it impossible. I wouldn't do the job a week, because that to me doesn't sound like a man that doesn't trust. It says to me that a man . . . is very insecure [and] doesn't feel comfortable with the job and . . . is going to every job saying, I wonder should I lift that job? I wonder, Shall I not? I mean, I would be honest, I would think they are talking crap because you couldn't taxi like that. *You are always aware, always watching,* but people get into the car, and you trust them until you have reason to turn against them (emphasis added).

Driver P-CC2 said he thinks more in terms of escaping from dangerous situations once he encounters them than in terms of screening. He said that he is in the job for the money and has to take fares even if they look a bit "iffy": "When you realize they have a violent disposition and are up to no good, it is too late—they are sitting next to you. So all you can do is find an exit solution, drive to the police, stop at a traffic light, and jump out of the car when you can."

Driving a taxi in a dangerous place makes it hard to be trusting, yet if one is untrusting, then one should not be a driver. That seems to be drivers' reasoning. There is an effect of self-selection that ensures that those who do drive a taxi will be of the trusting kind. Only driver P-CC12 seemed not to be trusting by nature and inclined not to trust customers until he had evidence to trust them.

You really do drive about alert most of the time. You have to be on top of it, because if there are three guys in the car and they say, "We're taking your car," there is not a lot you can do with it. So it is better to get it sorted at the start rather than end it somewhere where you can't get it sorted, because drivers have stopped and people have taken their car for joyriding. I have known drivers that the boys have said they were taking the car and the driver has taken the keys out of the car and ran off. [They can] do what they want to the car—and usually they don't do an awful lot—[but] once they know they are not going to get joyriding, they usually leave it and you can go back for it. It sounds really callous, but you have heard so many horrific stories of this and that [happening], so maybe you get a couple of rough guys coming towards you and one of those stories sticks in your head. I have sat at times going, "I've got to work." . . . My old saying is, "Everybody's a bastard unless they prove themselves different." So then I would think the worst of people, which is not a good thing but I think it is the safest thing.

Still, even driver P-CC12 was aware that paranoia does not get a driver very far: "If you started going into that much detail, you wouldn't pick anybody up. Although I have been saying you wouldn't do this and you wouldn't do that, 99 percent of the people are fine, and if you start looking for things, you will find them."

He was also aware that his attitude is less than optimal, even with respect to minimizing risk. Driver P-CC12 once rejected one hundred fares in a week, realized that he was not making enough money to meet his target income, and ended up picking up passengers who looked worse than others he had rejected.[1] And yet, "I pick people up, and I think, What have I done? And then they are fantastic. So you could be making the totally wrong decision at the start, but it is what you have to do. Better to be going home and thinking, I should have picked them up, than lying in the hospital thinking, I shouldn't have picked him up."

Screening Passengers

Once we start looking in detail at what drivers do, however, the evidence that they do not blindly trust but take signs into account, even if they are of a generally trusting disposition, is simply overwhelming. They may feel trusting, but in fact they are both focused and alert most of the time, seeking out any visible manifestations of the properties of passengers that they believe make passengers either trustworthy or untrustworthy. When they feel suspicious of a customer, they do sometimes refuse to pick up, or they probe and, in any case, raise their guard during the journey. Their screening depends on whether the passengers are callers or hailers, and it goes through a number of stages.

Screening Callers

All private-hire drivers get the majority of their customers through the dispatcher, who receives customers' phone calls and distributes them to the available drivers. Screening through a dispatcher has some advantages in that the callers are asked for information about themselves that is costless for honest customers to reveal but costly for the ill-intentioned ones. If the latter give truthful information, it becomes riskier for them to misbehave later, and if they give untruthful information, a considerable amount of mimicking will be necessary to make it credible. Driver C-CC1 put it thus:

> If somebody phones us for a taxi, generally you know their name, where you're picking them up, where you're taking them to, what time it was, what date it was. So [if] . . . you're going to their house to collect them, it's pretty foolish on their part [to misbehave], because I know who they are and it's all logged onto the mainframe computer at the depot. Obviously, if someone flags you down in the middle of the street, you're not going to know who they are.

Driver P-CC7 too showed a keen awareness of the advantages of taking on passengers who have called in to the dispatcher: "At least through the depot the job's booked in. They know where it was phoned in from, they have a phone number, they know the destination, and they know who was sent to it and at what time. Whereas, if you pick them up in the street, you have nothing. You don't even have a witness to say that you actually picked them [up]."

Some drivers avoid going to certain areas unless they get the call through the dispatcher:

> If somebody came and said, "Would you take me to Banbridge?" I would say no. If they were standing in the street, I would say no . . . but I don't mind if they give me a job going out to Banbridge, because they know who it is and where I am going. But they don't know if I pick them up off the street. I just put the meter on, and they just know that you are on a job, but I have no way of letting them know where I am going. (driver C-CCF3)

Dispatchers use a number of filtering rules, as driver P-C4 explained:

> Well, there's certain spots that they won't pick up from, they'll just say they're too busy—the ghettos, as I would call them. [For instance,] all over the Shankill Road. I don't so much mean ghettos but clubs where they're hard to get to, maybe somewhere where there's only one way in and out of it, and I generally wouldn't go in there. There's one up the Glen Road. We won't send cars in there because I think we lost one or two in the height of the Troubles. They would mainly be all Nationalists who drink in the wee club, or all Loyalists, and if they send the wrong person in, what if somebody recognizes them?

Driver C-CCF3 told us that, "if you phone from a phone box, they would just say, 'No, sorry, you have to have an address.' " However, matters improve slightly if a prospective fare calls from a cell phone, for it makes the caller more likely to be traceable. But a customer needs to offer other reassuring signals to offset the lack of a proper address:

> From a mobile [cell phone]? No. Now if you are *a regular customer* or an account holder, they would take it from a mobile, but, no, not off the street. . . . If you said, "Look, I am *a female*, and I am standing here on my own, and I am really *scared*," then they would send a driver round for you. But if you phoned and said, "Look, I am standing outside the Bot [a bar]. Is there any chance of a taxi?" they would just say no, they would say, "Go into the Wellington Park and lift the free phone in there." Any depot will take calls from a hotel, but not from a bar.

Driver C-WB4, an ex-Republican prisoner who works for a manifestly Catholic firm, has more reasons than most to worry about a sectarian attack. He said that his dispatcher's main rule is draconian: stick with the customers you know. "If you rang up from Central Station and said, 'This is Heather, I'm looking to be picked up,' they'd say, 'Ring a City Center firm,' whereas [if the customer says,] 'This is———[known local person],' they'd say, 'Right, we'll have a car down.' He would be known, you know, and we know exactly who we're going to look for—right. That's the difference."

If dispatchers are uncertain about a call, they try to put the customer off by saying that the firm is very busy and the taxi will take at least twenty minutes to arrive. Or they delay sending a driver and wait for the customer *to ring back* to ask where the taxi is. If the customer does ring back, his persistence is usually taken as a sign that he is genuine and willing to wait in order to ensure that he will get a taxi to his destination. Dispatchers expect attackers to be more impatient and to call another firm. Driver C-WB6 told us that on one occasion the dispatcher's misgivings were confirmed, for the caller did ring back, but to issue a threat: "We'll get you, you know." The attacker knew that the delay was a ruse resulting from the dispatcher's suspicions.

Dispatcher C-WBDF1 said that she selects not just customers but which drivers to send: "Well, basically you know who [the drivers] are, you know what I mean. So if a job came in that sounded even sorta dodgy, you wouldn't send someone who you knew was going to be a target there. You'd send someone that was unknown [to paramilitary groups]."

Once the dispatcher has passed on a call, the driver can still reject a customer. And he can do so before actually meeting the customer if he simply has a feeling that something is wrong. Not giving a precise destination to the dispatcher is just one such sign that warrants prudence:

> About two years ago, it came up on the data head, if anyone [wanted] a job at the depot going "as directed," which basically means a couple of guys

have come in and ordered a taxi and won't say where they are going, so it is fairly suspect. I did get a few of these jobs coming up. I just wouldn't do them. In March one of the guys I was sitting beside got the job on the computer at the depot "going as directed." I said, "Don't be doing that," but he said, "It might be a good one." Sometimes if you have multiple drops, they won't give a destination because you could be going [to] Lisburn Road, Antrim Road, Lenadoon, and then Antrim, so they just put "as directed." So he was under the illusion that this could have been a good job, and [he] was going to go round and find out anyway. I said, "I wouldn't do it," and I explained to him, but he went anyway. Half an hour later, he pulled in alongside me as gray as the sky. Two guys had jumped into his car, pulled out two hammers, and robbed him. Now, on the Sunday night the guy still had Saturday night's money in his pocket, and even when he had given them all that he had, he said the one in the back was foaming at the mouth with his hammer, and he said that "he still wanted to hit me," but the guy in front said, "No, let's go," and they went. (driver P-CC7)

Further Screening of Callers by Direct Observation   The driver can decide not to pick up once he observes the actual customer or otherwise perceives surrounding signs that worry him or that do not match the information given by the caller to the dispatcher. This second screening makes it harder for callers to lie about features that can be observed before pickup. Drivers' mental alarm bells ring loudly when they detect mismatches. For instance, while in West Belfast, Heather Hamill ordered a taxi from a local firm and gave Belfast City Center as her destination. By the time the taxi arrived, she had received a phone call from a friend that caused her to change her plans, and she asked the driver to take her to Protestant East Belfast. The driver was very reluctant to take her and immediately radioed the dispatcher to ask for advice as to what to do. He feared that she was setting him up, luring him into a trap. It took considerable effort to reassure him that she was not a threat. Heather named people and places in West Belfast that she knew, told him she was doing some research on taxi drivers (which made him even more suspicious), and showed him her business card. He finally agreed to take her.

The driver, however, was very unsure of his route because he was going to an area with which he was not familiar; when Heather offered directions, he radioed the dispatcher again to confirm the information she had given him. He questioned her the whole time she was in his car: What was she doing? Why did she want to talk to taxi drivers? Whom did she work for? Did she know who he was? At the destination he was very edgy, looking nervously around him as if expecting a gunman to appear from behind a tree or a parked car. He also told her that the only reason he took such a chance was because it was daytime; he would never have made such a journey at night. Later that evening he phoned

Heather on her cell phone (her telephone number was on her business card) to check that the number she had given him was truly hers.

This driver's response was typical of the case in which a driver finds a mismatch between the information the caller gives to the dispatcher and the actual customer or the customer's situation. If the driver expects a woman and finds a man, he is suspicious. If he finds more than one man when he was expecting only one, or is instructed to go to a different destination, again, he is on his guard. When getting customers through the dispatcher, drivers can also do a "dummy" drive by the address to check that all is in order; if they find that the address is that of a dilapidated house, they may fail to pick up:

> Now there are areas in Belfast, like the Lower Shankill and places like that, that what you will do is, whenever you pull up you will sit in your car with your engine running, because you are in a very bad area. You will watch who is coming out, you will watch as to what movements are about the place, and if you don't like it you will drive off before they ever get near your car. You will never let them get near your car, and that is only in extremely bad areas. That is in areas like the Lower Shankill and maybe Ballymurphy and places like that, where there is drug dealers in places and people who are in desperation for drug money. But as I say, whenever you pull up to the private houses . . . if you don't like it, you just drive away. But you will never get into the situation where you will talk to them, because once you are talking to them it is too late—they are in the car. (driver P-CC2)

Driver C-WB6 too said he would "swing by and have a look, and if it looks dodgy, I'll just keep on driving." This behavior may seem like taking a precaution, and in a loose sense it is. However, it is also screening in that the driver, having received a description of the caller from the dispatcher, checks for mismatches and worrying oddities or a mixture of both. In real-world incidents, precautions, screening, and probing may all be present and operating sequentially. For example, a driver may screen for a mismatch, find one, probe further, remain unpersuaded, and take precautions.

Getting customers through the dispatcher gives drivers information that helps them to double-check: "We've a safety thing built in so that every customer who phones from any area, their telephone number will come up on the screen. When he goes to dispatch a job, he knows who has phoned. If a driver arrives at that address and there is no answer at that door, he has a telephone number that he can phone. Maybe the guy's sleeping. It's a cross-check" (driver P-CC8).

By engaging in these further checks, the drivers are effectively, at some cost to themselves, probing the fare and trying to acquire more information over and above what was received from the dispatcher.

Even if the house looks safe, drivers are aware that a good address is easy to mimic: "Some guy would ring up and say, 'Go to 21, University Street.' He could be standing at the door when I come and I think he is from that house. You could give any address—just stand at the front gate or front door, and the taxi comes and you will get into it. Very easy—taxiing is probably the easiest job in the world to get set up in" (driver C-PH3).

On the whole, it seems as if getting fares through the dispatcher gives drivers greater opportunities to probe and filter customers. Drivers have prior information about customers, and it is possible to gather more information before having to confront customers face to face. Calling raises the cost to mimics who want to pass off as genuine customers.

An interesting point made by driver P-CC12, however, suggests that not all drivers regard calls as necessarily safer than picking up off the street: "Would I be more wary of picking up customers off the street? No, I would be more wary of the data head. Because picking up off the street, you can pick who you want . . . where the data head says you go and get the people, and that's it."

Judging by the successful sectarian attacks about which we have information, it seems that the telephone gives greater scope to determined mimics. In eight of the forty-nine cases, the attacker pretended on the phone to be a known *regular* customer, whom he must have stalked; such impersonation would not have been possible face to face with the driver. The attacker then ambushed the driver on his way to the pickup before he had any time for probing and detecting a mismatch. Also, if femaleness is deemed to be a reassuring sign, it would seem generally easier to have a woman make the call (and paramilitaries did exactly that) rather than to get a woman to agree to hail a taxi and risk being identified as an accomplice to a crime. The telephone, by filtering out certain cues that are transmitted naturally when contact is made face to face, may in fact make a setup easier, at least for mimics of the most dangerous and determined sort.

Screening Hailers

Public-hire taxis pick up only from street-hails; most of the private-hire drivers we interviewed also pick up off the street, to varying extents. When drivers pick up from the street, they first screen prospective customers by observation, noting their gender, age, dress, and any other observable feature, including the place from which they hail. Driver P-CC8 said: "You get all sorts of guys, you know, off their heads or steaming [drunk. They say,] 'Take me to such and such,' and I'll just say, 'Sorry, mate, I'm not allowed to pick up off the streets.' It just depends on what they look like, you know. If they look okay, you'll take them."

Looking "okay" encompasses many different signs that need to be unpacked. We consider them one by one as much as possible. We must stress, however, that drivers' assessments result from considering an array of signs rather than any one in particular. As driver C-WB5 noted: "I can look down a street and see what's going on and give them the slip if I need to. I can see things now that other people would never notice . . . how they walk, how they talk, how they glance, how they hold themselves, how they would get into the car."

Drivers' reasoning wrestles with the fact that although a sign might be mimic-proof, there is no single sign that is an absolutely reliable indicator of the underlying trait. In the language of signaling theory, there are only semi-sorting signals rather than perfectly sorting ones. It is often only a host of signs that, taken together, give a near-complete reassurance to drivers. Each sign is also given different weight depending on the type of peril the driver is most aware of or has reason to expect.

Known Customers   The strongest sign of trustworthiness a customer can give is to be known, either as a good previous customer or as a friendly local person. Drivers who are more at risk often deem previous knowledge essential, for so high is the perceived threat that nothing less will do. Quite simply, they will not pick up anyone whom they do not know. Personal knowledge is a very robust sign: the cost of impersonating a known individual, in face-to-face encounters at least, is close to infinity. Previous behavior is the best indicator of future behavior, and although a known trusted customer might suddenly act out of character and try to harm the driver, it would be highly unusual.

Being known by the driver offsets negative signs that a customer may display. Prior knowledge can even persuade drivers to pick up a customer from the other side of the religious divide. Or, as driver P-EB7 said, even a group of men can be picked up if they are known. Being known overrides negative cues for callers as well as hailers, though for the former it is a name or an address that reidentifies the customer rather than a face:

> I'd never have sent a driver if a call came from those hospitals unless you really knew the person that you were picking up. If they had phoned in and given a name, I'd have said, "I don't know that," and then if I'd have said to them, "Where are you coming back to?" and if they'd given me an address, well, then I'd have known if they were regulars. But if they had given me an address that I couldn't remember, then, no, I'd not send a driver to that destination, because you're not sure of who you're picking up. (driver C-WBDF1)

Customers can of course be known for being bad too, so prior knowledge also enables a driver to know whom *not* to trust: "The fella was a nuisance," remembered driver P-EB7. "One of the other drivers put him out too, so we just don't pick him up now." And driver P-EBF1 told us: "I can remember one—the reason why I rejected him was because he didn't pay me the last time. I wouldn't go again for him because this particular person had done this with everybody in the depot at some stage. So I felt that I had a justification."

Type and Style of Dress If a customer is unknown, drivers look for other observable signs. Driver P-PH5 pointed out that one can infer something, up to a point, from the type of dress: "Well, a guy in working clothes is probably wanting [to go] home in a hurry to get dressed to go out, so he's no problem. But you see the fly-men, it's like a con-man: a con-man is good at his job, which is taking people in." Driver P-CC4 felt that if he had the choice, he would "probably pick somebody up in a suit."

Driver P-CC12 also took dress style into consideration: "You do generalize with people if they are dressed in denim with short hair. It's a terrible way to be, but you do it." Still, they almost all agreed that the customer's attire is a weak sign of either trustworthiness or untrustworthiness:

One of the worse fares I ever got was a guy who walked out with a suit and shirt and tie on. He got into the car and said, "Glengormley." I said, "Right you are." Drove him to Glengormley, and when we got there he had fallen asleep, and I gave him a shake and said, "Whereabouts in Glengormley?" And he said, "Take me back to the town for a drink." I said, "Now, you realize that I have driven to Glengormley," and he said, "That's fine. Now take me back to the town." So we are in the town again, and I said to him, "Where do you want to go in town?" This was two in the morning, [and] he said, "I live in Glengormley," and I said, "Hold on a minute now," and by that stage he had started—"Who do you think you are?"—and I said, "I don't even want your money, now just get out of the car, you have wasted enough of my time," and he said, "I want you to take me home," and I said, "You see what's on the meter? You are going to have to pay this." I took him back up to the house, and he said, "It's usually six pounds," and I said, "Hold on," and he said, "There's six pounds. Do you want it or not?" And I said, "I don't, no."

So I just watched which house he went into and went down to the police and explained to them, and they said, "Take us to his house." So they rapped the door, and his girlfriend came out, and she didn't get off to a great start because the policeman said, "Is your husband in?" and she said no, and he said, "Excuse me, he just walked in two minutes ago," and she said, "I'm not married, but my boyfriend's here, though." And the policeman said, "Right, here we go." So he said, "You wouldn't get him out?" And she said, "He's sleeping," and the policeman said, "We are going to come in and arrest him for abuse of a public-service vehicle if he does not come down here now," and she said, "I'll see if I can get him." He came out with twenty pounds and said, "Will that do?" and I said, "That will do fine," and he slammed the door. The policeman said, "That makes a job worthwhile." I know I am saying denim jackets and all this, but this guy walked out totally respectable and became the worst nightmare of my life.

Driver P-CC12 concluded: "You can get the black penny coming up in the suit as well as you could in a leather jacket." Driver P-CC2 agreed: "I would just say that the boys that are going to rob you, or boys and girls that are going to rob you, they are not necessarily dressed as scruff-bags. They are not wearing training shoes, jeans, and looking thuggish—they don't always look like that. That is the facts."

Driver C-WB3 concurred with that view: "You might get a guy with a three-piece suit on him, and he could still be a bad boy and you wouldn't know. Or you could get a guy dressed up rough, and he could be a genuine guy. You just don't know. I take any type of people at all. You don't know until they put their hand in their pocket what is coming out next— it could be a wallet or a gun." Driver C-CC1 claimed not to be too concerned about how prospective fares are dressed because "I can dress like a wee bit of a slob sometimes, so it wouldn't bother me."

The general attitude is not to consider style of dress a very telling positive or negative signal. If someone is well dressed in a professional suit, drivers assess him as more likely to be a good customer, but not by much. By the same token, a customer dressed badly or wearing jeans is seen as somewhat more likely to be a bad customer. Down or scruffy dressing and even decorative tattoos are recognized as potentially just a fashion, and such dress provides little more than a first impression that may invite further probing.

However, that does not mean that drivers do not give *some* weight to dress, especially at the extremes of quality distribution:

> How somebody's dressed? Wouldn't matter. Although you can spot the uniform spidy characters or gangsters. Spidies? There's a standard uniform of young people. Young spidies would be wearing tracksuit trousers, dressed like they're going to football training, but there's no football about them. Baseball caps, street grime on the shoes, that sort of thing. You can tell, and the drugs. You can spot the junkies, the fly-men drug dealers, the shifty characters, all the Del-boy types. It's amazing, just what you pick up, the way you can read someone. A lot of it's stereotypical judgments as well. There would be a lot of people that I don't know who they are or what they are. This is just like a list of criteria that I would run through. (driver C-NB1)

Driver P-CC12 said: "I haven't the cheek to say skinheads." (Driver P-CC12 himself is a skinhead.) "It's a terrible thing to generalize, but if they come over in their Wranglers, their denim, and they are maybe staggering a bit and growling at people and all that sort of stuff . . . you get that. And you get an awful lot of sectarian abuse because you don't lift them."

Drivers do not seem to worry about customers with bags; on the contrary, said driver C-CC1, "if you see a guy with a big suitcase, you're going to try and pick him up because he's going to the airport. Simple." Driver P-CC7 explained: "The majority of bags would be carrier bags, and they normally end up in the boot—except for your old dears, and your old dears are not going to do too much. There is not too many people would carry bags apart from carry-outs [of alcohol], and the carry-out bags are normally sky blue and you can see through them."

Drivers tend to worry about things that are out of place, and for that reason clothing may arouse their suspicion more for what it hides than for what it reveals: "No, I am [not worried about bags]. It's the coats that worry me. The coats. A bag, you could have anything in it, but a coat, if it's zipped up the full way . . . and, you know, if it's a good day, if it's a half-decent day . . . and if it's a bulky coat, I'd want to know why he was wearing it, and I would tend not to take the fare" (driver C-WB4).

Not wearing a coat on a warm day is costly only to those who have something to hide. Gloves too can be regarded with suspicion for a similar reason:

> One of the times I was robbed a fella was standing at the City Hall, lovely job, going to Aldergrove [airport], and he was very well dressed—nice pair of gloves on him. Got into the backseat behind me, and then when he got into the backseat, as we were driving along, he took me into a side street to rob me. Certainly if you go into an area where there is trouble, where there is violence and stuff, you are in trouble generally, because they are coming at you [from all sides]. But if somebody is going to rob you, they are not necessarily going to be looking like a scruff, and this is a problem, and this is one of the things that people would meet normally. I would actually be watching now if somebody was getting into the backseat wearing a pair of gloves. A pair of gloves is something which people don't generally wear in Belfast. You go into that street, and I guarantee you stand there for two hours you wouldn't find someone with a pair of gloves. But if somebody gets into the back of your car, especially if they get behind you, sitting directly behind you with a pair of gloves, then you know you are in trouble, and the idea is then to get that journey aborted right away, even if you are wrong, even if you have misjudged the situation—get it aborted. (driver P-CC2)[2]

Drivers are on the lookout not only for suspicious items of clothing— for "bulges or anything that doesn't look right" (driver C-WB5) in terms of dress or other apparel—but also for unusual behavior. The most striking mismatch observed by drivers is *not being drunk on a Saturday night*: "The drunk ones, they're just out drinking, going wherever, and having a good time. But you get someone and he's sober at half past two in the morning, there you know. And you say to him, 'Were you out tonight?' 'Aye, I was out tonight.' And you know they weren't, you know what I mean? But there's something about them, something's not right" (driver C-WB6).

Gender Females are regarded as safer than males: "Would I have preferred to pick up women than men? Oh aye, as long as they're not drunk" (driver P-PH5). Driver P-CC7 concurred: "You will find in Belfast, in general, the women will get picked up first, because the driver stands a far less chance of getting turned over by a woman than what they would by a man, although sometimes. . . ." Driver P-CC12 agreed: "If two girls come over to me and say, 'Going to Bangor?' and two guys come over and say, 'Going to Bangor?' . . . you go for the girls, it's a safe sale."

Femaleness, insofar as it is a sign of trustworthiness, is a good sign of it, for it is hard to mimic the opposite gender, at least in face-to-face encounters. We return to femaleness later in the chapter.

Groups of Men If women are preferable to men, a man alone is preferable to groups of them. In the absence of counteracting signals, groups of men are viewed with circumspection by nearly all of the drivers we interviewed: "Two fellas might be bother. Three fellas is alarm bells, a warning" (driver C-NB1). This concern about three or more men was expressed by 80 percent of the drivers, partly because the chances of the driver being physically overpowered by three men are greater than with two. If there are three men, inevitably one has to sit behind the driver—the passenger position that makes the driver feel most vulnerable. Driver C-WB5, who used to be a robber and is now a taxi driver, also explained the technical importance of three men in a robbery:

> If you pulled up to a bar and seen two guys coming out, and then another one coming out behind them, that was even more hairy, as the two are coming out to cover the other one. Well, that's what I would have been doing. If I'd have been coming to do something—I often hijacked taxis myself, not to rob them but to use their cars for robbery—I'd have sent two men out to distract the driver while the other one came round and put a gun to his head.

The drivers who do not fear a sectarian attack may be inclined to pick up groups of men: "I'd pick up four fellas—not a problem," said driver C-CC1. However, coupled with other worrying signs, a group of men makes drivers wary. Driver C-CC1 added: "It just depends on what they're like. If they have big *swallow tattoos* and *love-hate across their hands,* then you're going to wonder."

Driver P-PH5 told us: "Well, if there's three or four of them with *Celtic scarves* [the Celtic football club is supported by Catholics], I'd just look the other way, as if I'd never seen them. Rugby fans are no problem. I would say that rugby fans are noisier, more boisterous, and they would drink more, but there's no trouble with them." Rugby fans are generally middle-class Protestants.

Driver P-PH5 has a theory on which type of man, in a group of men, one should worry about most. Size matters: "Usually if there's four fellas, there's always one smart aleck out of the four, and he's always the smallest. He's the one who starts the rows. . . . Now, you've very rarely any trouble with anybody who is six-foot-five. It's always the guy who is four-foot-six, and he'll be trouble all the time. Big giant men, you'll never have no trouble with them."

An interesting reasoning about the dangerousness of groups of men, apparently at odds with that of the rest of the drivers, came from driver P-EBF9, who had started taxiing only six weeks before we interviewed her: "Well, I actually had this discussion with a professional person, and he said to me that you are more at risk of one person really rather than two or three, because if one decides to do something, the other two could say, 'No, you are not.' You have to get the three people to agree."

This logic may look like the reverse of what is reasonable to expect: one would expect a group to be more threatening than just one or two men. However, the kind of peril driver P-EBF9 had in mind was sexual harassment rather than robbery or sectarian attack. Implicitly, she must have the following belief: like any other group attack, a sexual attack requires coordination among the perpetrators, but unlike with other types of attacks, coordinating a sexual attack is harder to achieve, and thus less likely to be both planned and carried out by a group of men. If a man in a group suddenly decides to make a sexual attack, chances are that his companions will object. This seems accurate in that rapes are, for the most part, solo rather than gang-perpetrated crimes.

Mixed-Gender Groups The simultaneous presence of a female with one or more male customers is perceived by 62 percent of the drivers to decrease the potential dangerousness of the fare: "I don't like picking up large crowds of fellas. I don't mind if there is a mixture making up five or six, but if it is all fellas, especially the way the times are, and the next minute they would say, 'Where do you live, driver? What is your name? Are you one of them then?'—and all that" (driver C-PH3).

For driver P-CC12 too, with some misgivings, a female presence makes a difference:

> It would make a difference [if there was one girl with two fellas], because what you are thinking is, right, there's a girl there, and hopefully it's one of

their wives. So hopefully it's not going to be guys out on a bit of a rampage looking for a free taxi home and to get the money from the taxi driver. But something you will find an awful lot is the guys will send the girl to stand on the side of the street and start waving, so once you stop the guys run out and you can't drive off without them. It does make a difference; I would be lying if I said it didn't. Better two fellas and a girl than three fellas.

Driver P-PH5 thought that "you usually find that a husband and wife are all right," but he also knew that enlisting a female to signal trust-worthiness is not that difficult. Seven or eight years before in Poleglass, a friend of his had lost his car:

> He picked up a fella and a girl going to Lisburn, and they said to take the back road, and they yarned away and yarned away and then: "Pull in here, driver." And the next thing is yer man pulled a Stanley knife to his throat—he actually had four stitches. And he held the knife at yer man's throat, grabbed his hair, and the girl got out, and she took his money and his wallet with his driving license and everything. And then she held the knife to his throat while the other guy got out, and then he ordered him out of the taxi. He never saw the car again, and he was lucky because where they cut him he had a double chin and they sort of cut the fat, but he never taxied again.

The weakness of the mixed-gender couple, or group, as a sign of trustworthiness is well illustrated by driver P-CC2:

> If, for instance, it was a fella and girl, you would stop, you would take them to wherever they were going to. But that by itself [does not] mean that because it is a fella and girl it is safe. It is not the looks of a person that makes it safe. A very innocent-looking situation can turn out to be the most awkward fare. I mean, how many robberies are there when there has been a girl involved? The one big decoy you can have is to have a girl on your arm. At least a fella standing with a girl on his arm looks safe when-ever they get into the car. The girls now are becoming more and more vio-lent. The girls now are taking drugs, and the girls are going over the top. You see there is a situation which any taxi driver coming along a street sees a fella and girl they will stop and that can be very dangerous. You can't judge it, and that is true. It can't be judged from the outside, it can only be judged whenever you get them in the car. Then you get the feel.

Driver P-CC7 warned: "Sometimes you can have them working together. I know on one occasion where a girl ran out shouting, 'Rape! Rape! Rape!' When the guy [driver] stopped, she jumped in, pulled a knife out of her bag, and stuck it to his throat. Two guys jumped in the backseat and robbed him. They took him to the cash-point and made him take the money out of the hole in the wall."

Those who fear a sectarian attack regard a woman's presence even more suspiciously:

> You might hear taxi drivers say, "I'll stop in the town and lift girls." I wouldn't lift a girl because girls can set you up as quick as a fella, and at the end of the day it has been proven that girls have done it. People would say, "Ahh, it's two girls, they're only going up the Ormeau Road, they're only going to the Shankill, I'll lift them." Girls can set you up just as quick as a fella. Or even, "Ahh, it's a girl and a fella, and the two of them's got a couple of drinks in them," but it can still happen they can still set you up. So you gotta be careful about exactly who you're lifting. (driver C-WB4)

Driver P-EB7 made the same point: "If there was a girl, would that make me feel safer? Not now, because, as I told you, I had a bad experience with a girl and two fellas."

Notice that with respect to gender we are dealing with three different signs. One is being a female rather than a male. Insofar as being a female is a property that connotes a good customer, as it seems to do most of the time, then femaleness is a reliable cue, for it is hard to impersonate the opposite gender convincingly, especially in person. The other sign is when a group of customers includes a female. Drivers consider two men with a female to be safer than three men or even two men. This sign, however, is not as reliable as femaleness alone, for it is not so difficult to recruit a female in order to make a menacing trio look like an ordinary quartet. Third, one or more male customers may use a real female as a decoy to hail or call a taxi. In this case, the real female mimics looking for a taxi when she is not. Again, this sign is not so difficult to display fraudulently.

In spite of these misgivings, drivers' overall preference structure is summarized by driver C-WB4: "If there is four or five fellas standing, I would drive on, because you are asking for trouble. I would prefer to pick up a couple of girls, not for any other reason, just because it is less hassle, or one couple rather than a crowd of fellas."

Age Older persons are regarded by approximately half of the drivers as less threatening than younger ones:

> I was sent to pick up a fare, and this man just came over and got into my car, and I said, "Look, I knew I was sent for a woman," because it was a Mrs. Mills, and she was a regular customer, and this man just opened the door and jumped in, and I says, "Look, you're going to have to get out." He says, "You can take me home." I say, "No, I'm not taking you home." He was a middle-aged man, I'd say about forty to fifty, so you don't expect somebody like that to give you any hassle. So I say, "You're going to have to get out of the car," again, and he says, "No, I'm not." So at this stage

there was a police Land Rover sitting about twenty yards up the street a bit. So I says to him, "Look, if you don't get out of my car, I'm going to reverse up, and I'll get the police to get you out of the car." He says, "No, you won't." I say, "Okay, well, that's all right." So I went to reverse up the street, and he opened the door and ran. If it had been a young fella, you would have been looking out for it, but with the age of him, you just didn't expect it. (driver P-CC4)

Interestingly, driver P-CC4 did not refuse to pick up this man because he was worried that he might be trouble. He refused because he wanted to get the right customer, the expected regular female; he did not expect trouble from this man, for he generally regarded older age as a sign of a customer's trustworthiness.

Drivers look first of all for easily observable cues and signs of properties that they believe can reveal whether a prospective passenger is trustworthy or untrustworthy. Unless drivers know the customer personally, however, there are few signs that alone can settle their trust dilemma either way. Rather, they form their judgment by taking a cluster of signs into consideration, for even if each sign could be mimicked, taken all together they may be too costly for a mimic to afford. A lone adult female, for instance, is a reassuring combination that encompasses a trio of features that are hard to fake: age, gender, and not being part of a group. However, drivers know all too well that in many cases appearances leave a large enough margin of error to their screening, and if uncertain they endeavor to probe the customer further, seeking to extract signs that are accessible only by a closer and more articulate interaction.

Chapter 5

Probing in Belfast

THE PASSENGER screening process described in the previous chapter relies either on dispatchers' filtering of information revealed by callers or on drivers' direct observations of signs displayed by prospective fares. This information may be sufficiently clear: if signs are starkly negative drivers reject the fare, and if positive they pick up the fare. However, that information may be—and often is—inconclusive. Our expectation is that, when in doubt, drivers probe further and try to extract more information from passengers. To do this they have to feel reassured enough to engage in closer interaction. Sometimes they may agree to pick up even when they feel suspicious but continue to probe the passenger in the car. At the same time, as Heather Hamill's experience (see chapter 4) reveals, both genuine and mimicking passengers who feel under suspicion volunteer additional reassuring signals. This further information exchange is described in this chapter. Particular attention is paid toward the end of the chapter to the strategies used by bona-fide passengers who give off negative signs.

Probing Before Picking Up

The next step drivers take when observing the prospective passenger at some distance has left them in doubt is to try to investigate further by getting closer and talking to him *before* deciding whether to take the fare on board. This enables the driver to "read" signs such as facial expression, politeness, tone of voice, accent, and intonation: "How someone was dressed would not make much of a difference to me. No, to me it would have been *what was coming out of their mouth*, what they were saying. And some people said nothing, which meant you never got to know them. Other people would have said quite a lot. There was always that element of uncertainty" (driver P-EBF1).

The Tone of Voice

What "comes out of their mouth" can be a number of things. Four drivers are mindful of politeness but not impressed by it alone. They focus instead on subtler, more elusive signs:

> If somebody was to stop me and say, "Where are you going? I am going to Ballysillan, mate," I would say, "Sorry, no." It is the tone. But if somebody turned round and says, "Look, excuse me, is there any chance of taking us up to Ballysillan?" I would say, "Okay." If they have a nice attitude . . . but *the tone of the voice* really determines whether I am going to take them or not. (driver C-PH3)

For driver P-PH1,

> it is subconscious. You can usually tell within the first sentence whether you are going to take to him or not, and it depends on his attitude how you react. Even given an address to go to, *you can tell from his voice*, the way he speaks to you—it is automatic. Honestly, I don't know what it is, it is just experience. You can tell if that guy is all right, he seems all right, or somebody can get in and *you know from the tone of the voice* that he is going to be aggressive or he is going to be friendly, you can tell that.

The Eyes

Unlike New York drivers who mention looking at a person's face (see chapters 9 and 10 and table 10.1), five Belfast drivers talked about an individual's eyes: "Ah, the madness in the eyes maybe! The madness in the eyes, you know" (diver P-EB8).

> The trust thing would be like a ritual. There's this brief moment of eye contact between the driver and the passenger, you know. It's a subconscious, automatic thing, a quick glance, quick eye contact. "Get in, I'm comfortable, you comfortable?" It's a subconscious checking each other out sort of thing. And if that doesn't work, then bang, you're on to something right away. What's wrong with this guy? What's he doing? What's he up to? (driver C-NB1)

Drivers also continue to observe eyes once the passenger is in the car.[1]

Gut Feelings

In eighteen interviews (40 percent), drivers invoked having a "funny feeling," an "instinct," a "gut feeling," or a "sixth sense," and they did not seem aware of what exactly triggered these feelings. Driver C-WB5 was adamant that such feelings should be heeded: "An instinct that's there—it's in-built. If you read it and you feel it, it's happening. You don't feel that for nothing. React to it, and I always did. . . . If I feel it, then I know it's happening, it's real. Why are you feeling it if it's not happening? I could be paranoid, you say? Could be, but it's better to be paranoid than dead!"

Judgments are arrived at by assessing a combination of signs, some observable, some derived from what the customer says, some less palpable:

> One night me and my wee mate were sitting outside Lavery's [a pub]. I was the first car, and he was in behind me, and this boy came up to me and says, "Take me to Banbridge. I've no money, I'll give it to you when I get home." Here's me: "No, not unless you have a Rolex watch on you." He says, "No," so I say, "No, I'm not taking you." But my wee mate, he went to him, he'd be what I'd call a greedy driver, and he says, "Aye, a twenty-five-pound fare," and he must have thought the fella was honest because he was up front and said, "Look, I've no money on me, but I'll give it to you when I get home." Well, he took him up to Banbridge, and sure and behold, he got out and ran. But there was just something about him—I says to myself, I don't trust him. I don't know what it was. I just had a funny feeling about him.

Interestingly, the runner in this story chose to reveal up front that he had no money, a confession that could have been taken as a sign that the young man was in fact honest.

Probing During the Journey

It is not always possible to do too much probing before a passenger gets in the car. Often drivers pick up a passenger they see or one the dispatcher sends them to pick up. According to driver P-CC2, the most consistently skeptical of our interviewees, one often cannot really see much of the passenger before picking up.

> [Drivers say] you can recognize a violent person, an aggressive person, by their looks, but you don't even get time to look into their eyes to see if their eyes are saying anything. . . . No matter what anyone says, you don't sit with your door locked and look out through the window to judge a person. . . . Your first game of taxiing is to make money, you are out to make money. So you want to take them even if they are a bit "iffy," you want to get the money off them, and you want to get going. So drivers talk—"I judge this" and "I judge that"—but I can tell you the facts, and the facts are that if you were a schizophrenic and you walked out of that door there, you'd have only about five to six feet before you are in my car. [In that distance] I don't see your face, I don't see your personality, I don't see anything at all about you until you are inside. That is not fantasyland, that is for real, that is the real taxiing.

Drivers of public-hire taxis in particular are often in the awkward position of having passengers get into their car before being able to do much screening at all, for they queue at taxi stands waiting for fares. Turning passengers away at the stands is harder and likely to prove more controversial than just driving by and pretending not to see a hailing passenger.

All six public-hire drivers we interviewed mentioned an interesting form of cooperation they resort to in one particular circumstance. On learning a passenger's *destination*—which is of course the minimal amount of information that a passenger cannot avoid exchanging with a driver—the driver can infer, so tightly segregated are the city neighborhoods, the passenger's religious affiliation. If the passenger is not of the same religion as the driver—and thus the destination rather than the passenger is judged unsafe—the driver can ask another driver in the queue who is of the same religion as the passenger to take the fare: "If it was my job next and they say, 'Shankill Road' [a Protestant area], well, the fella behind me would say, 'Joe, I'll take that Shankill Road job to avoid you going up there,' and vice versa. If there is any for the Falls area, I would volunteer, as I'm a Catholic" (driver C-PH3).

Whatever the reason that leads them to take a passenger on board, drivers do not lower their guard but keep monitoring him or her throughout the journey: "You always have your wits about you, watching every move. If people are too quiet, it could be a problem. If someone is too fidgety, they might be getting ready to run and you would hit the central locking. Even if an old lady gets in, you're worried that she might piss all over the seats" (driver C-WB8).

Once the passenger is in the car, the driver can pick up behavioral signs more easily and learn more from the increased verbal communication: "I think you can't really judge by appearances, because you can pick someone up who is like a nice old granny, and she could hit you just as quick [as] anybody else. I find once you have them in the car you spend the first five or six minutes trying to work out what way they think" (driver P-CC7).

Choice of Seating

One feature that 87 percent of drivers observe is passengers' choice of seating. They can sit in the front passenger seat, and they can sit in the back, either behind the driver or on the other side. A driver's unease about where a passenger sits depends on the type of passenger: "Two guys come [in the car] and they both get in the back, you do get wary of that, but mostly they don't, most people get in the front and chat away with you. A couple of girls get in the back, that's just normal, but if two guys come in and they both get in the back, then you have a wee glance and make sure there is nothing happening" (driver P-CC12).

Driver C-NB1 too expected passengers to sit in the front:

If they got in the back, I'd be wary. Then I'd be looking at dress, you know, if he was wearing a suit or . . . you just know, if somebody's sitting in the back, they're used to sitting in the back or they're doing something, they're looking over money or drugs or something. They're more comfortable in the back, and they don't want to talk to the taxi driver. You get a lot of that with professional people—they prefer sitting in the back—but I would see that as an antisocial thing. A single man getting in the backseat of a taxi is antisocial. A single girl is a different story. Girls are a different kettle of fish altogether—different conversations, different body language, different way of acting.

Driver P-CC4 was worried not so much about people sitting in the back but more about

somebody sitting behind you and not speaking. You get some people who, if you try to make a conversation, they'll just grunt at you, and then you just know not to say nothing. But I always hate people sitting right in behind me. I would sometimes say to them, would you move over to the other side, because you can't see them. You can't see them in the mirror, but you know they're behind you, and you get shivers up your back.

Driver P-CC7 agreed: "The only time you start worrying about people sitting in the car is if it is a [single] fella who would sit behind the driver because they know you can't see them. The majority of people who would get into your car, if they are on their own, will either sit on the passenger seat at the front or behind the passenger seat in the back. They do not sit behind the driver."

Eye Movements, Body Posture, Car "Temperature," and Other Subtle Signs

Some drivers may be more skilled than others at reading signs: "Well, somebody who doesn't know, who couldn't read the signs, he wouldn't know what a twitch was, or wouldn't know what a wee glance was, or . . . a wink, a nudge, and something else. But if you catch the first one of them, then you see the second and the third. If you aren't looking, you won't fucking see none of them. You'll get totaled, robbed, or battered." Driver C-WB5 here was speaking from experience from both sides, as he had been both a robber of drivers and later a driver himself.

The worrying signs may emerge as soon as the passenger gets into the car. Driver C-NB1 explained:

Upper body rigid, avoidance, they would be avoiding eye contact, they would be shifty, they wouldn't be comfortable. There's a way of getting in and out of a car. You can't have a rigid upper body structure if you're getting into a car. You have to relax to get into a car, and then to get yourself into the bucket seat of a car you have to relax, and if a person's not relaxed then they're up to something, and then the body posture is instinctively wrong.

What would make me worried? Again, [if they're] agitated—if they're agitated and bouncing about. If three blokes are in your car, and they're having a conversation that totally excludes you. Now, they're going to be talking amongst themselves anyway, which is fine, but there's a conversation amongst three passengers that doesn't necessarily include you but it doesn't exclude you either. But there is a conversation that completely excludes you, and the content of that conversation will let you know whether you're in trouble or not.

. . . If somebody's nervous, you'd be anxious, or if he is tense getting into the car, they've got all the symptoms that they're going to fight or they're going to run away, and that's the one you have to watch. They're going to run away, and if he doesn't start fighting in the taxi, he is going to run.

Still, with remarkable subtlety, the same driver acknowledges that the possibility of misreading signs is ever-present:

But then, you don't know, there might have been an incident outside of the car that has him in that situation in the car [and] that has nothing to do with me, or the journey, or anything else. He's actually running from something else, or he's angry about something else. You just don't know, but that's where the questioning comes in, the conversation that takes place. "What about you? How you doing? Where are you going?" That sort of thing. You know, I used to make it a challenge to actually create a conversation with the passenger. The silence is just too great. It's all just waffle, but it's creating it for the journey so this guy's talking, this person's talking, it's okay.

Driver C-WB5 too would read people's nervous signs: "playing with their hands, a wee bit sweaty, but then again, you do just get nervous people doing that. . . . You could be wrong, but it would click me on to having a wee look twice at somebody."

Driver C-NB1 stressed more elusive signs too:

It's not about looking in the mirror. You might give a quick glance in the mirror, but you know, because the *energy level* in the car has shifted, it's altered, it's changed. Whatever's happened, there's stuff going on, there's something going on, this isn't quite right. I never really thought as deeply about it before. . . . That intuitive stuff is essential, it is crucial, it is crucial, it is the stuff that works, the thing that works, that's how I can communicate.

Driver C-WB5 was aware of a similarly intangible sign: "The *temperature* lowers in the car if there's anything going on. It's not the same. If there's nothing going on and everybody's happy, the temperature is okay, but you really notice it if they get in and there's anything wrong. I notice it right away." Both drivers seemed to be speaking literally rather than metaphorically about energy level and temperature. Intuitively, we may grasp that they are referring to that state of suspended tension that precedes an attack, but it is hard to say whether a thermometer would really shift, since no experimental work to our knowledge has attempted to measure prestrike "atmospheric" variations as subtle as these.

Driver P-CC2 gave a good description of what he observes in a couple, a man and a woman, once they are in the car:

> You get a feel. Say, for instance, there is a couple, and you will watch them in the mirror, you will see them. They don't realize you are sitting watching them, and they are maybe giving each other wee eye movements—they are getting fidgety—things like that. So then, what you basically say [to yourself] is, Hold on, this just doesn't look right. If you get an ordinary fella and girl, and they are sitting in the backseat of the car, maybe they have just had a big night out, maybe [they] just sit there or maybe sit and kiss and get on like that. That is a safe situation—the two of them are interested in each other. But when you get them into the back of the car and you see . . . not necessarily words that are said but eye movements made to each other. It is body language; body language is what counts. You can see the body language, and body language tells you more than what comes out of the mouth.
>
> . . . What you see is, they are in the back, they are assessing you, that is what you will see. They are assessing you. You will see them looking over at each other, you will see them looking round the car in general to see what there is in the car. So what you are basically getting is a fidgeting, not a relaxed sort of sitting back and just waiting to get home. They are moving all the time, they are moving from side to side, they are looking around the car, and they are assessing the situation that is whenever you know [that it could be dangerous]. Always inside the car.

We asked driver P-CC2 if he could predict that someone was about to do a runner:

> Yes, very much so. Again, you will see them sit right up against the door, and they are feeling for the handle. So the next thing you will see is—you can watch it in the mirror—the next thing you see is the hands resting on the handle. Instead of your average passenger, who, as you come nearer to his home he will be going into his pockets for his money, the runner will be sitting with his hand on the door handle just ready to jump.

Driver C-WB5 was also very aware of seemingly innocent but somehow incongruous behavior: "Like somebody getting into the car in the passenger side and pulling the mirror thing down so he can look at his mates in the back and watch cars behind him in the back. Now, women do that to look at themselves in the mirror and stuff, but guys doing that are up to something. He's giving his mate the eye or a wee nod, because that used to be me."

Local Knowledge

Drivers also probe by asking about the customer's knowledge of the area of destination and their reasons for being there. Driver C-WB6 described how he became very suspicious of a customer who claimed to have a local girlfriend but could not tell the driver the name of the street in which she lived: "He's going with her for six months, and he doesn't know what the name of her street [is], and he doesn't know any of the clubs about, but yet and all he's drinking over here. . . . This isn't 100 percent, you know. As I say, I asked him loads of questions about this, that, and the other. 'Are you working away yourself and all? And where you working?' "

Driver C-WB8 was almost attacked by two gunmen who got into his car wearing gloves and leather jackets on a really nice summer day. He picked them up, but he was worried. When he asked them where they were from, they said, "Ballymurphy," but anyone who was genuinely from Ballymurphy would have said they were from "the Murph." He asked them if they knew anyone local; there were a number of high-profile residents known by everyone. They weren't able to give any names. The man who got into the back of the car sat with his arms folded, and then he slid across to sit behind the driver's seat. At that point, driver C-WB8 stopped the car and ran off. Later that day the same two men who had tried to attack him attacked another Catholic driver from a different depot. Driver C-WB8 had correctly surmised the situation.

Bona-Fide Customers with Negative Cues

Probing is designed, first and foremost, to avoid making a false positive mistake—that is, picking somebody up who turns out *not* to be a genuine passenger. At the same time, probing is aimed at avoiding the reverse mistake, namely, failing to pick up a bona-fide customer. This mistake does not have as bad a consequence as a false positive mistake does, but it still represents a loss of business for drivers. Moreover, it is a loss of service for genuine customers. Those who need to worry most are those passengers who cannot avoid displaying the "wrong" cues—traits that make them suspicious in drivers' eyes, particularly traits that for whatever reasons they cannot easily veil or remove when calling or hailing a taxi.

For instance, groups of two or three young working-class men in Belfast who are bona-fide customers face higher costs of signaling to drivers that they are bona fide, since drivers assess their manifest properties—being in a group, their age, their apparel—as negative. To be picked up they need to display reassuring signals or invite probing to offset the effect of these negative cues.

We investigated the strategies of this type of customer. To some extent this required looking at probing from the point of view of the probed—what they say or do when drivers investigate their trustworthiness. We also looked at those who expect to be rejected out of hand and at what they do, in anticipation of this response, to persuade drivers at least to stop and probe them. Several of their strategies, ironically, are identical to those used by mimics of the bad sort to persuade drivers to pick them up. We discovered that genuine customers possessing negative cues have a very good understanding of what worries drivers and what reassures them and that these customers go to considerable lengths to provide reassurance to taxi drivers.

Becoming Known

Driver C-WB5 said that when he is a customer he employs a cheap trick that takes advantage of callers who are more appealing than he is. Outside a pub or club at night, when everyone wants to go home, he pretends to be the customer who has successfully got the dispatcher to send a taxi: "[The driver calls] a name, and you go, 'That's me!' " This strategy is of limited and potentially troubled applicability, since it first creates a mismatch with the destination declared over the telephone and, moreover, some drivers have learned to respond to the possibility of such a ruse. Rather than call out the name of the person who booked the taxi, they wait for the customer to approach them, and then they ask for the customer's name rather than mention it first.

A far more promising strategy is to become a "regular" with a particular company, although this makes sense only for customers who envisage a repeated use of the service. We know that some local firms are unwilling to pick up fares unless they are familiar with the customer: "The only way to get a local depot round our way is if you use them regularly, and they know you, and they're more or less duty-bound to throw a car round" (driver C-NB1). Customers who experience difficulties in getting a taxi adjust their behavior accordingly. Although customer P-Cust5 is a respectable schoolteacher, he displays a number of negative signs when trying to get a taxi on a weekend night. He lives in quite a rough area, and when he needs a taxi most, he is often drunk and accompanied by three male friends who are also drunk—not a promising combination. He addressed this problem by consciously setting out to become known to a local taxi company and to build up a relationship with them: "At the start, when I first moved in here, I couldn't get a taxi to come round, but after about three weeks of ringing up [the same firm] and sometimes getting a taxi from them, they got to know me, and now I just ring up and give my name and address, and they'll come round."

As well as providing a familiar address, customer P-Cust5 also adopts a familiar weekend routine: "It's the same when I'm out at night: I drink in the same places almost all the time—the Duke of York, Lavery's, McGuinness's—so they'll always come, because they know that's where I always go, and who they're looking for, no matter what state [of drunkenness] I'm in."

Moving to a Safe Location

Customer P-Cust5 also arranges to be picked up at a location that is safe for both the driver and himself. This strategy was confirmed when we interviewed one of the taxi drivers from the firm regularly used by this customer. Heather Hamill asked him: "I have a friend who uses this firm. If he was out in Lavery's or somewhere nearby, he would go around to Donegall Pass—to the phone box." And driver P-EB7 replied: "Yes, that is a popular thing with us . . . away from the main crowd. How many people are going to be standing outside a telephone box at a police station? That is a popular spot for us to pick up."

Being able to convey this knowledge about a regular pickup location ensures that a taxi is dispatched, and being present at the location, away from the crowd, ensures that other opportunistic customers will not take the taxi.

Tipping

We did not set out to ask drivers about tipping. But it is interesting to report that we gathered some evidence that passengers who have unsafe destinations or who themselves look unsafe give more generous tips than regular customers:

> Most people regard West Belfast as a dodgy area. Most people who live there would be understanding enough and ask, "Would you go west, and could you take us?" I always find they are probably the best tippers in town. I mean, the Malone Road [a middle-class neighborhood] are not good tippers. Somewhere like West Belfast, usually people who don't have a lot of money, especially at nighttime, if you take them up they are usually pretty understanding and are pretty good with tips as well. (driver P-PH4)

Driver P-CC12 confirmed this, noting also that those going to the worst areas often tip the driver in gratitude for taking them:

> You will find that you will take people up Malone Road, and they will give you the fare, and that's it. Take somebody up to Twinbrook [a working-class neighborhood in West Belfast] and it's "Thanks very much for getting us home." It's like a challenge every week for them to get home, because they will go to the taxi and say, "Twinbrook," and the taxi will

say, "Booked, sorry," because they don't want to go into the rough areas late on a Saturday night.

Accounts of higher tipping by bona-fide passengers who are accepted despite carrying negative cues also emerged indirectly from several of the drivers' stories. These passengers may tip generously out of gratitude, rewarding the driver for overcoming his diffidence (which the passenger well understands), or in an effort to counteract the area's bad name by showing that not all its residents are to be distrusted. Driver C-PH3 told us, "I have taken people to the rough neighborhoods on the Falls Road or the Shankill Road, and they've told me, 'Don't worry, driver, if there's any rioting, just stop and leave me on the main road.' And when we got to their door and I asked for eight or nine pounds, they will give you an extra two or three pounds."

Driver P-PH4 also told us that passengers from bad areas tend to be more polite, hoping to encourage drivers to pick them up: "Guys from areas like West Belfast, which always had the worst name, they all come round and say, 'Would you take us to West Belfast, is that all right?' They are polite in asking you, because they know that people don't like going to West Belfast." (Driver P-PH4's statement—"I know that they know that we do not like going to West Belfast"—shows a sophisticated understanding.) Higher tipping could also be an inducement to help the driver remember the customer the next time round—part of the becoming-known strategy. As a new customer, P-Cust5 deliberately gave higher tips to enhance his emerging reputation with his local taxi firm.

Driver P-PH1 can also be persuaded by politeness: "If they are up front with me and they say, 'Any chance of a taxi? Look, I am going to the Falls Road—any chance?' I say, 'No problem, son, get in,' and it is all attitude, and whether they speak to you."

Once inside the taxi, good customers who appear bad may choose to continue to display signs of "goodness" in order to ensure that the driver takes them home. This may be as simple as sitting where the driver can see their movements—either in the back opposite the driver or in the passenger front seat—and appearing to be friendly by chatting casually to the driver. Silence can be interpreted as threatening: "The other day I got this taxi driver, and I think he was really uncomfortable with me being silent, and his body language and all was . . . and then I started getting a bit uncomfortable. I was going to try and rescue him and just say something stupid, but I just didn't want to talk, but obviously he wasn't used to the silent shit" (customer C-Cust4).

Female Baits

As we know, almost all drivers consider women customers preferable to men. We tested this preference a number of times with a little experiment.

We had two men stand on one side of the street and two women stand opposite and hail a taxi. Every time, the women were picked up first; taxis would ignore the men or even do a U-turn to pick up the female fare.

Customers know that femaleness acts as a positive signal. (It may be lust rather than trust that does the trick, though: "If you're female and you've got a coat on, you'll take it off, and that does work," said one female customer.) Even women who display some negative signs are successful in being picked up when they accentuate their femaleness. For example, customer P-CustF1, who has her lip, nose, and eyebrow pierced and sports a constellation of prominent tattoos on her arms and upper back, noted: "I've even found, when you phone a taxi company, if you change the way you're talking, if you do a wee girlie thing on the phone, you'll get it in five minutes. . . . My voice would go higher, and I'd be very polite and nice, and I'd get a taxi in no time."

Just as villainous mimics do, one or more bona-fide male customers often use a woman to hail a cab. The mimicry consists not in posing as a female when she is not, but in posing as a passenger when she is not: "I've also done that thing where the girl runs out into the middle of the road to get the taxi, and the fella comes out absolutely blocked [drunk] and being sick all over the backseat for a lift home" (customer P-CustF2). Stopping for a female passenger is also an opportunity to probe. The appearance of the real customers from a dark alley reveals that she is bait, but at that point the driver can ask whether she will join the rest as a passenger or whether she was only a bait. In the latter case he may drive away.

Taxi drivers are aware that this strategy is designed to make it harder for them *not* to pick up: "Something you will find an awful lot is the guys will send the girl to stand on the side of the street and start waving, so once you stop the guys run out and you can't drive off then" (driver P-CC12). However, as we have seen, the effects of a female hailer are eroded once a driver has experienced this trick several times at the hands of a mimic of the bad sort.

One for All

Given the reluctance of taxi drivers to pick up three or more men, often only one member of the group will hail a taxi while the others stand back and emerge from the shadows only after the taxi has stopped. The hailing man in this case mimics being on his own. The sudden appearance of more men can seem threatening to the driver, but once he has stopped the car it becomes harder to drive away:

> The other Sunday I was down at the bar down there, and a fella waved me down, so I stopped, and the next minute three of his mates came across to get into the car too, and here's me, "Oh no, I'm going to get grief here."

But it turned out they were dead on. They w.
home in the car. The fare was ten pounds and ten ₁
the fella gave me fifteen pounds. (driver P-CC4)

Many drivers are also reluctant to pick up a custom.
drunk, and so customers in a group will either try (often u.
to mask the extent of their intoxication or send the most sobe
the group to get the taxi before revealing the others. "If som.
incapable and you have time before they stagger over to your car,
you do then is just drive away," noted driver P-CC2.

Masking the Final Destination

Some customers may look no better or worse than any other customer,
but most drivers may view their destination as unsafe, and so they
struggle to get a ride in a taxi. Customers who want to go to troubled
neighborhoods try to be extra polite, as we have seen, and this may
sometimes suffice. By direct experience, however, we found that a strategy that included exhibiting signs of femaleness, hailing from a safe
location, being polite, and displaying a generally respectable appearance was not enough to get a taxi to take us to an unsafe destination.
Drivers would simply say, "I'm not going east," or, "I'm not going west,"
depending on their religious affiliation. "Trying to get up the Falls
Road—there's a lot just won't do it. Some won't go up the Falls, and
some won't go up the Shankill. It depends where you're from or where
the driver's from" (driver C-WB2).

To overcome this negative sign some customers give a safe destination first and do not reveal their final destination until they have secured
the taxi: "I'm going to one road, and the other person in the car isn't
going to that road, they're going somewhere else, but you don't say until
you're driving away" (customer C-Cust4). However, doing this can
make drivers wary: "If anybody had changed their story, I just wouldn't
have took them," said driver C-NB1. This well illustrates how bona-fide
customers with bad cues often fail to persuade a driver: there is no sign
that they can afford that a mimic could not also afford.

False Negative Mistakes

To conclude, we present seven stories in which drivers found many reasons to expect the worst but in the end were wrong, sometimes in a rather
amusing way. The stories give further evidence of what drivers look for
to assess passengers' trustworthiness, but at the same time they show that
bad signs can be only semi-sorting and may not reveal with absolute cer-
tainty the real type of the passenger. Just as drivers can pick up the wrong
passenger, they may be suspicious of and fail to pick up the right one.

Driver P-PH5

"Whispering in the back's a scary thing. If boys get in and they're shouting and roaring and bawling, that is fine, but if you get two boys or three boys in the back and they're whispering. . . . Now I was scared one night, but nothing happened to me. I got three boys in. I picked them up at Oxford Street where the old bus station was. I said, 'Which end?' 'This end,' they said, which is the Republican end. So I'm driving, and I got to the police station. 'Will it do for you here, lads?' 'No,' they said. 'A wee bit further, and turn in here to the flats.' By that time there was no lights or nothing round the back of the flats, and they were whispering, you see. I'm thinking, I'm in for it. 'Drive round,' they said, and I said, 'No, there's glass there,' so I stopped at the front of the flats, and two got out one side and the other got out beside me, and I was just ready to go when he says, 'How much do I owe you, mate?' I says, 'Two pound will do you.' He says, 'There's three pound, thanks very much.' I went home."

Driver P-PH5

"One of the biggest laughs I got one night was I got a boy who said, 'Can you take me up to Torrens in the Oldpark?' He said, 'There's a fiver, can I sit in the front?' I said, 'Sit in the back.' He said, 'Let me sit in the front.' It was a few years ago, and there were a lot of police checkpoints everywhere, and I says, 'Put the seat belt on, because if we're stopped, they'll be torturing me.' 'I don't use a seat belt,' he says. I says, 'Well, have you got a medical condition?' 'No, I'm carrying here,' and he pulls out a gun. And I says, 'Who are you working for?' 'I'm a hit-man for the UVF.' I says, 'Well, you're wild busy at the minute [*laughs*]. You've plenty of work to do.'

"So he chattered on, and we got off the subject, and I said, 'Have you been out for a drink?' 'Drinking all day.' I said, 'You're lucky. My wife wouldn't let me drink all day.' He says, 'I'm the king of the castle, nobody tells me what to do—nobody.' So I pulls up in Torrens. It was one of those streets, just a house and then a small footpath, no garden or nothing, and it was one of the older taxis that were noisy, they kind of rattled. He opened the taxi door, and this blonde appeared at the door, she was like Arnold Schwarzenegger with blond hair, and if you ever notice, people who have tattoos always wear skimpy tops, so she'd tattoos on both arms. So he turned round and said thanks, and as he turned round to her, she said, 'You cunt,' and he never got to answer because she just put a left hook on him, and the hit-man from the UVF hit the deck. I thought he had hit his head on the taxi and I leaned over to look, but she thought I was looking at her. 'What the fuck are you looking at?' Here's me: 'Nothing, dear.'

"Now, this is about 2:30 A.M., and I'm driving down the Oldpark laughing. If the police had stopped me, they'd have thought I was on drugs. The hit-man, the UVF, carrying a gun, drinking all day, king of the castle, hit the deck by a big blonde, and I wouldn't have tackled that woman with a hammer. At the same time, he could have been a hit-man for the UVF, you just don't know."

Driver P-CC7

"One time I was worried a bit because the guy I picked up at Central Station and was taking him to Randalstown, he had a plaster cast on one of his arms, and when he got in I made him put his seat belt on, and he said, 'Well, I will have to take my coat off,' and when he took his coat off and swung it into the car I could feel something hard hitting my hand from his inside pocket, so automatically your head starts going crazy. But, I thought, I can normally decide from a person within the first five minutes they are in my car what type of person they are, because I kind of joke about a bit with them, and if they bite on it, then I feel a bit more relaxed and they feel a bit more relaxed. If they don't, then I start asking questions. Why not? Because no one wants to get in a taxi where the driver just sits there, they like a little feedback.

"So the guy started to chat back, and I thought [this would be] a decent job out at Randalstown—but he was telling me he had been down in Dublin all weekend and had a great time . . . but when we came into Randalstown, I asked him, 'Whereabouts do you want [to be] left off?' There was a car park sign just about five hundred yards down the road on the left-hand side, and he said, 'Just pull into that car park.' So I pulled into a car park that didn't even have streetlights, had no cars in it, it was no-man's-land. I automatically started thinking, what is going down here? So then he says, 'Don't be going away, mate. I will be back in a minute,' which made me start thinking again, but all he did was he went out and went to the toilet in the hedge and then came back over [to] the car and asked me what the fare was, and I told him. He paid me, and then he lifted out some Irish money and said, 'Could you take this Irish money?' So I automatically assumed that he wanted me to exchange it for sterling and said, 'Right, okay.' But he didn't, he just gave me the money and said, 'I can't take this with me where I am going,' and walked away from the car. Now, there was twenty-odd punts, which was the equivalent, say, to fifteen pounds then, which he was freely giving away, so all my fear of what this guy was at was totally wrong."

"I did a job one night at the Harbor Bar, and the first guy who came out was cut just above his eye, and the blood was pouring out of it, and I said to myself, why did I even take this job on? I checked to see where the job was going, and it was booked to go to the Falls Road, and I thought, even more to the point, what am I doing here? But when he got into the car, the guy with the cut sat in the front seat, and these two big body builders got into the back, and I thought, what am I at? So I questioned where were they going to. 'Over to the Falls Road, and then we are going to the top of Broadway, and then you are going out by Shaw's Road,' and I thought, this is going to be a dead long journey. And then the guy started to say about how he had been hit on the head with a baseball bat, and these two guys were going on, don't be so stupid, you fell, you fell. 'You know who my big brother is?'—who was apparently a top IRA boy in Poleglass—'I will have them down to sort this out tomorrow.' Again [I thought,] why did I not go home?

"So then one of the guys in the back just happened to mention a punk group from the eighties to which I could have associated with, and right away I was in there. Me and Frankie are like big mates now, but he started rhyming off groups that I would have listened to, and it got to the point where he said to me, 'Let the first guy off,' and then we went to Frankie's house second, and Frankie said to me, 'Come on in, I have the LPs, we can listen to them.' So there, within five minutes I went from, what is going to happen to me? to he is inviting me into his house to listen to music. I said, 'No, Frankie, maybe some other time, but I need to get home.' So the last guy I was leaving off was the one with the cut, and Frankie shouts into him: 'This is Joe, he will look after you, he is a good man, don't worry about it.' So I felt comfortable.

"So when I got the guy up to his house, he then suddenly realized he had no money, but he was going to go into the house and get it. So you say to yourself, is it easier to let him go into the house and walk away? But he went into the house and left his Levi jacket sitting in the front seat, so I automatically thought I could get twenty pounds for the jacket to try and make up for it. But I thought, no, I will sit it out, and he opened the front door, and an Alsatian ran out, and I thought, what is going on here? And then he came out and paid.

"I know of two guys who to look at them they are just like eighteen or nineteen stone, six foot four inches, built like a brick toilet, tattoos everywhere, Mohicans, the lot, but they are the nicest two guys you will ever meet. It is like looking at a picture and seeing something totally different, but the minute they get in they always tip you well, et cetera, et cetera. So it is back to the same old saying: never judge a book by its cover."

Driver P-CC7's Friend

"I remember a friend of mine got this job one day going to Portadown, and the guy got into the car with a briefcase, behind the driver, which automatically he started thinking, going to Portadown is a really bad idea. So he started talking away to the guy when he got onto the motorway, and the guy never responded. So he automatically thought that there is something wrong here, with the guy had a briefcase sitting on his lap and the driver talking away and talking away but never gave him any comment. So the driver automatically thought, this guy is going, at any time now, to open that briefcase, pull a gun out, and clout me. So about four miles from Portadown he heard the *click-click* of the briefcase. He started to swear very heavily and wondered what was going on, and then the guy's hand came around the seat with a bit of paper, and he opened the paper. It said, 'I am deaf and dumb, sorry.' The guy had looked up and seen the driver talking to him in the mirror and realized that he had been talking to him and he hadn't replied. So he panicked the whole way out to Portadown thinking that he was going to get done and the guy was deaf and dumb."

Driver P-EB7

"I went to Newtownards one night, and the fella came out and said to me, 'There is a bit of a problem here, mate. I have no money, I will have to owe you it.' Now, I said to myself, you either leave him here—there was him and his girlfriend—you either leave him or else take him and take the chance of getting it maybe at a later date. Well, I took him, and I got paid about three weeks later."

Driver C-NB1

"I picked up four characters from the Wellington Park Hotel, and as soon as they got into the car, the first thing the guy in the passenger seat said was, 'Right, take us to God's country.' I'm thinking, where's 'God's country'? East Belfast, uh-uh-uh-oh! Definitely out of my territory altogether. Taking me away from going back up the Antrim Road again, and I swear the atmosphere in that car was just so unbelievably tense. . . . Four drunken Loyalists was what I had in the car, I was crapping myself. I thought, I'm going to get killed tonight. [*Did they know that you were Catholic?*] I think my whole 'Ahh, shit,' that's what everything about me said rather than me having to say anything, and when your taxi badge is hanging with your name and all on it. [I did not know where I was going.] Didn't have a clue. They took me down a wee dark street with a set of garages, and I thought, oh Jesus, I'm going to be killed here, but it just happened that they lived off this wee dark street with a set of garages. I dropped three of them off and took the other one out to Holywood. He opened up and started talking then, and he was friendly enough. He was going chasing [girls], and I started up a conversation about that. . . . It's amazing really, the vast majority of people are honest, they want to pay their taxi bill."

From these last two chapters, we have learned that, their mistakes not withstanding, Belfast's taxi drivers appear remarkably adept at negotiating their complex world of sectarianism while at the same time trying to earn a decent living. Much of their reasoning, some of which is sophisticated indeed, provides rich evidence of, among other things, an intuitive application of signaling theory in the real-life trust games that drivers play when deciding which customers to pick up and which to ignore. (We discuss in depth the central theoretical issues in chapter 11.) Yet the risks that drivers run in Belfast are relatively unambiguous: they are largely defined by the religious and political conflict, the geographical boundaries are clear, and there is only one predominant ethnic group. As driver P-CC2 pointed out, "Driving a taxi in Belfast is not rocket science, you can pick it up very quickly." As we noted in chapter 1, most drivers learn the basic "rules" by virtue of having grown up there.

In our tale of two cities, we now turn to explore how drivers fare in New York, where the risks of criminal encounters are more diffused and there is both greater anonymity and a greater variety of ethnic groups and types of areas.

PART II

NEW YORK

Chapter 6

New York and Its Taxi Drivers

T HERE IS hardly a city in the world in whose brand image taxis are more powerfully etched than New York. Among other large cities in the world, only London, with its black cabs, offers some competition in this regard. An icon of New York as much as skyscrapers or the music of Gershwin, New York yellow cabs appear everywhere in postcards, stories, films, and even as toys. They evoke the ceaseless buzzing of the metropolis and represent the at once nervous and light-hearted determination of all travelers in New York in negotiating obstacles to get somewhere. In a city in which a parking space for a private car is so rare as to be a reason to marry the owner of such a prize, many people, New Yorkers as well as tourists, have to use taxis regularly. They quickly get in and out of them at every corner of the city day and night.

By contrast, the drivers are stuck in their taxis for ten or twelve hours a day every day, and they see taxis with rather less romantic eyes than outsiders. Their work is not only monotonous, poorly paid, and nerve-wracking but also dangerous. Before describing their survival strategies in the following chapters, we provide a brief outline of the industry and its protagonists in New York.

Types of Taxis and Taxi Regulations

The New York City Taxi and Limousine Commission (TLC)[1] licenses and regulates over 50,000 vehicles and approximately 100,000 drivers, of which 12,187 are the yellow taxis.[2] Yellow taxis are the aristocracy of the industry, the only vehicles legally permitted to pick up street-hail passengers or passengers at taxi or airport stands in New York City.[3] They operate mainly in Manhattan and downtown Brooklyn, charge a metered fare, and have a roof light indicating whether they are available for hire, hired, or off-duty. Yellow taxi licenses (commonly known as "medallions") are transferable and in 2002 each fetched well over $200,000 in the market.

The rest—in fact the majority—of the taxis in New York are known collectively as liveries, or more formally as for-hire vehicles (FHVs). They are legally required to be affiliated with a for-hire base, a business that dispatches them via two-way radio or a computer data head and is responsible for handling complaints about the drivers or vehicles. Legally, livery cars are supposed to provide a prearranged service only.[4] They charge fares based on zone systems, by the hour or sometimes by the mile. They may not use meters and are not required to have roof signs or lights indicating whether they are a taxi, though they sometimes do have them on their windshields. The main way to identify these taxis is by the color, type, and brand of car. The FHV industry is segmented into "black cars," "limousines," and "car services."

Black cars are luxury cars that primarily serve business clientele. Under TLC rules, black cars are defined as FHVs that operate from bases organized as either a franchise or a cooperative. Limousines are generally stretch vehicles or so-called luxury limousines; passengers are charged on the basis of garage-to-garage service, and at least 90 percent of black car customers pay by a method other than cash.[5]

Our interest was focused mainly on drivers who work for the third type of liveries—namely, car services, which operate in the Bronx, Brooklyn, Queens, Staten Island, and northern Manhattan. Like the private-hire taxis in Belfast, they offer a neighborhood service. Although, by law, yellow cabs must take passengers to all five New York boroughs, since the mid-1980s they have limited their service to Manhattan. The pressing need for taxis in the high-crime neighborhoods of northern Manhattan, the South Bronx, and parts of Queens and Brooklyn has been met by the livery drivers, who work where yellow cabs do not dare to go. They form the proletariat of this industry, carrying the greatest number of passengers in the areas where risks are greatest. (We want to emphasize that "proletarian" does not refer to the conditions of their service or cars but to the areas into which they are forced to cruise.)

There is also a lumpen proletariat, a group of unlicensed and unregulated illegal liveries known locally as "gypsy cabs." It is often difficult to distinguish them by appearance from car service taxis, since both types of taxis use older Lincoln Town Cars. Their number is unknown, but the TLC reports that it seizes between four hundred and six hundred illegal livery vehicles per month.[6]

Livery cars are not allowed to pick up street-hail passengers, but they all do. A study commissioned by the Taxi Policy Institute measuring the prevalence of livery taxis illegally picking up street-hails in Manhattan shows that liveries account for 41 percent of vehicles (taxis or liveries) stopping for the testers (Schaller Consulting 2002).[7] However, picking up street-hails can be a very risky practice: for instance, 82 percent of the livery-cab robberies and six of the seven homicides of taxi drivers between January and April 2000 occurred after a driver had picked up a street-hail.[8]

Although livery drivers and their vehicles must be licensed and comply with TLC regulations, they are subject to far fewer regulations than the tightly controlled yellow cabs. City officials assume that New Yorkers and tourists need more protection when hopping into a hailed cab than when calling ahead for one. Unlike livery cabbies, yellow cab drivers have to attend an eighty-hour preparation course, get a physical examination, and prove they are proficient in English, and they are limited in what they can charge. They also have to retire their cars when they are three years old, install air conditioning, and post information in the cars to let passengers know their identity and show that they are licensed (Kennedy 2001a).

While the TLC regulates the taxi industry in New York, drivers are represented by two main organizations, both recently founded in 1998. The New York Taxi Workers Alliance (NYTWA) has three thousand members who are mostly yellow cab drivers, and the New York State Federation of Taxi Drivers (NYSFTD) represents eighteen thousand drivers, most of them livery.

The Demand for Taxis and the Impact of 9/11

The forty-one thousand livery cabs in New York service the city's population of over eight million people.[9] The NYSFTD estimates that its eighteen thousand members transport two million passengers every day. A report on yellow cab availability and ridership in New York City from 1990 to 1999 shows that taxis are the second-largest means of public transportation for traveling within Manhattan after the subway (Schaller 2000). Even though yellow cabs constitute 30 to 50 percent of traffic at many busy Manhattan intersections, in 1999 there was still a shortfall in taxi availability (Kennedy 2001a). As a result, liveries have increasingly been taking hails south of 125th Street. The yellow cab industry has complained that liveries are invading their territory and poaching their business, but the NYSFTD argues that livery cabs provide a vital service to people wanting to travel from Manhattan to the outer boroughs, where yellow cabs refuse to go.

In low-income neighborhoods livery cabs are often the only means of private transportation for residents. The NYSFTD has therefore proposed "Operation Green Zone" to the TLC, whereby livery drivers can legally provide a pickup service within the yellow cab "no-go" areas. At the time of writing, this had not yet been accepted.

We started our fieldwork one month after the September 11, 2001, terrorist attack. The impact of that event was being felt throughout the taxi industry, whose prosperity is symbiotically linked to the amount of disposable income. The yellow cabs, working in downtown Manhattan, were hit particularly hard by the combination of gridlocked roads, fewer hails, and, for some Arab American drivers and for those who simply looked as if they were of Middle Eastern descent, the fear of retaliatory violence.

We asked the livery drivers how the events of September 11 had affected them economically. They too had been feeling the financial pinch: "Well, this job is dangerous, but we make good money. Right now we don't make any good money because of what happened at the World Trade Center" (driver BX1). Now they had to work harder to maintain their income. Driver BR3, a livery driver in Brooklyn since 1995, said: "Before September 11, it was slow, but now it is more slow for me. It's very different from before. Before, you can make a lot of money easier than now. Now you gotta work fourteen or fifteen hours [to] make the same money when you worked eight hours before." Driver Q2, who is based in Queens, shared that view: "It's harder because fewer people are taking taxis, so drivers have to work longer hours in order to make their money." Working in an already poor neighborhood, driver BR1 was finding it hard to cover his expenses:

> So the people who got money, they scared. They don't wanna go out. They don't wanna dance like before. They scared to go to the store late at night. People want to save their money, and all that thing is killing [me] 'cause you gotta make money. If you pay six thousand dollars for insurance, you pay five hundred fifty dollars for the TLC and four hundred dollars for the taxicab. Plus, you have to fix your car if it's broke. There's a lot of things. You have to wash the car. Take it to the car wash, inspection of the car every three or four months. It's hard. You have to make at least a hundred fifty dollars. Situation like this, you never gonna do. Why? 'Cause this neighborhood [in Brooklyn] is a poor neighborhood. Most of those people go on welfare.

Since 9/11, he allowed that even on the colder days people still were not taking taxis: "They're freezing waiting for the bus. But they don't call the car 'cause they can't afford it. They don't make money; a lot of people are unemployed. So no business." He also believed that they weren't freezing after all and even the weather was conspiring against his ability to make a decent living: "There's no winter. If winter comes, they have to take cabs because it's cold out there." Driver BXF4 felt that the scarcity of fares had led drivers to be less discerning about the passengers they were willing to pick up: "Especially now after September 11 . . . we are not making the same money, so sometimes we have to just forget what the person looks like and just take them, 'cause we need the money. You have to do that." We return to the selectivity issue in chapter 7.

Drivers

The NYSFTD estimates that of the city's forty-one thousand livery drivers, three-quarters are Latino, and three-quarters of those are from the Dominican Republic.[10] In total, we interviewed sixty-three drivers. Twenty-eight (44 percent) originated in the Dominican Republic, sixteen (25 percent) were from other parts of South and Central America (Ecuador, Mexico, Puerto Rico, Peru, Colombia, and Argentina), eleven (17 percent) were from West Africa (Senegal, Ivory Coast, Ghana), and five (10 percent) were African American (see table 6.1).[11]

Finding work in New York is difficult even for skilled, educated immigrants, and driving a taxi has always been a popular choice among immigrants to the United States.[12] However, for many immigrants in New York the yellow cab requirements are prohibitively tough and a medallion's cost is well above their means. Driving a livery is a much more accessible and flexible option:

> I feel that it's better, this type of cab, than the yellow cabs. Yellow cabs, you know, it's more hectic than this. They are obligated to work those twelve hours. And this cab here, this is my cab. I can work whatever hours I want, and I can go home whenever I want. I can refuse a passenger if I want. In yellow cabs you can't do that. Although we are regulated by the TLC to oblige the customers . . . we do that. We get a call—we have to take them to where they want to go. But if that passenger gives us a hard time, we are also obliged to get them out, you know. (driver BX5)

Not to mention the traffic in Manhattan: " 'Cause in yellow taxis downtown [Manhattan] you got to be in a hurry all the time. Life is too complicated downtown. You got to hustle too much to make money there" (driver BX8).

Table 6.1   Area and Ethnicity of New York Taxi Drivers Interviewed

Area	Hispanic	West African	African American	Total
Bronx	12	—	—	12
Brooklyn	12	—	—	12
Queens	13	—	—	13
North Manhattan	2	11	5	18
(Yellow cabs)	5	—	2	7

Source: Authors' compilation.
Notes: Gender is not included in this table because there was only one woman in our New York sample; she was Hispanic and worked in the Bronx. Also not included in the table is one driver who was from New Zealand.

We asked the drivers why they chose to drive a livery cab despite the risks entailed. Their responses were similar to those given by the Belfast drivers: a lack of alternatives and the flexibility and independence of the job. Over 80 percent of the drivers we interviewed were married with children. Although their secondary motivations varied, they all drove a cab because they needed a job to provide for their families. Driver BR1 has five children: "I have to support them. I have to work." While the drivers are plying their trade every day, their families worry about their safety: "My family, they say, be careful. Because they see the news and see a lot of things happen. I was in so many funerals with my wife when a driver got killed. . . . They try to tell you be careful, and you get in your car, got to keep the window up and be alert in case something happens so you can defend yourself" (driver BR1).

For Spanish-speaking immigrants with poor English language skills, driving a livery is one of the most financially lucrative jobs they can get: "I make a good living. I earn more than I would on other jobs considering that I don't speak English, therefore I wouldn't be able to get a good job" (driver Q4). Driver Q2 studied economics at university in Peru and moved to New York twenty years ago. Unable to pursue a career in economics because of his limited English language skills, he began working in construction but makes more money as a taxi driver in Queens: "My wife was the one who kind of told me to get into the taxi business, because there was good money and because I didn't really know what else to do. It's very hard for a person, for an immigrant, when they come here, because of English. And that's the reason why I got into the taxi business."

Driver Q6 had been a lawyer in Mexico, but his English was too poor to practice law in New York: "My friend told me about the taxi business. When I tried it, I noticed that every day I would have money to feed my family. Every day I would have an income—every single day."

Other drivers stress the independence and flexibility that the job affords. Driver YC1, who has driven both yellow and livery cabs in Queens over the past fifteen years, trained as a chemical engineer in Argentina before he moved to New York: "So I came here, and I saw very fast that the taxi industry was able to offer me the possibility to do everything by myself. And in fact, I never liked to work for somebody, so the bottom line is independence." Driver BX2, who drives mostly in the Bronx, agreed: "I think it's a good profession for people that don't want a boss or want their time to be flexible and feel comfortable and feel secure about themselves and make the money that they wanna make."

Driver BXF4, a single mother with two children, also works in the Bronx and values the flexibility of taxiing:

> What's good about this is that while I am working I can be with the children. . . . I take them to school; I pick them up from school. If they have to

go to the library or they need to go to the doctor, I just stop working and go with them. If they have some homework to do or some project that they do in school, I just stop working and help them. This is what is good about this job. . . . I start working seven-thirty in the morning. I stop when my kids finish school. At two-thirty in the afternoon I stop, pick them up from school, take them home. I have my aunt in the house, so she lives with me . . . and then I go back to taxi for one, two, or three hours. So this is what's good about it. . . . That's the only thing I like about it.

Driver BX3 had been working as a mechanic but wanted to return to the community college course he started in 1993. He hoped taxiing would give him more free time to renew his studies. He told us that he was still working very long hours to make enough money, however, and was struggling to keep up at college.

Many drivers have a previous connection with the taxi industry. Some have friends and family who drive taxis and introduced them to taxiing in New York: "It's my first job in New York. I left my country. I have family in this job" (driver Q8). Driver BX1 said: "Yes, my father is a taxi driver. He helped me to get a car. He told me it's dangerous but you make money, you make a living." Others had worked as taxi drivers in their countries of origin. Driver Q1 had driven a taxi in Peru, and "when I came to this country, that was the only thing I knew how to do, and it was easier for me to start doing this than to go looking for a different job." Driver Q10 had driven a taxi in Colombia, and when he moved to New York, it was the only profession in which he had any experience.

During the course of the interviews, most of the drivers complained about the job: the traffic, the TLC, the police, the weather, and the customers. Asked whether he liked driving a taxi, driver BR1 replied: "No way. I do it because what am I gonna do? I need a job." Some, however, like driver BX4, genuinely enjoy meeting people and felt that they provide more than just a transport service: "Most of the customers, they talk. They take it like therapy. They like it. Sometimes there is people that they even talk about a problem and I don't have to do anything or say anything, or I think, this is a hard question. . . . I don't know why, but they trust me." For driver BX4, driving a taxi is like doing more than one job at the same time:

This job is like a bartender. People come in here, and they dump, they dump everything. So sometimes they will ask for, you know, how you say, prescriptions, you know. What can I do for this? What can I do for that? Oh, this hurts me. You have to be a doctor; you have to be a lawyer, a psychiatrist. Everything here. And if you know a little bit about some subjects, you know, you can help. I like it. This is a job that you have to like. If you don't like what you do, you're gonna have a hard time. With passengers, with drivers out in the street . . . I was cut out for it. This is my profession, and I try to improve it as I go on.

Not all of the drivers intended to stay in New York. For "the birds of passage," taxiing was a way to make some money before returning home: "I'm gonna drive for like three more years, and then I go back to the Dominican Republic for a while," said driver BX8.

The Dangers of Taxiing in New York

The crime rate in New York has been falling over the past ten years: the New York City Police Department has reported a drop from a total of 174,542 violent crimes in 1990 to 78,945 in 1999 (U.S. Department of Justice 2001). However, taxi drivers remain at risk of becoming victims of violent crimes because they work with the public, work with cash, work alone, work late at night or in the early hours of the morning, and work in high-crime areas (National Institute for Occupational Safety and Health 1996). Driver BR1 explained the hazards he faces every day:

Well, you have to be prepared for being attacked. It's a dangerous job. If you gonna do it, then you gotta know that you gonna have a problem at least once a week. Person who don't want to pay, person who want to pay less, people like that. Or people that wanna get money from you. Or people that wanna kill you. . . . It's a dangerous job . . . it's more dangerous than if you're the police. It's dangerous.

According to the National Institute for Occupational Safety and Health (NIOSH), more than 30 percent of the 510 taxi drivers killed in the United States between 1992 and 1998 were New York livery drivers (Sygnatur and Toscano 2000). The New York City TLC reported that between 1990 and 2001, over 250 drivers were killed in New York (see also Kugel 2001), and the drivers we interviewed told us that many of their friends and colleagues had been killed or injured: "I saw many, many people die in ten years working this job. I have participated in many funerals" (driver BX7).

Often the deaths and injuries arise because robbers turn violent. In a study of 280 murders of taxi drivers in the United States and Canada between 1980 and 1994, 91 percent of the attacks were robbery or suspected robbery, 85 percent of the fatal injuries were from gunshot wounds, and 64 percent of the deaths were from gunshot wounds to the head (Rathbone 1994/2002). The average take in a livery cab robbery is a mere seventy-five dollars (Martin 1993), and an attacker, whose perceptions may be distorted by drug use, may become aggressive if he is challenged by his victims or believes they are withholding money. According to the newspaper reports we examined, the livery driver Elhadji Gaye (an immigrant from Senegal) was murdered when his attackers became infuriated on finding only a quarter in his pockets (see Yardley 1997; *New York Times* 1999). Driver BX8, from the Bronx, told us:

> They are waiting for you to make mistakes. I mean, it's a lot of people who use drugs. They kill you for five dollars to buy drugs. . . . They like to use drugs, but they don't have the money for the drugs. They might say that we are easy pickings. They think, I know how to make some money, let me go out and get a taxi driver. They know that most of the time we got like sixty, seventy, seventy-five dollars.

Between January and April 2000, there were 269 reported robberies of livery cab drivers in New York. However, the actual number of robberies is likely to be much higher, since drivers are reluctant to report incidents to the police. Fernando Mateo, president of the NYSFTD, explained: "Livery drivers stopped reporting the robberies because they find that it is a waste of their time. . . . They end up sitting in a precinct or a courtroom, but almost never are the cases cracked. When they get robbed, they go home and sob a bit and go back to work" (Chivers 2000a).

A further danger faced by drivers in New York is being killed or injured in a car crash. A report on taxi and livery crashes in New York between 1990 and 1999 showed that yellow and livery taxis were in 16 percent of all crashes citywide, and in 30 percent of all crashes in Manhattan. In 1999 there were 17,127 taxi crashes (13,134 involved livery cars, and 4,270 involved yellow taxis), 13,126 of which entailed personal injury to a vehicle occupant, pedestrian, or bicyclist. There were 29 crashes involving fatalities (Schaller 2001).

Information Diffusion and Background Knowledge

In Belfast we witnessed how pivotal the exchange of information is in helping drivers cope with the daily hazards of their profession. In New York we were also made aware of the importance of information-sharing in protecting drivers. Because so many drivers in the New York livery industry are from South and Central America, they can communicate with each other in Spanish.

As in Belfast, drivers use their cell phones to report dangers or nuisances, such as suspicious-looking passengers or traffic buildup, and dispatchers broadcast this information over the radio: "All the time we are talking, and we talk about any passengers that we have, or any problems that we have with any passenger, and also we take warnings . . .

whatever" (driver BR2). Being constantly in touch with the base keeps the drivers abreast of what is happening on the streets and gives them a sense of solidarity and safety: "I feel more secure because there are people that call the base constantly. Yeah, the drivers, they protect each other. Say there's a driver with a person that didn't pay them, or they think it's not a good person. They'll [call the base] and say that they picked up at what time, the building, and the driver warns others" (driver BX2).

The New York drivers also have their own radio program, one resource that does not exist in Belfast. Every evening between ten o'clock and midnight, drivers can tune into a program broadcast from a Spanish-speaking radio station and dedicated specifically to livery drivers. The NYSFTD uses this program to spread information about its activities, and the announcers, who were themselves taxi drivers, provide information, advice, and warnings on a range of topics, including car mechanics, insurance, avoiding roadwork, fares, attacks on drivers, and whether or not to participate in a certain research study. (Heather Hamill was told by a driver in Brooklyn that he had been waiting for the opportunity to talk to her about his experiences since he had heard the research being discussed on the radio program.)

The West African drivers working in northern Manhattan, who are neither Spanish-speaking nor members of the NYSFTD, do not have access to this resource but keep in touch with each other by using their cell phones or by talking to each other as they wait for trains to arrive at the Metro North station at 125th Street and Lexington Avenue. "We meet each other every day, and we got our phones. . . . Anything that happens in a particular neighborhood, after a few hours we all hear about it" (driver NM13). These drivers keep a watchful eye out for each other: "Sometimes, they see me parked somewhere, they will stop and ask me, 'Are you all right?' Sometimes I could have a flat or maybe the car could break down, and if they can help, they help. You know, if I need a jump, sometimes the battery can die. You can help in different ways" (driver NM17).

With one exception, all of the drivers we interviewed in Belfast originated in Northern Ireland, and most in Belfast. They had gained their knowledge of the city—the characteristics and pitfalls of each area—by virtue of growing up and living there. Much of this information was acquired before they started taxiing, and the depots provided little or no structured training.

In New York almost all of the livery drivers in our sample were immigrants to the United States from Central and South America and West Africa and had been living in New York for an average of fifteen years. Whereas yellow cab drivers operating in the safer environment of Manhattan have to attend an eighty-hour preparation course, livery cab drivers do not have any formal training.

When a livery driver first starts taxiing, he has much to learn, and it must be learned quickly from family, friends, other drivers, and personal experience. New drivers can pay a heavy price for their inexperience on the job. Driver BR1's friend had been working only two weeks when a passenger murdered him. In a separate incident, in January 1998, Konstantine Kondratenko was in his second week of work as a livery driver when he was killed on his first night shift by the only passenger he picked up that evening (Jacobs 1998).

As in Belfast, we asked the New York drivers the questions "What do you need to know to drive a taxi in New York?" and "How do you know it?" Driver BX9, one of our first interviewees, believed that above all a driver needs survival skills: "They need to know a little bit of survival. The most things that he gotta know is survival. He's gonna get every situation, and every situation is different. And at different times different days . . . and unfortunately some of them don't know the way to come out of that situation." Driver Q10 was more specific:

> When someone is starting as a cab driver, they should consult with other people who have been taxi drivers for a long time. They should get familiarized with how the industry is, with how the insurance is so high. They should make sure that they know what they are getting into, because it's a lot of money to pay. They should have the partition—that's very important because of all the criminals. They should know the language well because it's very important. They should know their way around. They should be familiar with the streets close to the base and things like that.

One of the first things a cabby must learn is the topography of the areas in which he works—where streets and buildings are and the most efficient routes to take. "We need maps, we need to know how to get there, is the first thing," noted driver BX4. "We need to know distance, we need to know how much to charge and not to overcharge. We need to know how to drive, what to do if there is an incident. And also we need to know about people, about the passengers. It's hard . . . your brain is doing three, four things at the same time, you know."

Driver BX2 agreed: "Well, the first thing is a map. There're many drivers that don't have a map. They don't know where they're going, and they have to ask the dispatcher, or if they go somewhere . . . they get lost. A map is very important."

Because of the risks that accompany the job, a driver must quickly get to know which areas are more dangerous and which buildings to be especially careful of. Driver BR3, who works in East New York, a notorious area of Brooklyn, will not pick up from certain residential buildings that he has come to learn can be very dangerous: "I know the area. 'Cause I live in this area, like eight years. I know the buildings what are trouble, what the buildings that are not trouble. I know everything in the area."

The primary source of knowledge acquisition is the close-knit community of Dominican drivers. Driver BX9 was fortunate to have a father who had been a livery driver and had taught him a lot: "My father was a cab driver at that time. He give me some advice, a lot of advice. But when you're on the street, the way to learn is to be on the street. That's the way to learn. People tell you advice, but until you got a bad experience you won't get it." Driver BX1's father had also been a driver: "My father, he have a lot of experiences. He's been driving for like twenty years. . . . He told me a lot of things before I got into this. Especially he don't want me to work without a partition. Every time he sees it open, he tells me. But he got a lot of experience."

Driver Q10 had worked as a taxi driver in Colombia. He moved to New York to join his father, who owns a base, and was made to do an apprenticeship, learning the business from the bottom up: "My dad has a base. First, what I used to do was clean the office and help out, like with the taxi drivers. Then my father lent me some money to buy a cab, and I bought one, and then I started working as a taxi driver. In Colombia I used to work as a taxi driver, so I knew about it. And when I came here, working with my dad, I was able to become familiar with it quickly." Driver BX4 got a lot of advice from other drivers at the base where she worked:

> They help me a lot. I know how to drive in the city, but I didn't know how to take the routes and how to take people places that I never been before. Sometimes drivers used to come and they say, "Follow me when I take you to that place." I was the one making the money and he just helping me. There is a good relationship between taxi drivers. They're great to work with. It's a very beautiful relationship. If something happens, there's always people there to help.

Driver BR2 was helped out by a taxi-driving friend: "You have to know the place, the streets, the area, you know. Because when I started, I knew a lot of the area. Because I went with, like I told you before, a friend of mine, and he told me." Although the more experienced drivers pass on their accumulated knowledge to "rookies" ("I just look at them and say, 'Oh, this guy is never gonna learn.' But this is the world. You tell other people, they don't listen, what can we do? That's a life, you can't help everybody. Some people listen" [driver BX10]), there is little substitute for experience, especially bad experience. The best way to learn is by doing the job, as driver YC1 noted: "[Things that happened to me before], they will never happen again, because I know about it. But you never know about that until you work four or five years. You don't remember overnight." Driver BX5 agreed: "The more you do this job, the more, the better you get at judging people, judging situations."

The New York drivers are disadvantaged in ways that the native Belfast drivers are not. As immigrants to the city, they must learn enough English to understand customers' directions, and they must also quickly absorb a great deal of information, not least New York's large geographical spread. As in part I, how drivers use such knowledge to screen and probe customers is discussed in the last two chapters of part II.

Chapter 7

Mimics in New York

A PART FROM drunken customers, many of whom cannot hide their state even if they want to, Belfast drivers are exposed to three insidious perils from passengers, or rather, from mimics of them: runners, robbers, and, worst of all, paramilitaries intent on hijacking their car or harming them for sectarian reasons. In addition, drivers who are breaking the industry laws and regulations fear undercover DOE agents who pass themselves off as passengers in order to try to catch them in flagrante delicto.

In New York drivers also worry about runners and robbers, though not about sectarian attacks. This does not make their lives any easier, for, as table 2.1 shows (see p. 50, this volume), the threat from *violent* robbers is greater in New York than in Belfast, both because robberies are committed more frequently in New York and because robbers there are more likely to become violent. Occasionally, New York drivers have even been exposed to mindlessly violent attacks. Finally, drivers, especially yellow cab drivers, have had to contend with undercover police and TLC operations in recent times. These are intended to deter and punish discrimination against African American passengers. Here we review the threats that these various characters pose.

Runners

In New York drivers seem less preoccupied with runners than in Belfast; they do not even have a name for this category of troublesome passenger. It is not that runners do not exist in New York—in fact, all of our interviewees had been victims at least once of passengers who did not pay them—but in the face of the much greater threat from violent offenders, a runner is regarded as a minor frustration. The drivers sounded almost relieved if the worst passenger they picked up during their shift was someone who ran off without paying the fare: "So you gonna lose two dollars, lose two dollars. People run away, that's it, don't be so sensitive," said driver BX10. Driver BX5 expressed similar sentiments:

> I picked up a guy here—a suit, tie, everything clean. It was on a Sunday about nine o'clock in the morning. I picked him up by Lincoln Hospital. I took him to 175th Street, and there's a new building over there. He tells me he was gonna go inside, get somebody, and then he was gonna go to 125th Street and Broadway. I say, "No problem." I trusted him. He was all right. He went into the building and never came out. And I don't mind that. Better than to pull out a gun, take my money, or maybe pistol-whip me, you know. So that's how you got to take it as it comes.

Although we cannot estimate the exact incidence of runners—neither drivers nor depots, not even the NYSFTD, keep a record of that—all of the drivers we interviewed had suffered from them: "When I pick up somebody, it is fifty-fifty whether they are going to pay me or not," said driver NM3. Driver Q9 estimated that he is the victim of runners three or four times a week. Driver BR4 said that it frequently happens in Brooklyn, where he works: "In this area, yes, we complain a lot about it. The way that I see it, suppose you're a person who has no money to eat or uses drugs or something. If you have to pay ten or five dollars, you prefer to jump out of the car and keep the money."

The stereotypical New York runner is a teenager of any ethnicity and either sex: "Anywhere from around age fourteen up to around eighteen . . . they're gonna rip you off. . . . And not only that, but they'll write on the partition in the back. They'll write their names with magic markers and all that, yeah, yeah. Then they'll open the door and run out. It's crazy. That's their kick, you know. I understand that. I not gonna get out and chase them" (driver BX5). Driver BXF4 picked up three teenagers, and when she stopped at their destination, "all of them were out of the car, and they started running like crazy. I just looked back, and I was laughing. I knew it was going to happen to me, it happens with the teenagers all the time."

Not all runners are teenagers, though. Some look like ordinary, respectable customers and need to do little extra to persuade a driver to pick them up: "Sometimes they're Spanish, they look okay, they're clean dressed, but you never know. In this city nobody trust anybody" (driver BX7). Driver Q9 told us: "I have the experience where the person wears a nice suit and a nice tie, and then he run away, he don't pay me. You can never tell. It's very hard to say . . . it can be anybody. I just open the door, and they just run away."

Runners are literally free-riders: they want to be taken to a specific destination free of charge. In this sense, runners are passengers rather than robbers pretending to be passengers. Their distinctive mimicry act is aimed at persuading drivers that they are going to pay when they plan not to. They mimic not so much a genuine passenger as a *paying* one. There are those, of course, who need to persuade drivers to pick them up in the first place, for they have bad signs about them that make drivers suspicious. For instance, aware that drivers are reluctant to pick them up, teenagers call a dispatcher and pretend they are not teenagers. The young people whom driver BXF4 was dispatched to pick up pretended to be one man seeking a ride with his child:

> These teenagers, they know nobody gonna pick them up. So they made a call, and one of them tells the dispatcher that he was a guy with his baby and he needed a taxi. I took the call. So . . . when I get to the building . . . I looking and waiting for the gentleman and his baby and I see three teenagers. They come beside the car and they say, "Oh, I was the one who called." And I say, "No, the one who called was a gentleman with a baby." "Oh no" [he said,] "I called, but because I'm young I knew you wouldn't come, but I'm not going too far, I'm a nice guy coming from school." So I called the dispatcher and another car and say, "I'm not picking up no person with no baby. It's three teenagers." And he said, "Make sure that you are careful. Those fellas are not to be trusted." So I took them, and they was nasty, and when they got out of the car, they say they not gonna pay.

Once runners succeed in being picked up, they must make sure not to give their true intention away until the taxi reaches their desired destination. If the driver smells a rat beforehand, the runner may fail on both counts: he can be dropped elsewhere *and* he has to pay. The moment of truth—or rather, of mimicry—comes when he reaches his destination, since at that point he has to signal to the driver that he is about to pay and then make off before the driver has a chance to stop him: "Sometimes you get a nice-looking woman, oh man, slow the cab, then get her. I get her, then pull away, and when I get there, she'll give me a story, 'Oh, I forgot my money. Oh, I got no money, I have to go and get it,' and then she never comes back" (driver BX5).

Driver BX8 was duped by a woman with a young child:

> Friday I took a black girl from here, from the Bronx to Brooklyn. She had a child, like a six-year-old child. And when we get there, she say to me, "I'll be back in one minute. Let me get the money from my husband." And she never came back. You know, I lost three hours from the Bronx to Brooklyn, 'cause in the weekend you take like an hour because of the traffic over there. And she didn't pay me.

Driver NM3 laughingly told us about having the most unlikely runner:

> It seems funny, but elderly folk don't really run off, they give you some kind of excuse like, "I'm going upstairs to get the money." You might not

believe this, but I picked up an elderly man in a wheelchair and his wife. The wheelchair was in the boot, and when I stopped, the wife insisted on getting the wheelchair, and she quickly got her husband out of the car, and they took off. I thought they were going to get the money. I couldn't believe it when they didn't come back.

A frequently used strategy among those who do not want to pay is to tell the driver they are leaving a package in the car, as a guarantee of their return, while they go and get the money to pay him. All too often the package is bogus: "The type of problems are when people run away with the money. Sometimes they get in conversation, they're friendly and don't look nervous. But if they try and make conversation about anything, they would say, 'Oh, I'm gonna go back in and get the money. I'll be right back,' and they left a package there. And you think, they left the package, they're coming back, but it turns out the package is empty" (driver Q4).

A runner once left driver BX5 with an odd pledge—a fake gun he pretended was real:

One time a guy had a fake gun. A fake gun, you know. And he tells me he has to go into the store to go and get the money to pay me, you know. So he comes back out, and he asks me to lend him twenty dollars. "What, I can't lend [you] twenty dollars." The guy says, "I not gonna rip you off. Here's my gun." He shows me a gun. To me that gun looks real, and I'm not gonna touch the gun. I'm gonna leave it under the seat. So he says, "Lend me the twenty dollars, I'll go inside, I'll be right back with your money." So he put the gun [under the seat], and I lend him twenty dollars, and the guy didn't come back. . . . It was a fake gun, plastic. But you can't tell. That was early in the morning, around five or six o'clock in the morning. So it just goes to show how they rip you off. One way or another, they rip you off. I just chalk it up to experience.

Driver BR3 told us of incidents in which female passengers went as far as to pretend to leave their baby behind in the car: "Because you're picking up the lady, you think everything is all right. They say, 'Let me go try and pick up the money'—they never come out. And sometimes they got a kid, and they go inside and never come out. Sometimes they say, 'I'll leave [the baby] in the back,' and they go inside, and you go in the back and there's nothing there. They fake the baby."

Driver BX5 met another inventive, if forgetful, runner twice:

Around six o'clock in the morning, I picked up this guy, he was supposed to be deaf-mute. I say, "Where you going?" He say, "Mmm," and he gives me a note that says, "181st Street and———." I say, "That'll be seven dollars." He says, "Mmm." He's a big chubby guy, and when I get over there, he opens the door and runs. And the way he was running, I could have caught him, you know. He was giant. I gotta laugh, I really laughed. Now, a week later, I pick up the same guy again with his little note, and him saying, "Mmm." This guy, I don't know, there's something wrong with his eyesight or something. He got in. I took his little note and said, "Don't you remember me?" and he jumped out. He only got one leg outside, and I pulled away, and he landed on his back. It's crazy, it's crazy.

All New York drivers, even more so than Belfast drivers, are adamant that it is not worth giving chase: "Nah, we just leave it. Because, you know, a lot of my friends have lost their lives trying to get money. And I think that life is more important than money, because you can get the money back someplace else, but you cannot get your life" (driver BX8).

Robbers and Killers: Profiles

Drivers in New York are most fearful of robbers, and for good reasons: 18 percent of the drivers we interviewed had been robbed, and 50 percent had been attacked at least once, sometimes by innocent-looking passengers. Driver BX9 told us: "The first time it was two old guys. I smelt that they were drinking, and they were older, about forty-five, fifty years. I never thought that they would do that, and when I saw the guns, I thought I was gonna [die]. They took my wallet, my license, seventy dollars. I was told that they could have killed me right there."

We collected data from the *New York Times* and the *New York Post* between 1990 and May 2002 on all the reports we could find regarding individuals who had attacked drivers. We found fifty-nine instances in which the attacker of a taxi driver had been charged with a serious offense. The newspapers do not reveal the ethnic background of the attackers. They do, however, tell us the age and gender of the attackers, as well as whether they acted solo or in a group.

Age

Among the fifty-nine individuals accused of violent crimes against taxi drivers in New York City between 1990 and May 2002, the youngest attacker was fourteen, the oldest was forty-five, and the average age was twenty-two. As table 7.1 shows, nearly half of those accused of attacking taxi drivers in our sample were teenagers.

Table 7.2 further reveals that all age groups in the sample appeared to be seriously bent on using violence, but those age fourteen to nineteen were even more likely to be charged with murder and attempted murder than those in the older age groups. Robberies are almost certainly underrepresented, partly because many do not even get reported—as noted by Fernando Mateo, president of the NYSFTD, in

Table 7.1   Age of Accused Attackers of Taxi Drivers in New York City,
             1990 to 2002

Age Range	Number of Cases	Percentage
14 to 19	27	46
20 to 25	16	27
26 or older	16	27
Total	59	100

Source: Authors' compilation.

chapter 6—and partly because violent crimes are more likely to be pur-
sued by law enforcers and to be reported in the press. Still, if we assume
that robberies are equally underrepresented in all age categories, the
finding that the younger the deadlier still holds.[1]

There is a further feature to be considered. Some of the fifty-nine
attackers were charged for the same attack, which they carried out
jointly. Table 7.4 shows that twenty-eight were charged for a solo attack,
while thirty-one were charged for a group attack, of which fifteen
involved two individuals and sixteen involved three or more individuals. In addition, the proportion of group attacks is higher the younger
the age of the attackers: 69 percent of those twenty-six or older acted
alone, as opposed to only 33 percent of teenagers.

These data closely reflect the finding of the National Center for Juvenile Justice that in the United States juveniles are twice as likely
as adults to commit serious violent crimes in groups (Snyder and
Sickmund 1999). In 1999 homicides involving multiple offenders
represented 28 percent of the homicides committed by offenders age
fourteen to seventeen, 23 percent of the homicides committed by
offenders age eighteen to twenty-four, and 10 percent of the homicides
committed by offenders age twenty-five or older (U.S. Department of
Justice 2001).

Table 7.2   Number of Attacks Against Taxi Drivers in New York City, by
             Type of Offense and Age of Accused Attacker, 1990 to 2002

Age Range	Murder or Attempted Murder	Assault	Robbery	Total
14 to 19	19 (70%)	1 (4%)	7 (26%)	27 (100%)
20 to 25	10 (63%)	5 (31%)	1 (6%)	16 (100%)
26 or older	10 (62%)	3 (19%)	3 (19%)	16 (100%)
Total	39 (66%)	9 (15%)	11 (19%)	59 (100%)

Source: Authors' compilation.

Table 7.4   **Percentage of Multiple Attackers Against Taxi Drivers in New York City, by Age Range, 1990 to 2002**

Offense Committed . . .	14 to 19	20 to 25	26 or Older	All Ages
Alone	33% (9)	50% (8)	69% (11)	48% (28)
With one other	30 (8)	25 (4)	19 (3)	25 (15)
With two others	26 (7)	19 (3)	12 (2)	20 (12)
With three others	11 (3)	6 (1)	0 (0)	7 (4)
Total	100 (27)	100 (16)	100 (16)	100 (59)

Source: Authors' compilation.

Gender

Attackers are overwhelmingly male. According to the National Center for Juvenile Justice, between 1980 and 1997 the large majority (93 percent) of known juvenile homicide offenders in the United States were male (Snyder and Sickmund 1999). Once again, this finding is reflected by our data: fifty-one (86 percent) of the fifty-nine individuals accused of an offense against a taxi driver in the cases gathered from the newspaper archive were male. Furthermore, almost all of the drivers we interviewed who had been attacked or robbed had been the victims of men. Two drivers told us their stories:

> I had actually two major bad experiences. First it was four men tried to rob me, and they had knives with them, and they try to attack me. They did rob me, but they ran away. The second one, one guy tried to rob me, and we started fighting because the guy wasn't armed, and the police ended up arresting him. (driver Q1)

> Once, I was attacked by two men. One was white and the other was black. They had a gun, and they put it to my head. They were trying to shoot me. They were gonna rob me. But I was mad, and I started fighting against them, and the car had an accident with another car because I was fighting with the guy. [When the car crashed,] one of them got out of the car and came round the car and attacked me in the neck. I don't know how I had the strength to push them away so that they couldn't shoot the gun. And then the police came, but the robbers took all my money and got away, and the police didn't catch them.

> The second time I was attacked by two white men. They just put a knife to my neck. They didn't do anything, they didn't harm me in any way, they just took the money and ran off. (driver Q2)

Driver Q7 was robbed by a group of men and had to plead for his life: "In 1990 I was attacked by a whole bunch of men. I was taken to a building, and they took all my money, and all I was asking for was for them to leave me alive."

The eight females accused of attacking livery drivers were all between the ages of fourteen and twenty-three.[2] None had acted alone; all of them had attacked a driver together with another female or a male. Although the number of females was small, their dangerousness was proportionally higher: five out of the eight were accused of murder, and the others were accused of robbery. The chances of being attacked by young females were lower than they were for being attacked by young males, but the consequences were more likely to be lethal.

Two of the females, Marta Cassiano (also known as Marta Nelson, age fourteen) and Erica Colon (age twenty-two), worked together and were charged with robbing and killing the livery driver Elhadji Gaye (an immigrant from Senegal) in Spanish Harlem (Yardley 1997; *New York Times* 1999). Nancy Gonzalez (age seventeen) and Dasha Sanchez (age nineteen) were charged with first-degree robbery and criminal possession of a weapon (Rashbaum 2000a). The others, all involved in separate incidents, acted with male co-attackers. Rosa Ocasio (accused of murder) had one male accomplice (Fries 2002). Jasmine Valentin (accused of second-degree murder; Strunsky 2001), Felicia Field (accused of murder; Rashbaum 2000b), and Carolyn Brown (accused of criminal possession of a weapon and unlawful imprisonment; Gardner 2000) all acted with at least two male accomplices.

Another reported incident we found mentions three black girls, age sixteen to nineteen, who were being sought by police for the murder of Carlos Uzhca, a livery driver from Ecuador who was shot in Brooklyn in 1994 (James 1994). They are not included in the fifty-nine cases because the police never found them.

Attacks by Neighborhoods

We also collected any article from the *New York Times* or the *New York Post* concerning cases of drivers who had been killed or injured in an attack between 1990 and May 2002. This yielded 128 cases: 93 murders (out of a total of over 250) and 35 violent assaults. Figure 7.1 illustrates the distribution of the neighborhoods where the attacks took place, as identified in these reports.

The largest percentage of attacks on drivers over the past twelve years have taken place in the Bronx (33 percent) and in Brooklyn (32 percent), in particular in the South Bronx and East New York, Brooklyn.

Recently, there were fifty-eight livery robberies between January and April 2000 in the northern Brooklyn neighborhoods of Prospect Heights, Bedford-Stuyvesant, and East New York (Chivers 2000b). Both the Bronx

**Figure 7.1   Areas of New York in Which Livery Drivers Were Murdered or
Violently Assaulted, 1990 to May 2002**

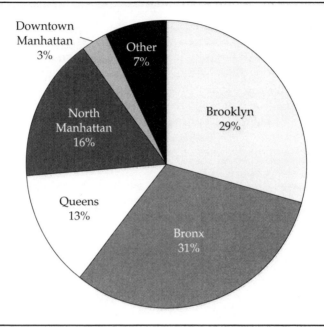

Source: Authors' configuration.
Note: n = 128

and Brooklyn contain a higher concentration of government housing,
and drivers have grown wary of certain buildings in these neighborhoods: "The projects, the government projects—you got to be careful
with them" (driver BX10).

Time and Season of Attack

In 95 of the 128 cases we collected from our search of the newspapers,
the article reports the time of day the attack occurred. Sixty-four percent
of the 95 drivers killed or injured were attacked between ten o'clock in
the evening and six o'clock in the morning.[3] Drivers are aware of this:
"You know in the night shift you deal with the delinquent" (driver BR1).
Driver BX5 told us: "If a bad person really want to do something bad to
you, they'll do it at night. The majority of time is at night. They also do
it at daytime, but not as much. At night they have too much cover. And
then, not only that, but they jump out of a cab, [and] nobody can get
their description 'cause it's dark." Yet more than 50 percent of our New

York interviewees chose to work at night because, with less traffic, they can make more money (see chapter 10).

We were also able to plot the number of attacks by month for all the 128 cases we found described in the newspapers (see figure 7.2). We did not find a particular month or months in which attacks were systematically (and statistically significantly) higher or lower than in others. This suggests that we are not witnessing a seasonal effect (although we did find that in 1990, 1992, 1993, and 1999 the largest number of monthly attacks took place in April, "proving" that for livery drivers, as for T. S. Eliot, April can be "the cruelest month"). Rather, we found that attacks took place in waves, with a sharp increase followed by a steep decline (see figure 7.2). The pattern is reminiscent of the short-lived adjustment effect of a prey-predator dynamic cycle: drivers in the months following an increased number of attacks raise their guard and become more selective of passengers, thereby lowering the number of attacks by foiling more attempts until they relax their guard again and the number of attacks soars.

The number of attacks has declined somewhat in recent years along-side the general decline in violent crime in New York, as we noted in chapter 6. This decline is visible in the increasingly longer intervals between the peaks (the longest being between 1996 and 2000) and in the fact that after the bad peak in 2000 there has never been more than one attack a month. This decline may be due to the fact that drivers take longer

Figure 7.2   Number of Taxi Drivers Killed or Injured in New York, January 1990 to May 2002

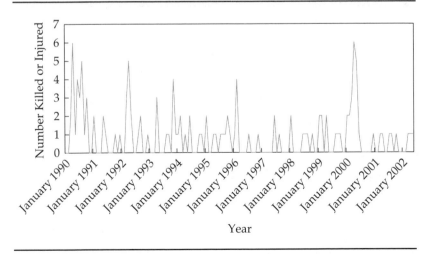

Source: Authors' configuration.

to lower their guard when deciding whether to pick up suspicious-looking passengers, but it may also have something to do with specific deterrent devices that drivers were required to introduce in 2000, such as partitions and cameras (see chapter 8). Livery drivers may have also benefited from undercover police operations. In 2000 detectives posed as livery drivers in the hope of catching attackers red-handed, thereby deterring future attackers. Using Lincoln Town Cars (the livery car of choice) equipped with partitions, hidden cameras, and audio recording devices, the police deployed as many as ten decoy cabs every night in certain "dangerous" neighborhoods. Backup teams driving close by in several unmarked vehicles supported these cabs in case the "drivers" were attacked (Rashbaum 2000a).[4] They used mimics to catch other mimics.

Robbers and Killers: Strategies

The drivers emphasized how difficult it is to judge whether someone is intent on harming them: "They're smart, they know what they're doing," said driver Q10. And robbers often do not look like robbers: "It could be somebody dressed the way we are now, very neat and very nice," observed driver Q2, "and it could be somebody who has a bad mind, that's out to harm me." Robbers make an effort to look like trustworthy passengers: "So you have a bad man who says, 'Okay, I gonna do something tonight, I gonna dress like this.' You don't even know, you know. There is some [bad guys] who dress very nice, and you don't know what they're gonna do to you" (driver BR2).

Unlike runners, robbers are not necessarily particular about reaching a given destination. If the driver gets suspicious and stops the car, he may be robbed anyway, wherever he has stopped. The chief preoccupation of the robber is to persuade the driver to take him in the first place by looking like a trustworthy passenger. Robbers have learned to manipulate the "safe" signs that drivers look for in a passenger. First, they need to give a credible destination: "If they give me a strange direction, I'm going to know [what they are up to,] but they know what they're doing. So they give me somewhere that's not so far away, because they know . . . that I would think that that was 'okay, I'll take you there.' But in the middle of [the journey], that's when they get me" (driver Q12).

Robbers also manipulate the manner and location of pickup, choosing locations that they believe look safe to drivers. A high proportion of attacks (82 percent of the livery cab robberies and at least six of the homicides between January and April 2000) occurred after the drivers had picked up street-hails (Chivers 2000a). Picking up in the street is much less safe than picking up through the dispatcher: "90 percent of the bad people is picked up on the street" (driver NM3). Some attackers, however, choose to call the dispatcher and try to get a cab through the taxi base, especially those who know they would not stand a chance of being picked up as a hailer. Mimics pose as a different type on the telephone and gamble that once the driver has been dispatched to the fare, he will be more likely to accept it.

In other cases mimics have brazenly walked into the base and requested a taxi. At 9:20 A.M. on Sunday, February 22, 1998, Stanley Meinero walked into a taxi base in Brooklyn asking for a taxi. Shortly into the ten-minute journey, he attempted to rob the driver, Gregory Abramson (Cooper 1998). Jean Scutt was killed in Brooklyn when he agreed to take a young man who walked into the base at two o'clock one Saturday morning in April 2000 (Forero 2000). By voluntarily showing his face to potential witnesses, the mimic encourages the dispatcher and drivers to trust him.

Other robbers present themselves as being trustworthy by moving to a "safe" location before hailing a cab. Lakhwinder Singh picked up Jondale Willis (age twenty) and Joedale Willis (age eighteen) outside the Long Island Railway station in Jamaica, Queens; the brothers then shot and robbed him. Mr. Singh said of them: "These two guys, they looked good to me" (Feuer 2000).

Besides the location of the hail, another strategy—or at least a decision that may be a conscious choice on the part of robbers—is the time of day. Although robbers tend to target drivers predominantly during the night, some choose to attack during the day, when drivers may not be as vigilant as they are at night. Roder Minchala was robbed and shot dead by two passengers he picked up at five o'clock in the afternoon in Queens (Newman 1999), and Carlos Uzhca was shot at four-thirty in the afternoon while sitting in his cab in East New York, Brooklyn (James 1994).

Over 50 percent of the attacks were perpetrated by groups of people (see table 7.4). For instance, thirty-two of the fifty-eight livery robberies between January and April 2000 in the northern Brooklyn neighborhoods occurred in taxis carrying multiple passengers (Chivers 2000b). Since the majority of passengers travel alone (two-thirds by drivers' estimates), this implies that multiple passengers are proportionally more dangerous. Drivers know this and are wary of groups, especially groups of men.

Male attackers intent on jointly attacking a driver therefore resort to mimicry to induce drivers to pick them up. A classic trick is to get one member of the group to flag down the taxi before the others reveal themselves: "You know what happens sometimes: one guy stop the car, and three more is waiting on that guy to stop the car. When he opens the door . . . the other three come" (driver BX7). Driver NM8 told us: "The one that looks most presentable will come and stop you, so you think it's okay. As soon as he's stopped you, the other guys will arrive. Then he says, 'Don't worry, they are my brothers.' "

A variant of this is to do the same using a woman, exploiting drivers' positive bias not only toward solo passengers but also toward females: "So sometimes they use the woman to attract the driver, you know what I'm saying?" (driver BR2). Driver BX7 remembered "one girl, about thirteen years old, she stopped the car, and over there was two more guys. Because one girl will get the taxi to stop, because the driver sees the girl, but the danger is the man."[5] Occasionally a child is added as well: "One of my friends, he almost got killed with a knife. One woman and a male with a child, and they almost killed my friend. So you know . . . in this job you trust nobody" (driver BX8).

A different ploy is for a single female passenger to lure the driver to the location of her accomplice:

> It was a girl, seventeen or nineteen years old, something like that. And she asked me to take her somewhere in Yonkers, and the idea was to hold me up. She had another person waiting for her there. But when I got to the place, I realized that the guy in the other car was looking back all the time. So I could tell something was wrong, so I just made a U-turn right off the parking lot and went to the police station with her in the car. I wrote down the plate number of the car. I told my base. They sent two guys to wait for me on the highway, and they were there. So it was nothing more serious than that, but it could have been. I don't know what, maybe they just take my money. Maybe kill me, I don't know. (driver BX4)

Some of our interviewees, however, were not taken in by such a ploy: "Yeah, there's a lot of bad girls over here. Over here there's a lot of girls who grow up with a single mother. The mother got a boyfriend on junk. By the time they are fourteen years old, they have seen a lot of things and are very wild. . . . We know what is a bad girl here, we know how the bad girls look" (driver BX10).

Driver BR4 even distrusted well-dressed women: "I learned this, I heard this a long time ago: be careful with the ladies, because they come up very nice, beautiful, they may be something else. So I always be careful with the ladies." Driver BR5 told us:

> I was this close to getting mugged. . . . I was supposed to pick up a young woman, and out of the blue these three guys, they jump in the car. They completely surprised me, and they told me, "Just drive down this way, and you make a right after this street." And that's this industrial park. It's late at night, so what are they gonna do at these factories that are empty? The streets are empty, and it's dark. What are they gonna do there? There's nothing there. There's no houses, there's no stores, there's no buildings, there's nothing there. So there's no way that I'm gonna go there. But they say that after that we gonna go to this other place which is

far, so that means a big fare. And I said, "Really?" And I said, "No, and you better get out of the car."

Undercover Agents

In Belfast private-hire drivers are faced with the threat of undercover agents from the DOE who are intent on catching them illegally picking up street-hails. In New York yellow cab drivers too have faced undercover agents from the police department and the TLC whose aim is to catch those among them who do not pick up a certain type of hailing passenger, notably African Americans.

In November 1999, the actor Danny Glover accused the yellow cab industry in New York of discrimination following a series of episodes in which he was refused a ride on Adam Clayton Powell Boulevard and 116th Street. In another incident on Second Avenue in the East Village, when a taxi did stop for Mr. Glover and his daughter, the driver refused to let him sit in the front seat despite his request to sit there because, with a bad hip, he needed the extra legroom. Taxi drivers are required to let passengers sit in the front if they have a physical need (Graves, Parascandola, and Camplinile 1994; Lueck 1999). The considerable furor surrounding these incidents sparked a series of controversial "sting" operations by the police and the TLC designed to root out discrimination and racism among yellow cab drivers. The TLC refused our request for an interview about this and other issues, so our information about these operations comes from taxi drivers' reports and newspaper accounts only.

The sting operations take the following form. Police and TLC officers pose as customers in multiracial groups of three. A black officer and a white officer stand near each other, black first, and attempt to hail a cab while being observed by a supervisor. If a taxi passes the black officer in favor of the white officer, something black customers say happens all the time, the driver's hack license is suspended, and he can be fined between $200 and $350 (Bumiller 1999). Driver YC1, one of the three yellow cab drivers we interviewed, picked up one of these mimics:

> The bad thing is, in many cases they are dressed in a very bad way. One time I will never forget. An undercover policeman approach me with a look that said to anyone driving a cab, "Lock your doors." See, and any person, even if you are the commissioner, you're gonna lock your doors. So he approach to my car, and he ask me to go to a bad area of Brooklyn. So I just put on the destination, and then two blocks later he said pull over and got out.

Even though drivers claim the results of these sting operations are skewed against them because many of these undercover agents are poorly dressed and request "dangerous" destinations, in fact the results reported thus far reveal very few cases of drivers refusing to take people because of race or ethnic background. Mayor Rudolph Giuliani announced in 1999: "Sure we'd make twenty, twenty-five arrests, but that would be out of like 1,500, 1,600, 1,800 actual tests that we do. And when we didn't announce it [the sting operation], we had exactly the same percentage" (Ciezadlo and Janison 1999). These results seem to indicate that the vast majority of yellow cab drivers do not discriminate by race. As we shall see in chapters 9 and 10, however, both livery and yellow cab drivers (including black drivers) say that they do discriminate, especially against African American hailers.

The high rates of robbery, violent assault, and murder encountered by New York livery drivers prove just how vulnerable they are to dangerous mimics. Drivers are therefore extremely aware of the need to protect themselves by taking precautions, screening customers, and probing customers further, as discussed in the following chapters.

Chapter 8

Precautions in New York

NEW YORK drivers, like their Belfast counterparts, do not rely solely on screening but act to limit their risks by taking general precautions in addition to the specific cautions they take with certain passengers. And like their Northern Irish colleagues, they keep in mind a menu of remedial actions to be taken in case they let in the wrong customer. These remedial actions depend on the customer's type—for example, whether they are drunk or violent or have no money to pay the fare.

Precautions and Deterrents

Before they pick up a passenger, drivers take measures to limit both the extent to which they need to worry about a passenger's trustworthiness and the damage in case their screening fails to detect an untrustworthy one. These measures, which include safety and warning devices as well as an array of rules and practices, only partially overlap with those employed by Belfast drivers (see table 8.1), and to some extent this is explained by the differences in the perils they face. In other parts of the world, taxi drivers do face problems similar to those that come up in Northern Ireland. For instance, in Macedonia, drivers and passengers are wary of Albanian passengers and drivers, respectively, and act in ways similar to their Catholic and Protestant counterparts in Northern Ireland (Mark Starbuck, personal communication, February 6, 2003). New York drivers, by contrast, are subject to neither sectarian violence nor, generally, violence triggered purely by their "type." They are not attacked because of their religious beliefs or political affiliation, and only very occasionally because of their ethnic origins. There was only a brief interlude after September 11 during which Arab or Arab-looking drivers feared that could happen. In New York drivers have thus no need to mask or alter the signs of their affiliations. Moreover, certain

Table 8.1   Precautions and Deterrents Practiced by Taxi Drivers in
Belfast and New York

Precautions and Deterrents	Belfast (N = 45)	New York (N = 50)
Do not wear a seat belt	98% (44)	100% (50)
Mask cues that give away their religion	91 (41)	N/A
Drive only in their local area	58 (26)	N/A
Do not display a TAXI sign	51 (23)	100 (50)
Work for a religiously anonymous firm	40 (18)	N/A
Carry a weapon	36 (16)	0 (0)
Look fierce, make threats, or match aggression	36 (16)	0 (0)
Do not work at night	16 (7)	38 (19)
Drop off cash takings	9 (4)	24 (12)
Avoid provocation or prevent violent escalation	20 (9)	98 (49)
Have a partition	18 (8)	68 (34)
Be selective about pickup location and destination	60 (27)	52 (26)
Have a camera	N/A	28 (14)

Source: Authors' compilation.
Note: N/A = not applicable.

areas being dominated by particular religious, ethnic, or other groups does not raise safety concerns for them. Their concern is mostly with neighborhood crime rates. As we described their experience in the preceding chapter, they worry about petty crime turning violent, a possibility that is of only partial concern to Belfast drivers. Several other differences in the precautionary and remedial practices adopted by taxi drivers in the two cities are discussed in detail in this chapter.

Choice of Locations

Because yellow cabs control the market in the choice locations in Manhattan, livery drivers have to make do with servicing the other neighborhoods—the Bronx, Brooklyn, Queens, and north of 125th Street in Manhattan, where the vast majority of attacks occur (see figure 7.1). "The first guy who robbed me, robbed me in the Bronx in a place where nobody was around. In the city usually they can't rob you in Manhattan in daytime, they try to take you to a remote area" (driver NM17). Livery drivers quickly learn which neighborhoods are dangerous, but they cannot afford to be too picky and to avoid those areas entirely. Many drivers accept pickups in a dangerous area provided it is *their* area, while refusing to pick up or drop off in other dangerous areas. Detailed knowledge of their turf refines their screening feelers:

The drivers in Brooklyn don't want to go to the Bronx, and the drivers in the Bronx don't wanna come to Brooklyn. . . . Like we have this area, it has its reputation, and the Bronx has its own reputation, and if you go there it's bad. And sometimes, *if you live here, you don't look at it as being bad.* You know the guys who deal in drugs, they say hello to you [*laughs*]. So it's like the same in the Bronx, the guys know each other. So there are certain areas that you don't wanna go . . . it's like that. I wouldn't stop in the Bronx. I know some people would do it, but I don't think it's a good idea. (driver BR5)

When drivers do pick up or drop off in bad areas, they increase their precautions and the intensity of their screening. Driver BX8 told us that he would not get out of the car even if the passenger ran off without paying and left the door open. Instead, he would drive to a safe location before exiting the car to close the door:

South Bronx is more dangerous, and East New York. You know a lot of taxi drivers have been killed over there in East New York, Brooklyn. We pick a passenger and he tell us to go there, we don't wanna go there, because there are some areas that you don't wanna go to, and then they don't wanna pay you sometimes. They just open the door and they leave. They don't pay you, and they don't close the door. And if you get out of the car, they might shoot you. So it's better to just drive with the door open.

Drivers who venture through notorious locations prefer to stay in well-lit areas, and they avoid dead-ends: "If they tell me, take me to 122nd Street and Amsterdam [in northern Manhattan], if you only have a dead-end, it means that you cannot go nowhere. So what you do is you leave it right there, 122nd and Amsterdam. And you go nowhere [else]—you stay right there on the corner. You stay where light is, where people is. You don't go to places where there's no people and there's no light. You gotta be aware what you're doing" (BX6).

If driver BR3 is suspicious of a passenger, he takes main, well-lit, and more populous avenues: "[When] I pick up people who look like trouble people, I take the avenue. . . . It's better for me, you know."

Partitions and Cameras

In the recent past livery drivers have introduced a number of security devices to their cars. Partitions, cameras, emergency radio codes, and flashing lights are all intended to protect drivers from passengers who are intent on harming them. None of these systems, with the exception of radio codes, are in use in Belfast.

As we anticipated in chapter 6, since April 2000 the TLC has required that all livery vehicles and yellow taxis install either a bullet-resistant partition or an in-vehicle digital security camera:

> You know, before [partitions were introduced], a lot of people have been killed. If you wanted to use [a partition] before, that's up to you, but now it's the law. You gotta use it now. You don't have a partition now, you got a ticket. So before, in 1993, 1992, they killed thirty-five taxi drivers. I know you heard that in England—thirty-five. So after we have started using the partition, the crime in taxi driving went down like 90 percent. (driver BX8)

Thirty-four of the livery drivers we interviewed (68 percent) had partitions in their cars and preferred it to a camera. (Only one driver had both devices.) "I have the partition . . . because I think the partition is more sturdy, because a camera only records the guy. But the partition can save your life" (driver BX7). Driver NM3 pointed out that customers who are high on drugs "don't notice the camera, and by the time they found out it's too late—they already killed you." Driver NM8 added, "People who really want to harm you, they will harm you. They don't give a damn when they are under the influence of anger." Most of these drivers, like driver BR4, feel more secure with the partition than without it: "I always drive with a partition. Even when the crime dropped out after Giuliani started working in the second term, at the beginning of the second term, I always have my partition because I feel safer." Driver BX9 told us that he used to be very anxious about picking up passengers in the Bronx, but having the partition has eased his mind: "Those two or three years I didn't have [a partition], and that's when the more times I got really scared. . . . When I picked up someone, I said, now I am in trouble. I was scared of them . . . you could feel that something was wrong. . . . Now I wouldn't buy a car without a partition."

Although most drivers approved of partitions, some expressed reservations about their efficacy and side effects: "The [partition] was installed on every car, but it's not like it's real strong or is going to protect you. It's not. It's just there to show that we comply with the law" (driver BR5). People assume that partitions are bullet-proof, but in fact they are only bullet-resistant, and five of the drivers felt that they give a false sense of security.[1] "If I see somebody pointing a gun at me through the partition, I would try to get out of those situations without getting shot through the partition. You're supposed to change the glass every two years, and nobody does it. So I don't know. I don't trust it" (driver BX9).[2]

Driver BX5 pointed out that, "with a partition or without a partition, they can still hold you up. They can still take your life. This is not a deterrent to getting held up. The deterrent is over here; you gotta use your brain. Once you use your brain, that's what it's all about." Driver BX7 observed that at night the partition obscures his view of the passenger: "In the day you can see the face of the people. But in the night it's different because I have partition. Sometimes we can't see the face." Other drivers complained of back problems caused by long hours spent in seats made rigid by the partitions, and they were concerned about the increase in serious and fatal injuries sustained by passengers in collisions (Schaller 2001).

The partition offers the most protection, of course, when kept closed.[3] However, drivers' practices in this regard varied; while some kept it closed all the time, others, like driver BXF4, said whether or not he keeps his partition closed depends on the passenger: "Like I said, you never know. Win or lose, you don't know nothing. I leave this closed if this person is moving around and uncomfortable, I just leave it closed. The person who is calm, then sometimes I open it." Driver BX1, on the other hand, said that he "almost always leave[s] it open. Nothing has happened to me yet, and I started five years ago. A lot of drivers tell me, close it, close it . . . but I just leave it open." He believes his instincts will keep him safe.

According to driver BX7, another problem with the partition is that it encourages passengers to come to the driver's window to pay, an approach that he considers potentially dangerous: "Until you have partition, you have to be careful because sometimes the passenger comes through to this door to tell you and it's dangerous . . . many times. I don't want money for the trip if they pay at my window. Because many drivers die because they come round to the window." Driver BX7's fear that passengers coming outside to the driver's window to pay can more easily shoot the driver is warranted. Souleymane Diallo, originally from Guinea, drove a livery car with a partition but was killed when he was shot from outside of the car (Rashbaum 2001). Driver BR1 described an incident that happened a few years ago: "Two or three guys come, and they wanna go someplace. All of them get out without paying me. One of them came and looked like he was gonna pay me at my side of the car. I put the window down. As soon as I put the window down, he said, 'Gimme the money. It's a holdup!' "

Partitions are also unpopular with some passengers because they restrict the amount of room in the backseat. Driver NM11 told us that "we got some people get in the cab who are very big, you know, tall and fat. In America there are some very fat people. The partition makes it very small in the back, so without it you can just push the seat forward and they can get in." According to driver BX9, some customers request a car without a partition, and driver Q2 added, "The partition can go against me because not all of the customers want it. They feel uncomfortable. And I have to please the customers." Driver BR1 told us that many of the black cars with a more corporate clientele prefer to install a camera rather than a partition. That way, "if anything happens, the police know, they gonna find out. 'Cause you got a picture." Although most passengers in these cars are low-risk businesspeople, some black car drivers supplement their income by picking up street-hails, thus making themselves vulnerable to attack. However, drivers BX2, BX3, and BX6, who all drive black cars with a camera only, work during the day and are reluctant to pick up hailing passengers.

Warning Systems

The drivers who have radios also use a radio code to alert the base if they are in danger, and some have cell phones on which they can call the police quickly. Most also have an emergency flashing light on the back of the car that can signal to a passing police car or taxi that they are in trouble, unbeknownst to the passenger. Two drivers explained:

> We have a code on the radio. We use numbers. Like you see somebody dangerous, we say like, "We got a ten-thirty-eight." Like the police, we use a code. And we have a light here. If I press that button, we got one light in the front and one light in the back that start flashing. So the police, or anybody, see the light flashing, they know we are in trouble. So they might help us. The Federation want to help with the light. (driver BX8)

> You see that yellow light, that's a trouble light. All the cars have that light. And I know, if you had a problem, if you turn on the light, I know I would check him, and all the drivers would check him too. You . . . turn it on, I know something happened. It could be just something that could lead to a bigger problem, but you already know people who want to do something bad to you. . . . So we able to help a lot of people with that light. And now we have cameras on the car, and now we gonna have phones so we can contact the police right away. Some cars is using them already. So it's changing. Now we feel more secure. (driver BX10)

If drivers get into trouble, they contact the base or the police if possible and hope that help will come quickly: "If I see some dangerous people, I have to let [the dispatcher] know at the base so they can send a couple of cars over there to where I drop [the passenger] so I can cover myself" (driver BR1).

> Oh, if I don't feel good, I call the base. For anything, you have to call the base. Let them know what is going on so they call you every certain time. Two or three minutes, "How are you doing?" whatever. . . . Or let's say a guy's giving problems and I want him out of here—I tell the base. Four or five cars come, drivers, and will take him out. If he's still giving trouble, we'll call the cops, but we'll try to talk to them and tell them to get out. If things get difficult, then we call the cops. (driver BX1)

However, as driver Q7 pointed out, a driver might not want to alert the passenger to the fact that he is calling the police, since that might aggravate the situation: "And by the way, you cannot call the police, because the passenger is gonna find out that you are calling the police. So you try to find a police cabin [cruiser] on the street. You have to park beside it . . . leave the car and find them. . . . If he's a suspicious passenger, you have to frame it right."

When driver BX9 once had a very bad feeling about a passenger, he too went in search of the police: "One time it happen to me that a guy just came into the car, and the second the guy sit down I say, this is wrong . . . I just go, that's not the way. . . . You are lost right there, you don't know where to go. But saying that, most of the time you know you are in trouble. I was looking for the police. When I see the police, I stop in front of them." Noticing the police, this passenger got out of the car.

Aguelgasi Khoghali managed to thwart his robbers by running a red light and crashing into a police car when his passengers pulled out a gun and demanded his money (*New York Times* 1998).

Behavioral and Attitudinal Practices

These various devices, which provide drivers with some protection in case of trouble, are supplemented by a number of behavioral strategies that protect drivers from attacks, deter attackers, or prevent an attack from becoming life-threatening. These strategies have almost all been developed out of the experience of doing the job and from knowledge passed on from driver to driver (see chapter 6).

Limiting Robbers' Payoffs and Temptations

Most attacks on livery drivers involve robbery, and the average amount of money taken from the driver is a pitiful seventy-five dollars (Martin 1993). In part, robbers' take is low because of drivers' meager earnings, but drivers also limit the amount of money they keep with them during their shift. "When I leave my house, I make sure that I don't bring with me more than thirty, forty dollars, just for change, you know" (driver BXF4). Twelve of the drivers (24 percent), like Q10, prefer to drop off their precious earnings in case they get robbed. "I try not to keep a lot of money in the car. I go to the bank, or I put it away and am careful not to carry too much money with me," said driver NM13, who also makes daily visits to the bank. "Anytime I make about one hundred dollars, I make sure that I make a deposit at the ATM before I start back again."

Driver Q10 also deliberately removes any jewelry or visible possessions that might tempt robbers: "At the beginning, I would wear a lot of jewelry, like rings and bracelets and chains. And one time they got in the car, and they were commenting about how they wanted a ring, and I was nervous because of that because I thought they were going to do something to me. From then on, I never wore jewelry again."

Similarly, driver BX10 said that "some drivers, they wanna use nice watches, nice chains. They wanna look too fancy. That's not good for business. You try to look too fancy, you gonna draw attention from other people. That's no good. And I see some people doing it."

Avoiding Provocation and Calming Passengers

In contrast with the pugnacious attitude of their Belfast counterparts, all of the drivers we interviewed in New York pursue a line of appeasement with passengers, and they all believe in trying to stay away from trouble as much as possible. Not only do New York drivers not carry weapons or fighting implements in their cars, but they generally advocate being acquiescent, staying calm, and being patient and polite. "In order to survive in this industry you have to be patient with people. You have to have good relations with people. You have to be cordial," said driver Q4. Driver BX8 concurred:

> You got to know how to talk to people. . . . You cannot have a bad attitude with people, 'cause they might have a gun. Maybe they don't have the gun for you, they have the gun for somebody else. And you try to fight with words with that person, you might get hurt. So in this job you got to know how to treat people. 'Cause in this city people live with a lot of problems. You got to be polite with people, with any people—it doesn't matter what color they are.

When sensing possible dangers, drivers try to calm passengers by soft means, even by playing music: "Sometimes they don't look so good. But you can talk to them, turn the music how they like it. Get some conversation, and they let you go. Sometimes they got it in mind to do something to you, but if you are smart and try to go along with them . . . they believe that you like them and they leave you alone." Driver BR4 mentioned a similar practice:

> Okay, sometimes when I go to pick up, I try to put the music for the people that is coming to the station that they want. I want them to feel fine, because I just want to take them to their place and pay me. Suppose they come into the car and they have a bad attitude. Another example with the music—"Put the music!" They don't say, "Please," they just say, "Put the music!" Okay, no problem. I approve of music. If they start smoking, I say, "I'm gonna crack the window just a little bit so you can smoke." Like I approve of smoking. This is the way that I try to avoid contact . . . confrontation. I turn up the music.

Driver NM13 once tried to get rid of some passengers as calmly as possible by using the same trick some Belfast drivers use: pretending his car had broken down. "At the red stop light, I put my car out of gear and I cranked the engine. I cranked it three times, and I said, 'Man, my car won't start. I think there's a problem. Can you pick up another cab?' "

When a passenger refuses to pay the full fare or runs off without paying at all, as we know from chapter 7, most drivers believe that it is better to let it go rather than get involved in an argument or a chase:

> I am the type of person who never makes any trouble. You don't want to pay me, then fine—go your way, I'll go mine. I don't make trouble that way. I prefer to stay away from those types of things. I let them go.

> Somebody say the fare is ten dollars, and they say they only got nine dollars; I don't want to fight for that dollar. Other drivers fight for that dollar. . . . And the passenger say, "I give you a dollar, but I gonna break your window!" [The driver is] gonna pay 145 dollars for that because he don't wanna let somebody go with a dollar. You have to use your mind; you have to know how to deal with and who you deal with. (driver Q3)

> Because I'm a calm person, I don't like to argue, I don't like that. So one of the problems the drivers have is those kind of guys using the service that don't wanna pay. If you try to get your money—ten dollars, fifteen dollars—you gonna lose more, 'cause they gonna break a window. Maybe they gonna shoot at you. Maybe they gonna do a lot of things that you gonna lose. They gonna break a window, then you gotta pay for it. The window cost more than the twenty dollars you gonna get. So I think that way, and I let him go. You know what, okay, fine! I open the door—just go. (driver BR1)

Handling drunks also requires maintaining careful composure. Driver BX5 told us:

> I don't advise you to take drunken people, people that are drunk. I never have any problems with people that are drunk. I mean, that's why they call a cab. Because they can't drive . . . they leave their car, they call us. I never have any problems with that, but you have to be very careful with drunken people. Because one wrong word could send that person to go berserk. So you gotta really know how to handle them. If you can handle a drunk person, pick them up. If you don't know how to handle them, don't pick 'em up.

Preventing Violent Escalation

When an attack occurs, virtually all drivers offer no resistance. Attackers almost always use the threat of violence to force drivers to hand over their earnings, generally resorting to actual violence only if the driver seems inclined to resist. Drivers advise compliance with a robber's demands.[4] "[If they say,] 'I just want the money, give me all the money,' 'Okay,' [I say,] 'here's the money, it's in my wallet. Go, I don't have no more money.' Okay, they will tell you what to do. Just do whatever they say—whatever they say, do it. Don't try to be a hero, okay, or you gonna end up in the hospital. A lot of my friends in the hospital because they want to be a hero" (driver BX10).

However, even when a driver complies with robbers' demands, they may still become violent. Lakhwinder Singh escaped with his life during an armed robbery because he put his foot down hard on the accelerator, throwing his assailant off balance just as he fired his gun: "I said, 'Please take the money and don't shoot me.' . . . And they took the money, and they shot me anyway" (Kugel 2000).

If held up, a driver who genuinely does not have any money knows that this will be interpreted as a refusal and aggravate an attacker further. So while drivers try to drive with as little money as possible, they avoid driving with none at all: "It's better that we have some money, because maybe, we don't have that, they might kill you. If I don't have money and they don't believe me, they might think that I'm lying to them, so it's better always to carry your own cash" (driver BX8). Like driver BX8, many drivers have taken to carrying "mug money": "You have to have something with you always, because the money can save your life. You have to have with you always a hundred dollars. Sometimes if you don't have money, they'll kill" (driver BX7).

When faced with an aggressive passenger, a driver must try to prevent the situation from escalating into something more violent:

> The important thing is, don't panic. They just doing a bad job. Don't panic, they just doing it. They're doing a holdup. And I know when a person have a knife or a gun on you, they got a bad thing in their head. It's not normal. Sometimes they drink . . . or they have some drugs or heavy problems. So you don't want to have problems. Do whatever they say, and you'll be better off. Next day you forget about it, and you're happy on the street. But don't try to be a hero. You have to be quiet. They just human. They doing that, but they're human too. And you're cool, try to be cool. (driver BX10)

The most difficult and frightening situations are those in which the aggressor has a gun. Driver BX5 told us what happened when he was held at gunpoint: "I sweet-talked the person. I don't come out like, 'Hey! What you doing? You can't have my money!' That's when you are in trouble. All they want is your money. Give them your money. You look [at] them good, and then when the police comes, you tell them what the guy looks like, and you should have no problem. But when you get tough, that's when you have problem."

Driver NM17 had been robbed twice at gunpoint, and on both occasions he handed over his money immediately: "You want my shirt, you want my coat, I will give everything to you, because life is precious. Maybe that's why I'm still living, because a lot of my friends are dead and gone. Some have been shot, some have been killed over two dollars, five dollars." His strategy is to comply and pacify:

> First of all, they don't want to get caught, period. They want to rob you and get away with it, you see, without being caught. So . . . you make it easy for them. Don't make them panic. When they panic, they try to shoot you, but you let them know, if they want money, you give it to them, you see. You make it easy for them. You comply. If you comply, they will not hurt you, because they are after the money. They are not after you, they don't need you. I think that is the bottom line to save your life.

With one exception, the drivers all said that they believed in staying away from trouble. Driver BX9, the odd one out, claimed that sometimes he bluffs a willingness to fight, which is an essential "survival skill" in his view. "Sometimes you gotta be aggressive, even though you are not willing to do anything. Yes, bluff, yes. Sometimes people come and tell me: 'You don't know what I have.' And then I say, 'You don't know what I have either.' " Even driver BX9, however, realized the problems with this approach, which most drivers would regard as high-risk. For one, "we cannot carry even a screwdriver in the car," he noted. More interestingly, he knew that drivers signal their weakness by the very fact of being in the job: "If I would be willing to do anything, I wouldn't be driving a car, I would be robbing a bank, I would be willing to die. That's why I think a lot of cab drivers is being abused. They know that the driver is not a criminal and doesn't want any problem. They try to take advantage of that."

The self-image of New York drivers differs markedly from the self-image of Belfast drivers and is evidenced in the differences in the precautions they take and the deterrents they apply (see table 8.1). This self-image seems to reflect the New Yorkers' position as well as their perception of the city in which they work. Since most of them are immigrants, they do not have a sense that they own the city—it is not their turf. They do not have a paramilitary past, nor do they have any links with men of violence that attackers need to worry about. The big anonymous metropolis conceals perils toward which they feel powerless.

The difference in self-image also reflects a different perception of the nature of the aggressors. The overall impression one derives from the New York drivers' accounts is that they conceive of their assailants, even those who simply free-ride, as potentially very dangerous, unpredictable, and prone to irrational violence. ("In this city people live with a lot of problems," in driver BX8's words.) So they act as one does with mentally ill patients and deranged junkies (at least as seen on American TV)—trying to be calm and to pacify the situation. Belfast drivers, by contrast, consider attackers on the whole to be rational and collected, no matter how violent they are. New York drivers have an image of attackers as being prepared to do anything to get what they want, no matter how calm and rational they may appear when trying to dupe the driver. Not only does this image make the need to take precautions all the more salient, but it also, as we shall see, puts heavy pressure on drivers to develop effective screening and probing strategies.

Chapter 9

Screening in New York

I N CHAPTER 4, we documented the ways in which Belfast drivers, in addition to taking many precautions to protect their safety and making contingency plans for handling dangerous situations, pay a great deal of attention to the cues and signs displayed by prospective fares. In chapter 5, we also described the array of actions that they take to probe suspicious fares, both before and after taking them on board. We expect New York drivers to engage in similar screening and probing efforts. Our goal is to uncover the logic that governs their "street-level epistemology" (Hardin 1993). A key feature of it, we hypothesize, is drivers' search for signs that are significantly more costly for a mimic to fake but affordable enough for the genuine passenger, given the benefit that each can expect in the situation.

In the previous chapter, we found both similarities and differences between the precautions adopted by drivers in the two cities. In this chapter too, we find that the signs New York drivers look for follow the same general logic as, but are only partially similar to, those that drivers in Belfast look for.

The comparison between drivers in the two cities vividly shows the validity of a crucial theoretical expectation that prompted our research: the reasoning that sustains trusting decisions is both governed by the same general principles and instantiated by a distinctly specific semiotics that reflects the differences in the environments and the perils associated with them.

Drivers' Dispositions to Trust

In New York as in Belfast—as indeed everywhere—taxi drivers face a trade-off. They want to maximize their earnings by accepting as many fares as possible. However, they need to minimize the risks by being selective about the passengers they pick up. The New York drivers reiterated how very difficult it can be to differentiate a good customer from a bad one: "Look, man, you can't tell. He could be a nice, good-looking person and he still robs you, and sometimes be a bum guy and he gives you money and he'll even tip you. The bum likes you, and the nice-looking guy robs you, which means that you can't tell anymore" (driver NM7). Although screening is no doubt valuable in avoiding some mistakes, it does not suffice to identify all mimics: "There's always room for being wrong and making the wrong judgment," said driver BR5. Driver Q2 told us:

> It is very hard for me to say, I'm not gonna pick them up. Because one, everybody deserves a fair chance, and two, if I was to decide that, then I would lose money. Okay? I don't look for skin color, race. It's very difficult for me to tell, that's what I'm telling you. I can't judge by the clothes they are wearing or by their skin color because it's different and it would be very difficult for me to tell.

Driver BXF4 agreed that it is very difficult to judge: "This is hard, to be honest. And I'm talking about everyone. Not everyone who is dressed sloppy is a bad person, and not everybody who's well dressed is a good person."

In their study of yellow cab drivers in New York, Camerer and his colleagues (1997, 414) found that drivers work about nine and a half hours per day, take between twenty-eight and thirty trips, and collect almost seventeen dollars per hour in revenues (excluding tips). The drivers in our sample too estimated that, to make a day of work worth their while financially, they need to pick up thirty passengers on average in each shift, which is usually about twelve hours: "Most of the drivers, I say, they have to work twelve, fifteen hours a day to maybe bring home 135, 150 dollars" (driver BXF4). To make a living in this business drivers face a trade-off: they either work longer hours or are prepared to take more risks.[1] Despite the possibility of being attacked, drivers therefore approach their customers inclined to pick them up rather than not. Driver BX5, who has been driving a taxi in the Bronx for thirty years, said: "I have to do my job. I just pick up the person, you know. . . . You cannot prejudge nobody out there. You can't. . . . The only time you don't feel safe is when you see they have a gun." Driver NM3 has to overcome his fear in order to continue working: "If you have too much nerves, you gonna fear everybody. You not gonna want to pick nobody ever again. Anytime I get nervous, I just go back home for a while until I feel better again." The tension between the pressure of working and that of staying safe is well expressed by driver Q4, who said that, "if you wanna make money, you don't have the time to look at a person. . . . But many times you can tell by appearance. What the person is wearing. What the person looks like. Their eyes. But mostly taxi drivers don't usually have the time."

As in Belfast, some of the New York drivers were less aware of prior screening and more focused on coping with or escaping from a dangerous situation once it arose. "At least when you have an idea that they are bad you have something on your side, because you're already prepared for that. Nobody gonna catch you like this, you know. You know how to slow down, you know how to defend yourself, you know when to stop. . . . But you don't like somebody, don't pick them up. If you already have them in, tell them to get out" (driver BX10). Driver BX5 agreed: "Like I say, it's a judgment call. You say, 'Okay, I'll take you,' then you got them and you have to pay the consequences. But you got to be prepared for it."

For nine drivers of West African origin, a priori trust turns into faith, not so much in passengers' trustworthiness as in God's: "One thing I do know is that God sees me and protects me. When I consider the danger that is involved in driving cabs, I would not want to do it. But because I have this strong faith in the Almighty, he protects me, he guides me, and I dare go anywhere on earth. He will save me if I am in danger" (driver NM8).

While most drivers in Belfast pick up passengers in a reasonably relaxed fashion because of a generally trusting attitude, the drivers of New York, who also pick up quite liberally, frame this disposition as unavoidable risk-taking. "I see some kids, I have a *double judgment*. I look at them: 'Should I?' Okay, sometimes I take the risk. But before I take such risks, I have already prepared myself in advance should it be the other way round" (driver NM8). The New Yorkers' manner is much more guarded and fatalistic: "I'm extra, extra careful when it comes to picking up customers—I'm very, very careful" (driver NM17). This attitude reflects, one can surmise, their higher likelihood of being attacked and the somewhat more irrational kind of potential attacker they expect: "Yeah, somebody look okay, they clean dress, but you never know. In this city nobody trust anybody" (driver BX7). Still, just as in Northern Ireland, much consequential screening does go on.

Screening Callers

The majority of the livery drivers work through a dispatcher who receives customers' telephoned requests and distributes them to the available drivers. The dispatcher's role goes beyond that of taking and distributing calls. First, this person offers a point of contact—a safe, understanding voice in the perilous metropolitan sea. Being in regular contact with the base during their shift makes drivers feel more secure. If their suspicions are aroused about a passenger, they call the dispatcher to ask for more information, advice on how to proceed, or backup from other drivers or the police. Above all, as in Belfast, the dispatcher screens callers before contacting a driver. The dispatcher does not, for the most part, mindlessly connect a caller with a driver.

The screening is partly built into the automatic recording system. Increasingly, the bases have introduced computerized systems that log the customer's name, telephone number, and address. Not only does this system allow callers to be traced more easily, but the system recalls the customer's details if he phones again. It works as an identity archive for matching new callers with past callers: "I trust the dispatcher because it's all computerized. When they call, the address is computerized, their phone number. That way you can get a person easier" (driver Q4).

More screening is done as the dispatcher registers and evaluates those details of the caller's request that are essential to providing the service—location and destination—and those features of the caller that are unavoidably revealed in a telephone call—gender, tone of voice, accent. Even more screening is accomplished when the dispatcher asks a caller to supply further information that will make it harder for that person to misbehave later, such as phone number, name, and number of passengers.

Even though calling a taxi through the dispatcher is considered a moderately positive sign in itself ("A person that would rob the taxi drivers wouldn't call the base. They would just be in the street waiting for someone to pick them up," said driver Q2), dispatchers use a number of filtering tools, and for good reasons, since ill-intentioned people do sometimes call for a taxi rather than hail a taxi. Luis Soto robbed the taxi driver Yovanny Grullon by ringing the base and asking for a taxi. When Mr. Soto, at once incautious and unimaginative, called the same taxi base a week later, the dispatcher recognized his telephone number, and the drivers, led by Mr. Grullon, set a trap, resulting in Mr. Soto being charged with attempted murder and criminal possession of a weapon.[2]

Like several of his colleagues, driver BR5 switched between working as a dispatcher and as a driver, and he screened for regular—hence known—customers: "I was working as a dispatcher, and we get these calls from these houses at certain hours, because they going home, because they were visiting the girlfriend, boyfriend, or they're leaving to work, or they're coming back from work, whatever, okay. So we got the usual customers, and the usual customers call from certain places."

Driver BX2 agreed: "If you pick up somebody in the street, you don't know who you're picking up . . . but just by hearing the voice, [the dispatchers] know the address. They're constantly with the passengers every day . . . and some people call for like ten years."

Dispatchers issue both reassurances and warnings to drivers regarding certain fares. For example, Mr. Miranda, a livery driver whose trust decisions are reported in an investigative article in the *New York Times*, said that if he hears a call for a pickup in Harlem or one of the rougher neighborhoods in the Bronx, he does not take the fare unless the dispatcher says something reassuring, like the coded message "11-4 positivo." That means the passenger has used the car service before (Kershaw 2000). Driver Q4 told us that, "if the base knows firsthand of people just trying to get taxis to harm them or attack them, they would warn the taxi drivers: 'If they are on this corner, don't pick them.' " Sometimes, however, the drivers do not take the dispatcher's advice: "As a dispatcher, I recommended a couple of friends not to take the fare. One of my friends, I told him, 'Go and see—if these people is not standing in front of this house, don't take them.' And he didn't listen to me. So he went there, and the people were not in front of the house, and he picked them up, and he got robbed" (driver BR5).

Driver BR5's suspicions were aroused in part because the callers were not regular users of his taxi base. But he also had a "gut feeling": "Now, if I get a call from somebody who never calls, right, that's one sign. And, I dunno, it was something, just something"—presumably something the caller said, or how he said it. Driver BR5 told us about another occasion when his concerns about a fare were proven correct. This time two men came into the base to ask for a taxi: "I went and looked at the guys and said, 'I dunno.' I didn't want the driver to take these people, but he did and he got robbed—they took his car."

Further Screening of Callers by Direct Observation

Accepting a call through the dispatcher does not prevent drivers from using their own judgment; they will reject a fare if, by direct observation, they pick up negative signs that escaped the dispatcher. Cabbies cannot be complacent, as driver BX8 pointed out: "I don't trust [dispatchers] 100 percent, but it's like 85 percent. Still, you got to be alert, 'cause in New York you never know what a person is going to be like."

The drivers therefore do not wholly rely on dispatchers' screening. Their level of dependence is partly determined by their understanding of the dispatcher's dispositions:

> Well, they are human beings. To err is human. People make mistakes. They can give you the call, and sometimes the person is no good. They can't even tell you. So I use my own discretion. I don't depend on the judgment of the dispatcher, because a similar case happened in the Bronx, by the Bronx Zoo. The guy pick up the call from the base, and you know he went and pick up the guy, to pick up the guy by Bronx Zoo, and the guy was killed. (driver NM17)

Driver BR4, who was more critical, believed that some dispatchers in noncomputerized bases are rather slack in their screening and could do more to help out the drivers. He understood very well that asking for identifiers might deter ill-intentioned callers by raising the cost for them of mimicking a bona-fide passenger and thus make them desist: "They have to play their role and be more responsible and ask the passenger for phone number. It's up to the passenger if they want to give the phone number. They don't have to give any information. . . . If it's a bad passenger or a dangerous passenger, if you start asking them, 'Name? Telephone number?' they don't like that. They will call another place, or they will catch a cab in the street."

Driver BX9 felt that the dispatchers are primarily interested in making money for the firm and consider drivers' safety a secondary concern: "Sometimes the base wants you to pick up people at the location, at the base. And when you see them, you say, 'No way! I not gonna pick up those bad persons.' Even they trying to make the business, they want you to pick up."

Driver BX5 even went so far as to suggest that a dispatcher who knew that he had worked a double shift—and was therefore likely to be carrying more money than most drivers—had set him up to be robbed: "Because the dispatcher knew that I worked a double shift. Nobody else knows that, but the dispatcher knows that. And then they have, you know, your account right there. How much you already made. . . . So I think it was a setup. Any dispatcher could set you up. They know how much money you already make."

Apart from their dispositions, dispatchers' ability to screen, while better in some respects, is also constrained by the medium of communication they use. All they have to go by are the caller's voice and the verbally transmitted identifiers, which may be backed up by stored information on the computer. Moreover, the person who phones for the cab is often not the intended passenger: "Sometimes you go to a restaurant because you get a call from the dispatcher, and they don't see the passenger. Right? I see the passenger. Sometimes they put a woman to call, and then when the passenger come he's drunk or whatever, and that's why I trust my own judgment" (driver BR2). Drivers therefore do not blindly accept fares that have been called in: "The dispatcher is behind the phone. He can only hear the voice. And I can see the person and can see the appearance," said driver Q1. Driver BR4 also said he has "to see the passenger, every time."

Ultimately, drivers rely on their own ability to identify trustworthy passengers by direct observation. "I always have the choice of whether to pick up a person or not," observed driver Q4. Driver BX2 agreed: " 'Cause there are people who, you know, the way they act, or when you look at them you see that they're not a nice person, I wouldn't pick them up. I would call the base and tell them, 'They don't look good.' " There are limits to this strategy, however, as driver Q4 then pointed out: "If I don't pick up too often, I can also get suspended by the base. I cannot do whatever I want."

Screening Hailers

Drivers' screening by observation becomes naturally more intense if they are picking up street-hailers rather than callers. All of the drivers we interviewed did that despite the law about picking up street-hails.[3] "I have to pick up passengers in the street because the phone calls that I get from the base are not enough. They don't give me enough money to support myself and my family. And I have to do it no matter what," explained driver Q2.

As in Belfast, New York drivers take a good look at prospective customers before deciding whether to pick them up: "You see, you look at people, and you get a good idea how, or what, they are about" (driver BR5). Driver Q7, who said that he would never take "suspicious-looking people," explained: "It takes me about thirty seconds. I drive up, see them, see what's going on. I can tell, no matter who they are, what they look like." Driver NM17 relies on the screening strategies of other drivers as well as his own: "If I'm following two taxis on the Avenue and I see those two taxis refuse to pick up customers, it makes me wonder: why did those two taxis not pick up the guy? So I slow down. I'm very, very careful, because two taxis didn't pick up the guy. But I want the business, and I want to know why they didn't pick him up, so I let the window down a little bit—not all the way down, just a little bit that he can talk to me. Then I ask him, 'Where do you want to go?' "

As we did in Belfast, we questioned drivers in an attempt to identify which factors they take into consideration in deciding whether a fare looks suspicious. In this chapter, we consider signs displayed by customers that can be effortlessly observed even at some distance. These include categorical signs (age, gender, ethnicity), signs of status (dress and other apparel, the quality of the housing or establishment near which the passenger is hailing), and signs of the state of mind of the prospective fare (displays of "street etiquette," way of walking, general demeanor). In the next chapter, we consider signs that can be perceived on closer inspection or by probing—signs, that is, that require an effort on the part of the driver.

We found several differences dictated by the dissimilarities in the two cities. For instance, unlike drivers in Belfast, who work in close-knit neighborhoods, New York drivers cannot count on reidentification of previously known hailers for the very good reason that the likelihood that they have already met them is small (see table 9.1). Regular customers are likely to call the base for a taxi, while hailers are almost invariably strangers. The city is just too large. We did find one excep-

Table 9.1   Screening by Taxi Drivers in Belfast and New York

Screening Practices	Belfast (N = 45)	New York (N = 50)
Screen for attitude	87% (39)	76% (38)
Avoid groups of men	80 (36)	74 (37)
Believe mixed-gender groups are safer	62 (28)	20 (10)
Screen for dress	56 (25)	66 (33)
Screen for age	51 (23)	84 (42)
Believe females are safer	44 (20)	20 (10)
Prefer known or regular customers	42 (19)	2 (1)
Drive past to check fare before pickup	38 (17)	88 (44)
Screen for drunkenness	20 (9)	28 (14)
Screen for skin color	N/A	26 (13)

Source: Authors' compilation.
Note: N/A = not applicable.

tion, though. Driver NM13 had bypassed the dispatch base and given his cell phone number to favored customers, who called him direct. When we interviewed him, he was waiting for one such regular passenger at the Metro North station at 125th Street and Lexington Avenue in Harlem. The interview ended when his white, professional-looking, middle-aged male customer arrived.

Table 9.1 allows us, at a glance, to see that there are a number of other differences between Belfast and New York—above all, differences of race and age.

Street Etiquette

Appearances, even at a distance, reveal a wide range of information, some of which is good enough to form a considered judgment of the quality of the fare. One can see whether a hailer looks disheveled, has bruises or wears rags, or shows signs of being mentally or socially dispossessed by how he walks or looks and whether he behaves in an agitated way on the sidewalk. Drivers do, of course, avoid picking up people who display these signs of severe social marginality or cognitive impairment: "See, when the hail stands in the middle of the street, waving at any car and acting stupid, I don't stop for them. But if they see me and [calmly] wave me over, and they look normal, I'll pull over and pick them up" (driver BX5).

Although taxi drivers cruise the streets looking for people who want a ride, they are wary of people who seem too keen or desperate for them to stop. Driver NM7 explained: "Sometimes the person who is waiting for the cab isn't even paying attention to you, he's just waving his hand.

I feel comfortable with him, to pick him up. Sometimes the person be meaning to stop you, he's grabbing the door, and that kind of person I refuse him right away."

Driver BX9 would pass by a fare if he felt that the individual was using drugs, was drunk, or was homeless. Any such person is beyond any ability to mimic being an ordinary passenger, since these conditions are hard to veil:

> There are people who you know from far away that they are on drugs. You can see from far that they are dirty, or homeless, or whatever. . . . If I see a drunk people, no way. I have two or three experiences in the beginning where I picked up drunk people. That was terrible. . . . Sometimes they don't know where to go. They don't want to get up from the car. It's really, really a problem—drunk people. And sometimes they call two, three, four times a day, and I say, "No way, he's drunk."

Driver Q1 was also careful not to pick up drunks: "[What] I look for, first of all, is their appearance. I might look for things like if a person is drunk—he looks drunk or he looks like he doesn't have balance—or I looks to see if the person is probably on drugs or, if not, you know, normal." Driver BR1 told us: "Sometimes you can see those guys who are dirty, their clothes are dirty, and they are smoking marijuana or things like that, with a bottle of beer in the hand. You can see it's not a decent person. 'Cause I never gonna be out in the street with a beer in my hand. 'Cause I got respect for the people, I got respect for myself."

However, knowing that fares are often looking for a ride because drinking has rendered them unfit to drive, one of our respondents from the Internet taxi newsgroup, a Chicago taxi driver, has developed an uncanny knowledge of the signs of various types of drunkenness. He noted that whether he picks up a drunken fare depends on what type of drunk he is: "If the drunkard has a hard time opening the door to get in, he will more than likely vomit. If the drunkard is waddling, like a duck, he will probably pass out in your taxi. If they got kicked out of the bar, they will tell their 'sob story,' give you a decent tip, and stay awake for the ride" (e-mail communication).

Type and Style of Dress

Drivers also take dress and other aspects of physical appearance into consideration. Thirty-three (66 percent) believed that one can "read" criminal or antisocial disposition into a person's style of dress: "Sometimes I see people and I say, 'These people are good for nothing,' " noted driver BX3. "I watch the shoes, the clothes." It was unclear, however, what exactly it is in some people's shoes and clothes that raises driver BX3's suspicions.

Driver NM13, working in northern Manhattan, was much more specific: "People that mostly do the robbings don't dress that nice. They don't present themselves so clean. People that mostly do the robbing have tattoos on, they [have] roughneck dressing with some hoody, trying to hide some part of their face, because they know they don't want to leave no witnesses when they do stuff like that." His observations were based on evidence from the footage of robberies taken from the cameras in livery cars: "Because cameras, from the taxi base that I work at, the cameras in the car that will review the people that robbed our people, we saw them. They didn't have anybody in a suit and tie or any shirt, casual shirt. They were all wearing a sweater, a hoody with jacket, trying to put some hood on or a cap or something like that." In his experience, robbers do not bother to differentiate themselves from the stereotypical villain. Another driver, however, had been robbed by a man wearing a business suit: "He was well dressed. He was very nice-looking, he called me 'sir,' you'd never think he is a thief, but he robbed me." In contrast, he told us, "I was behind another taxi, and the guy didn't stop to pick up one guy, about forty years old, because he was so dirty, not knowing he was a construction worker. You see construction workers tip more than people in an Italian suit because they work hard and they want to get home. I picked him up, and the fare was like eight dollars—he gave me I think thirteen dollars" (driver NM17).

Driver BX2 avoids customers who have "real baggy pants . . . you know, when you see them, you know, it's the way they dress—people that hang out in the street mostly." Driver Q4 checks passengers to see "if they're not dressed very smartly," and he is particular about hairdos: "The hair, if it's all wild and different colors, I stay away from that." Driver BX1 also looks at physical appearance: "How they're dressed, how they move. Guys with hands all grubby—I don't like to take them." Driver BX10 screens for dress *and* age at the same time: "When you see young people and you see how they look in their face, and how they dress, it tell you a lot how they are like. . . . the way they talk."

However, apart from taking into account extreme signs of undesirability in an individual's appearance, New York drivers do not consider style of dress much of a guide to passengers' quality. In Belfast there is a great deal of homogeneity in the style and type of dress of many customers. Working-class Protestant and Catholic males dress in a similar style, and it is very difficult to distinguish between them on that basis. In terms of status, where differences do exist, drivers are mindful of the style of dress but not overly reliant on it; it is too easy to make a mistake either way. New York is much more ethnically and stylistically diverse. The ample, sometimes extravagant variability of styles and the absence of clear dress codes make it difficult to distinguish types of people from their dress alone. Driver NM13 told us: "Tattoos, ear piercings, tongue piercings, some people have three or four rings, earrings in his face. Sometimes it's fashion, but sometimes you get scared." If in Belfast styles of dress vary too little to be of value, in New York they vary too much. Driver Q6 explained:

> Since in this country there is such a freedom of expression, it is hard to judge the way a person is dressed, and it doesn't mean that they are a bad person or a good person. . . . If I were to decline somebody because of the way they were dressed, I would lose a lot of money because of that, because here there is freedom of expression. And if I was to do that, then I would discriminate [against] a lot of people, and as a result I would not make as much money as I can.

Still, dress may be of some use, though not as a sign of status. According to driver YC1, dress can indicate where a passenger's final destination is likely to be. A man wearing a suit, for example, is probably going downtown in Manhattan, and driver YC1 would pick him up. He uses dress as an indicator of destination rather than of status as such, so dress anticipates information that he would otherwise have to stop to acquire from the passenger.

Dress also leads to another type of inference based on "mismatches," a reasoning that is triggered when two signs convey starkly contrasting messages. Belfast is a city with a relatively static population and well-established customs and patterns of behavior. Drivers are therefore well attuned to things that appear out of place or behavior that seems odd. In contrast, New York's fluctuating population spawns a greater diversity of "normal" behavior. Nevertheless, drivers are on the lookout for suspicious oddities. Driver BR4, for example, is wary of a well-dressed man in a bad area, because "they don't match—a well-dressed man in a bad area, something has to be wrong. Or someone who comes very nice, so nice that something has to be wrong." This reasoning is the mirror image of that of Belfast drivers, who, on weekend nights in pub-ridden areas, are suspicious of sober men when everyone else is staggering around drunk. Both use the "too good to be true" rule for detecting mimics.

Finally, dress is taken into account not for what it says but for what it may hide. In Belfast the drivers screen for clothes that hide passengers' features or may conceal a weapon, such as a heavy coat—especially in a warm season, which makes it odd as well. In New York we found fewer drivers who interpret the dress of prospective customers in this way. One was Mr. Miranda, who said he would never pick up a person wearing a ski cap, which he sees as a potential robber's mask (Kershaw 2000). And driver BX8 is wary of people with "glasses, [or] like a hat. You know that you don't see [them] clearly. You know, driving a taxi is more dangerous in the winter. Because if you are passenger, I know how you look now, though I don't know what you got in your belt or something."

But if I see you from outside, I see that you don't have any weapons. In the summertime it's less dangerous."

Age

Belfast drivers do not have a univocal reading of age. They are somewhat wary of younger customers, who could be minor troublemakers like runners or muggers, but at the same time they fear older males more because they are more likely than teenagers to instigate a sectarian attack. Drivers in New York, by contrast, are very distrustful of young people hailing cabs (see table 9.1). They were adamant that age is *the* trait they notice most:

> Okay, the way that I select my customers, if I'm seeing the customers for the first time, I see the *age*. The age is very important. . . . I've been learning that [for] all the people, no matter race, color, boy or girl, don't matter. It's the *age*. It is teenagers that are definitely the problem. They sometimes—not all of them—they don't wanna pay for the fare, and sometimes they destroy the car 'cause they write stuff. (driver BR4)

Driver BX9 agreed: "Young people. It doesn't matter which race they are. Young people—no way. . . . Young people are troublemakers. I have a lot of experience with young people. . . . They want to not pay. . . . If you charge them in advance, you got two enemies right there. So most of the time it's not good to pick up young people."

Driver BR2 felt that teenagers are the most dangerous passengers because "they got nothing to lose. That's what I think. And sometimes they are drunk or on drugs, whatever, and you don't see it when they are gonna get into the car, you don't have a way to see if they have a gun or a knife." Drivers therefore prefer to "pick up more mature adults, older adults" (driver Q10), or people with younger children.

Judging by the profile of the attackers we presented in chapter 7, the screening out of young people is not just the result of drivers' prejudice—a bad case of ephebophobia. The strategy is based in reality: teenagers *are* the passengers from whom a driver might statistically expect a higher likelihood of attack.[4] Difficult to disguise and easy to observe, age seems indeed a very telling correlate of dangerousness.

Gender

Youth is in fact such a strong warning sign for drivers that it not only breaks through racial divides—white youngsters being thought of as potentially as bad as blacks or Hispanic ones—but also silences the generally positive sign of being female. Most drivers are particularly wary of teenage girls: "Before it was the men, but now even the girls are doing bad things" (driver BX10). Driver BX9 believed that "males and females, it doesn't matter, they are the same." Driver Q8 told us that in separate incidents a girl robbed both him and his friend at gunpoint. Victimization studies suggest that drivers are right to be as wary of young females as young males. Lawrence Greenfeld and Tracy Snell (1999) report that juveniles account for approximately 28 percent of female violent offenders and 26 percent of male violent offenders.

Despite a strong suspicion of young females and a stronger reluctance than in Belfast to accept femaleness as a positive sign at face value, New York drivers perceived *adult* women as safer: "I don't mind about females. It's hard for a female to do something. It happens maybe about once a year" (driver BX1). From the following account, we can infer that, coupled with the "right" ethnicity, femaleness still works.

> Another fare comes over the radio: "St. Nicholas and 145th," the dispatcher shouts—a corner in Harlem. No one responds. There are about one hundred drivers cruising the streets on the overnight shift. If none of them presses the button on their microphones indicating they want a fare, the dispatchers shout out the location again, up to five or six times. After the fifth broadcast of "St. Nicholas and 145th," the dispatcher clarifies things: "*Hispanic female.*" Another driver quickly takes the call. (Kershaw 2000)

Mr. Miranda, the same livery driver in whose car this episode was recorded by the *New York Times* reporter, was also quite relaxed about picking up hailing women alone or in pairs off the street, even at night, something most drivers would not easily do with men.

Still, drivers looked for concomitant signs of trustworthiness even with women. Mr. Miranda was happier picking them up when they emerged from reputable nightclubs. For driver BX6, "it all depends . . . lady with a Bible, I'm sure you got no problem. If you see a lady with a bottle of beer, I'm sure you got problems." Another sign is whether the hailer has a young child with her: "Maybe if a woman has a baby, then I'm gonna know that that woman is not gonna do anything to me. . . . I have more faith in women. . . . I just feel that that type of women represent more safe people" (driver Q2). Driver BX7 concurred: "Before I pick up, I check the passenger, always. If I had two passengers, I see their faces. You find you can check what is better. If I see one lady and one baby, I know that's not a problem." As we discussed in chapter 7, some mimics realize that drivers have this expectation and try to outwit them by carrying a baby, real or fake.

Mixed-Gender Groups of Passengers

Belfast drivers perceived the presence of a female with one or more male hailers as decreasing the potential dangerousness of the fare. Between

1993 and 1997, only 1 percent of male violent offenders in the United States committed the offense in the company of a female offender (Greenfeld and Snell 1999). Yet New York drivers are more circumspect than Belfast drivers (see table 9.1). Driver NM8 told us that, on the one hand, the presence of a female can help to prevent a potentially violent situation from escalating because "the girlfriend, she will say, 'Don't do it.' She will talk to him and tell him to be calm." However, he pointed out, the converse is also true: a passenger may become more aggressive in an effort to save face in front of a female: "The high-risk people will take your life because of a girl. . . . They don't want you to embarrass them in front of her. So, to avoid all that, they become aggressive, they become violent."

In general, in New York the presence of a female is viewed with caution: "They work with their men to rob you. You see, anytime you hear that a woman has robbed somebody, about 80 percent of the time they are with a man. The woman can't do that all by themselves. Always they are with their men" (driver NM17). Driver Q1 agreed: "Females have attachments to men, and they lie to try to harm drivers." Driver BRF4 said: "Sometimes I see couples, but with them you have to be very, very careful."[5] The drivers told us of a number of incidents in which women had been used to lure drivers into a trap (see chapter 7), and three of the eight women who attacked taxi drivers as reported in our newspaper archive co-offended with men. One of them, Rosa Ocasio, lured the driver Ousmane Diallo out of his car and into a building where her male accomplice shot him (Fries 2002).

Groups of Men

In Belfast groups of men are immediately viewed with suspicion, and in New York drivers are also wary of groups of more than two men unless they display some neutralizing signal. Driver BR1 told us that a colleague of his was killed by "a bunch of young guys, and they were drinking and smoking and dealing like that about five o'clock in the morning."

Driver Q9 pointed out that sometimes picking up a group of guys is unavoidable: "Well, unfortunately, I prefer not to pick up sometimes, but we have to." In such cases he tries to make the best of a bad situation: "I mean, you have to show them that everything is going to be okay, or right away they say, 'What's the matter?' I mean, you're gonna make them feel bad. Not everybody is bad. Personally, three persons can go in the back, but I don't like to have anybody in front."

Driver Q4's practice of trying to "stay away from people in groups, like in groups of more than three," was shared by many of the drivers. If the men are black, then driver BX1 will not even take two: "If I see like two guys, two dark guys, I don't pick them. Usually they give problems, so I prefer not to." Driver Q10 also told us that he does not like to pick up groups of guys because "he doesn't feel safe with groups of guys, and I try to avoid them." Once again, their concern seems to be well grounded: the statistical probability of being attacked by a group is proportionally greater than it is of being attacked by a solo passenger.

Often, however, drivers do not mindlessly reject a group but evaluate a cluster of signs before making a decision, and a good sign may be enough to offset many bad ones. Mr. Miranda stopped when a group of young men flagged him down at four o'clock in the morning. They were disc jockeys who had just finished a job at a party. The men offered him fifty dollars to take them and their equipment to Valentine Avenue in Bedford Park. The men, speaking in Spanish, told him they had called fifteen car services, and all had refused to come to the neighborhood (Kershaw 2000). This is an interesting case in which direct observation yields information of better quality than is conveyed in taking a call. Even if they had informed the dispatchers that they were honest, hardworking DJs, words over the phone are cheap. When these men called by phone and could not be observed in person, no one agreed to take them. All signs conveyed over the phone were discouraging—where they were, where they wanted to go, the time of night they called, the fact that they were in a group, and the fact that they were men. Yet when Mr. Miranda saw them he picked them up, because they had an additional sign, the DJ equipment. That signaled to him that they were very likely to be true DJs rather than phony ones going to the trouble of looking like DJs just to rob him of his few dollars.

Drivers are also mistrustful of racially mixed groups, especially if young, not just because they are in a group but because they are so rare and thus trigger the mismatch reasoning. Driver BX10 said: "Be careful when two people are together, like African American and Latino. When you see a Latin person and an African American together, I say be careful, that is really something. I don't really know [why], . . . but it's true. They are too different, and they young too, they could be up to something."

Driver BX8 had the same reaction: "I'm Hispanic, but if I see a white standing with a black, I don't take them. When they are together, it's no good, it's no good. . . . When they're together like that and they're drinking, they're using drugs."

Skin Color

One trait for which drivers in Belfast do not screen passengers is skin color. They could not do so even if they wanted to, for nearly everyone there is white. This is not so in New York City, of course. The sting operations we described in chapter 7—the police department and TLC acting together to have black officers pose as customers and to fine any yellow cab driver who did not stop to pick up those "customers"—revealed that most yellow cab drivers do not discriminate against black customers. Whether this outcome is reliable is not so clear, for as we shall see in the next chapter, African Americans' experiences with hailing yellow cabs indicate that discrimination does occur. Perhaps yellow cab drivers got wind of the operations or at least knew that, after the publicity of the Danny Glover case, the spotlight was on them, and so they behaved better than usual.

Our interviews with Hispanic livery drivers also reveal that discrimination does occur. Livery drivers were not included in the sting operations, since they are not supposed to be picking up hailing passengers in the first place. Ironically, this gives them more freedom to screen by skin color, for if they do not pick up they are, as it were, simply respecting the law. Because of the high-voltage sensitivity of the issue of racial discrimination, however, drivers were guarded in their responses to questions about screening on the basis of overt signs of race:

> The United States is made up of many different races who come from different places. Yes, a black person can walk away without paying you, and the same thing can be done by a white female person or by a Hispanic person. It's different, it depends on where you are, the place that you are at, and you can't say that there are people who do this more . . . 'cause the population is so diverse that you see people everywhere. (driver Q6)

Driver BX9 pointed out that many of his customers in the Bronx are "black and Hispanic and some white people." "If you wanna work up here," said driver BX6, "and you wanna make good money with the kind of people up here, it doesn't matter. I know black or Chinese or Dominican—I don't care. I drive anybody."

On the night Mr. Miranda drove around with the *New York Times* journalist, he drove past several people hailing him, all young men of different races, explaining that they "just didn't look right." Mr. Miranda said that Hispanic drivers are generally more comfortable with Hispanic passengers (we discuss a reason for this in the next chapter), although, he added, drivers at his service generally do not discriminate through racial stereotyping. In dangerous neighborhoods, he said, drivers simply avoid people who look threatening—and threatening people can be of any color.

Maybe so. But our investigation yielded far more realistic results. Less coy drivers admitted to screening on the basis of skin color: "I going to say, because we are alone in the interview, I don't like to take the black people because they give me, or us, a hard time" (driver BX3). Some drivers discriminate not on the basis of black skin alone but only if this sign is combined with youth and negative signs in terms of dress: "I don't like to pick up black people. Not to the extreme, just black people that don't look too well dressed maybe . . . or teenagers, 'cause I know that sometimes the incentives of teenagers are not very . . . you know. So mostly I try to prevent picking up those people" (driver Q10).

Most drivers who confessed to using skin color to screen passengers were eager to justify the practice lest they appear racist, and they provided a number of arguments. Driver BX8 said that fear dictates his preferences: "Some black people—not only me, a lot of my friends too—we're scared to take them sometimes. I don't say that all black people are bad people, you know." Many drivers justify their attitude as the result of learning from bad experiences: "I have had a lot of bad experiences with black people, so whenever I see a black person in the street I look the other way, because I have had bad experiences. It's not just a racial thing. Very often they're very picky. They will drive you crazy with directions. Oh, turn here, go there, take this lane, go into that lane" (driver Q3).

Although drivers are aware that the actions of a minority should not make it difficult for the majority of black people who need taxis to go about their daily business, they are still influenced by the actions of the offending few: "Let's say you're a good person, but the good person shares the consequences for the bad person," argued driver BX8. "That's my theory. It's like, sometimes you take a passenger. They tell you, 'Take me to Manhattan,' and they say, 'While you wait, I gonna go upstairs and get the money.' You know sometimes we do it, and they go upstairs and they never come back."

Driver YC1, who drives a yellow cab, argued that it is not race per se that makes him more guarded with black customers. The drawback, he said, is that there is a much greater chance that a black person's destination will be in an area that is undesirable for him because it is either unsafe or financially less lucrative, since he is less likely to find a fare to drive back into Manhattan: "It's basic, not much more than economic reason. I mean, I'm not justifying the fact that the guy was not picked up. But I just want people to understand that it's not a racial issue. It's an economic issue, which has nothing to do with this. Even black passengers sometimes tell me that black drivers do not pick them up."

We could not find data on the race of the individuals who attacked taxi drivers in New York, so we cannot say for sure whether drivers' "statistical discrimination" is well founded or a racial prejudice. Still, drivers share the generalized knowledge that, statistically, young blacks are more likely to be dangerous. The National Center for Youth Justice, for instance, found that over half of known male juvenile homicide offenders in the whole of the United States between 1980 and 1997 were black (Snyder and Sickmund 1999, 4). Provided that it is not unconditional, their response seems to reflect reality.

Drivers' attitudes are not always tempered, however, or rationally thought through. For some drivers, their racially driven choices are gender-blind. Driver Q3 and driver BX3, for instance, were even more wary of black women than of black men, an attitude that does not seem to be justified by crime statistics and may be motivated by their perception of black women as a generic "nuisance":

> Women are worse. One time I take three ladies, old ladies, in New York to Brooklyn on the Prospect Expressway. They were black, and it was a street where there was no traffic whatsoever. But the speed limit was thirty, and they were fighting with me because they wanted me to go sixty, but I couldn't, so they started banging on the car and . . . all sorts of things. (driver Q3)

> For example, the black women, when we see black women out on the streets, we don't want to pick up, because that kind of women going to give me problems because they never work. That kind of people that stop you on the street, they don't use the car company, they don't have money to call you. That kind of people are no good. I don't pick up because I know that kind of people are going to give me problems and then no pay the money. (driver BX3)

Driver Q12 candidly revealed that although both blacks and whites have robbed him, he now only discriminates against blacks: "Before I would take everybody, I would take black people, white people, everybody. But now, because the people who threatened me, the people who robbed me before, were black people, I don't take black people, even though the people who put the pistol to my head were white but I still takes them."

Yet most Hispanic drivers were at pains to show that they are not racist and argued, as driver YC1 put it: "There are also black drivers who don't want to pick up black people. So this is black on black at this point, you not talking about discrimination." The case of Steven Holmes (1999), a black journalist with the *New York Times* who worked as a taxi driver in the 1970s in New York City, seems to confirm this point. After being held up twice in three years by young black men—once at gunpoint and once at knifepoint—he reported that he too started screening his customers on the basis of race and age:

> I became more choosy about who I let in my cab. I still picked up black women, older men, couples, families and men dressed in suits. But my sense of tolerance and racial solidarity was tested every time a casually dressed young black man, especially one in sneakers, tried to hail my cab. Most times, I drove right by. I sometimes wondered about their reaction, but I kept thinking that if I guessed wrong, I could pay for my mistake with my life. Like it or not, I was engaging in my own form of racial pro-

filing. But I rationalized. Racism, I told myself, would be to decline to pick up every black person who hailed my cab. What I was doing was playing the odds, playing it safe, taking no chances.

Holmes's experience echoes Reverend Jesse Jackson's controversial statement: "There is nothing more painful to me at this stage in my life than to walk down the street and hear footsteps and start thinking about robbery—then look around and see somebody white and feel relieved" (Herbert 1993).

But is it really true that black taxi drivers screen passengers on the basis of color as well? We interviewed eighteen black drivers who work in the predominantly black neighborhoods of northern Manhattan, where, if they were to discriminate on the basis of color alone, they would never pick up anyone. However, we did find that, at least for thirteen (72 percent) of the drivers, color is an important sign.

The drivers' responses to the questions on race varied according to their own ethnic origin and that of the interviewer. The three African American interviewees were very reluctant to engage in any discussion on race. Driver NM1's reply was typical: "People is people, some of them is a little darker, and some is a little lighter. That's it. But we all basically the same." In contrast, the West African drivers were much more forthright—except when being interviewed by our African American research assistant, with whom they steadfastly avoided answering questions about race, preferring to play down any differences: "If I work in a black area I have more trouble with blacks, if I work in a Spanish area I have more trouble with Hispanics, and if I work in an Irish area I always have trouble with Irish guys who are drunk," offered driver NM10. Driver NM13 said, "We have white people that robbed us, we have Spanish people that robbed us, and we have female white girls that robbed us. They come from all kinds of races, not just black people." Driver NM17 was keen to point out that the attackers are in the minority: "Once in a while you run into trouble, you know. That doesn't mean that black people are no good. They are very good, they are my people; I love them. But once in a while one apple spoils the whole bunch." Driver NM8 felt that any two taxi drivers may screen the same customer for different characteristics and hinted that some may view skin color as an important feature: "No doubt any cab driver has different ways of looking at the person he is going to pick up. Me, I don't mind picking white, black, purple, yellow, green, whatever, any color. If I think I'm going to feel comfortable with him, I'm going to pick him up."

In contrast, those interviewed by our white researchers (Heather Hamill and a white British male) were willing to discuss the issue, and four of them introduced it unprompted while replying to other questions. For example, when asked about runners, driver NM3 said, "It's 99 percent blacks—young black guys who run off and don't pay." Other West African drivers agreed that black passengers are more likely to not pay them: "With respect to race, I have not picked up any white man that never pay me" (driver NM8). However, working in Harlem gives him many more opportunities to pick up blacks than whites, and his chances of meeting a white runner are reduced, a point made by driver NM17: "I work in Harlem, so there are more blacks who rob me and jump out of the car without paying than the white people because I don't work in the white neighborhood." Nevertheless, driver NM8, who is from Guinea and had worked as a taxi driver in New York for nine years, also made the distinction between African Americans and those he called "foreigners": "Even foreigner, foreigner blacks, they don't do it, you know. I'm sorry, it's a shame for me to say, but I have never picked up any white Americans that never pay me, only black Americans."

The West African drivers also expected black passengers to more readily become violent: "Yeah, they like to fight you, they curse you, they will hit your car—it's risky, risky. There is no respect in this job, it's risky. One black guy, when I came up to the red lights and he started cursing and saying, 'You motherfucker, just go,' I thought he was going to hit me" (driver NM6).

Given that most passengers in northern Manhattan are black, drivers screen for color plus at least one other sign, usually gender and age: "It's always the black man that threatens you. From age twenty to twenty-seven, and always black" (driver NM3). Driver NM6 agreed: "Man, I drive past all kinds of people and don't pick them up. It's mainly black people, all guys, but normally it's black guys. Sometimes Spanish guys, the young ones."

The West African drivers also expressed some solidarity with yellow cab drivers, who at times may be unwilling to pick up black passengers. Driver NM7 reiterated one of the arguments used by Hispanic drivers about risk calculation: "If I'm a black person and I'm in Manhattan, yellow cabs are supposed to stop and take me no matter what color I am. But he must go by his sensitive feeling also, but me, sometimes I refuse him because I risk my life. I work uptown, where bad people are hanging around. So I don't refuse him just for his color. I'm scared for my life, and for five dollars you can get killed for no reason." Driver NM2 reiterated the Hispanic drivers' argument about profit maximization: "If I was a yellow cab driver, I wouldn't pick up black guys going uptown or out to the Bronx. Where they going to get a fare back into the city? They're losing money right there."

Because of New York's vast geographic size and large population, drivers rarely get to know their customers. So even though they, like Belfast drivers, look for easily observable cues and signs of trustworthiness, they are more likely to look for clusters of signs that together are more reliable than any one sign taken singly. However, the diversity of New York's population in terms of ethnicity, dress, and demeanor makes sign-reading very difficult. In New York more so than in Belfast, appearances can be deceptive, and drivers do not relax when they pick up customers but continue to probe for additional and less easily observable signs throughout the journey.

Chapter 10

Probing in New York

*A*S WE REPORTED in the last chapter, New York drivers glean some information from their initial observation of potential customers. All of the drivers agree, however, that there is no foolproof way to establish a passenger's trustworthiness by first appearances only: "You can have trouble from anybody. You never know when you have trouble. Sometimes you look at the old lady, you have trouble. Sometimes you look at the young man, you got trouble . . . you never know" (driver BR3). Some learn the hard way. One driver was shot in the shoulder after he picked up two men who robbed him of fifty dollars: "I always try to pick up nice guys, guys who don't look like they will give me any trouble. . . . These two guys, they looked good to me" (Kugel 2000, B1).

Savvy drivers, once they have absorbed the easily observable features, may reach an open verdict and thereafter engage in additional probing and screening: "Mostly drivers, they see the appearance, and they drive away because they see trouble. But many people can be dressed very nicely and they have a gun. There are other ways to find out if you are smart about it. If you get into conversations, then you may get your money if you take the fare" (driver Q6). Driver BR4 works through a mental list: "I do it like this—check, check. Because you get real mad when something happens to you—you say, I knew it, I knew it. So I start discriminating and checking in the beginning."

Probing Before Picking Up

Once a passenger enters the car, it becomes much more difficult for a driver to rescue the situation if he feels unsafe: "You gotta feel it out. Like I say, if you're taking them, you're taking them. If you're not, [don't let them in the car,] don't take them" (driver BX5). Further investigation therefore takes place before drivers agree to take the fare. In this regard, livery cab drivers have a slight advantage over yellow cab drivers: they can, and do, exploit the fact that their fares are not metered. Instead, driver and passenger agree on the fare before the journey begins, and often before the passenger enters the car. This is a critical moment when drivers have an opportunity to obtain a plurality of additional signs before committing to the fare.

Seventeen (34 percent) of the drivers judge passengers by how they respond to the cost of the journey. If driver BR1 sees "some person that you suspect, like you see they're dirty, smoking and things like that, you ask for the money up front. He doesn't wanna pay, you leave him right there and you got no problem." If in doubt, driver BR4 deliberately *increases* the fare to test the person's reactions: "It's something with my instincts. For example, if I see a person that look like maybe they don't wanna pay. Suppose the fare is ten dollars and I say, 'That's gonna come to thirteen dollars,' and the person don't complain, that means they don't care, they are not ready to pay anyway." One other driver mentioned this ruse, adding, "If he wants to rob me, he don't mind if I give him a higher price, he just wants to get into the car so he can rob me. If I give him the higher price and he refuses, that means he don't want to do nothing with me, he just wants to go somewhere and not pay that much money" (driver NM7). This trick may help to confirm the driver's suspicions already formed on the basis of other signs. On its own, however, it seems an imperfect strategy. The driver refuses to pick up the passenger who is too ready to accept the higher fare, interpreting his agreement as a sign that he does not care because he is not planning to pay it. For such a passenger, it costs nothing to accept the higher fare. However, this assumes both that the good passenger is not under some pressure that leads him to accept the higher fare and that the bad passenger who says yes to the higher fare does not realize he is being tested. Otherwise, he too might not accept the higher fare in order to pass off as a good passenger and be picked up.

By absorbing extra signs through the first direct contact with potential passengers—signs, for instance, that come from a verbal exchange—drivers can gain not only something that may be telling in itself but also information that they can compare with signs they collected at first sight. Driver BX9 told us that he checks whether a person's style of dress and speech match: "When people is well dressed, you pick them up easily. But sometimes if they are well dressed and then the way that they talk—you know that it is not the real them. So right there something comes to you that something is going on. So they look good, but they don't sound good."

A mimic can easily find good-looking clothes even if he does not wear them to start with. However, as the phonetics professor Henry Higgins in *Pygmalion* knows very well when he undertakes to tutor the very

Cockney Eliza Doolittle, the refinement of one's accent and manner of speech is much harder to achieve. It is thus a more reliable signal of the underlying type of customer than clothing. By itself speech may not be enough for a driver to reject a passenger—there are plenty of uneducated but honest passengers—but the mismatch raises the probability that the customer may be intent on duping the driver. With a lowly accent or manner of speech, a well-dressed customer looks better than he sounds and thus may be too good to be true.

Mimicking only one sign of a cluster that would identify a good-quality passenger while not bothering to conceal those that cannot be changed may thus backfire for the mimic and lower the probability that the driver will deem him trustworthy. Yet with drivers who are unable to judge accents and speech quality, as is often the case with immigrant drivers, the trick may work.[1]

Facial Expression and Eyes

One feature that drivers can observe on closer inspection is the hailer's face—the expression, the eyes, even the skin. And they do take notice of faces: "Yeah, I look at the people before I pick them up. You know. I look at the fare. . . . I know the things about whether people are good or they are trouble. The people *you look in their face* there's something wrong, I never pick up. Sometimes I'm confused, but not too many times" (driver BR3).

It is not always clear what exactly drivers "read" in the face; some would simply say, as driver NM13 did, "When you look at their face, they look weird; you don't want to pick them up." Paul Ekman (2001) and his associates have found that most of us are not very good readers of facial expressions and that few people do better than chance when judging whether someone is lying or not. However, there are a few exceptional people who can spot the deceit in someone who is lying. Ekman (2001, 162n) has noted that he does not yet know whether "such people are naturally gifted or acquire this ability through special circumstances." We cannot rule out the possibility that some drivers, like some police officers, either already have or develop special skills in this regard.

In two cases, the drivers themselves made clear the exact nature of the inferences. Driver BXF4 is acutely aware of the importance of eye contact:

> When a person is trying to do something, they always have to keep from your sight. You looking at them, and they look somewhere else. They think that if you look at me, you gonna know what I want to do. So the eye contact . . . and you know, as a taxi driver, I look at them. When they realize that I'm looking at them, they try to look away. That's when I know something could be happening. You know. If I look at another person and

he's looking at me, then I'm fine. 'Cause I know, that person, nothing is wrong. He's looking at me. We having an eye contact. He knows that I'm looking at him, so he will be looking at me. Nothing is wrong. You know he doesn't avoid my view.

While driver BXF4 looks for the emotional and behavioral signs of lying that she believes can be triggered by eye contact, driver BR5 looks for physical signs of drug use and prostitution:

You see, you can pick up [or identify] a junkie or a woman doing something, a hooker, right away. Sometimes people get in the car, and right away they try to hide it. Okay, they think that you won't be able [to notice,] because the other people, they don't notice. Okay. But I've seen so many junkies, so I can tell their faces. I can tell. [Not their eyes so much,] *it's the skin,* the skin. The people who use heroin, they look like Keith Richards, they get like that. So, yeah, as far as that, you get very good at that, at telling what they're like.

Gut Feelings

A number of Belfast drivers spoke of experiencing "gut feelings" or having a "sixth sense" that alerted them to something being wrong. Even though the exact stimulus for these feelings was not obvious to the drivers, they paid attention to them and modified their behavior accordingly—by, for example, deciding at the last minute not to take a passenger. The Chicago driver contacted via an Internet taxi newsgroup described how this works: "Cab drivers somehow manage to get a form of ESP. Like homosexuals and 'gay-dar,' like radar, I like to call this 'cab-dar,' you just know. You know when a fare is going to make a break for it. You know when someone is going to pass out, vomit, or just be abusive, before they get in the taxi. This *gift* does take time to master" (email communication, November 8, 2002). Another driver who works in Melbourne, Australia, wrote: "I've been driving cabs for eighteen years and have a very well developed sixth sense of what is danger, but then I can be wrong, as I was one year ago when I picked up three well dressed young males and ended up in hospital" (email communication, November 11, 2002). Similarly, in New York the drivers spoke of "premonitions," "instincts," "vibes," and "funny feelings," all of which would prompt them to change tack. Driver BX9 explained: "Like something tell you, you are in trouble right now." Driver NM7 believed his "sensitive feelings" were of fundamental importance in keeping him safe:

When you come to be a cab driver, God gives you that sensitive feeling. Sometimes the person who stops you gives you a look, and you get that sensitive feeling. You must have that sensitive feeling, because you could pick up someone who looks nice and he hurts you, he robs you. And maybe you could pick up someone who looked like a bum and you find that this guy, he pay you and he gives you a good tip and he is nicer than any type of person you could take. So it's a lot complicated.

Driver NM8 told us that, "when you are in the danger zone, you have body signals." Driver BXF4 was vague about the exact nature of her hunch: "Most of the time I feel like my heart tells me. Let me tell you, my heart is telling me what to do, and I do what my heart wants to do." Driver BR4 said: "Sometimes the people I don't like, I say good-bye." Driver YC1 gave us a more articulate example of his intuition in operation, though the exact stimulus still eluded him:

I was driving in my taxi in Manhattan, and somebody flagged me down on 96th and 3rd Avenue for a very short trip. When the guy flagged me down, I looked at the guy, and part of my judgment said, this guy is not dangerous. But right away, immediately, it came to my mind, he's gonna cheat me. But I said to myself, I am overjudging people, I shouldn't be like that. The guy said, "I gonna go to the grocery, and when I come back I pay you." So the guy went to the grocery, and then when he left the grocery, he never came back to my car. So my judgment was correct. He didn't look dangerous, but he cheated me.

As it happens, driver YC1 shrewdly knew that this experience provided him with a valuable lesson: "And I was very happy when this happened, because for only three dollars twenty-five I was able to check my senses, which is great. I would have to pay more than three dollars twenty-five to call a technician and see if my alarm system works. Right? I feel very happy about that." However, despite another driver's assertion that "sometimes something will tell me, be careful with that guy who is in the car," his instincts let him down when he was robbed by two men: "I felt comfortable with them. I thought they'd be all right—you know, they will pay me—and all of a sudden they surprised me" (driver NM17).

Probing During the Journey

Most drivers, like driver BX9, pick up passengers only if they are reasonably confident of their trustworthiness: "The better way is before they get into the car—be ready." However, even after accepting the fare, drivers do not necessarily relax but continue to monitor the passenger carefully: "You take them by looking at them and then the first thing they say, you know you are in trouble, you know what kind of person they are" (driver BX9). Driver NM2 closely watches the passenger approach: "Say somebody just came out of the building and they already in a fight, even two men and a girl. I won't stop, because I think it gonna continue in the car, and perhaps in their confusion they might not pay me, not that they mean to, one is mad with the other and they just get out. If the beginning [of the journey] don't look good, I don't want to take it for granted that the ending will be good. I don't know what the ending is gonna be." Many of the drivers believed that knowing how to read the signs makes it possible to deduce the passenger's intentions: "You see a lot of things on the faces of the person when you look at them. On the way they dress, the way they talk . . . they always let you know something when they get in the car. Like about who they are or what they are going to do" (driver BX10).

General Demeanor

The drivers pay close attention to passengers' attitudes and behavior as they enter the car: "I don't care what you wear, but the way that you act with me when you get into the car and the way that you talk, that's what I look for" (driver NM7). Driver BR5 told us, "I don't pick up people who has a bad attitude. People who get in the car and instead of telling you where to go they just bark a direction. It's not nice. That kind of people you try to avoid. . . . For me, [I don't care if the passenger] is just like a sack of potatoes or something sitting in the back, but they have to show some respect."

And drivers continue to focus on passengers' manner and style of speech during the journey: "The way they order you something. That's when you already got them in the car. The way they talk, you can tell. When a bad person comes to you, you can tell. They talk bad. Like they order you to do something: 'Stop here, man! Why are you doing that?' Like . . . they want a confrontation" (driver BX10). Driver NM13 started to get very worried when he picked up two men who had been playing basketball:

> The kind of language they were using, and the kind of things they were talking about, like they were talking about drugs and some guy who hasn't brought back they money and they were going to fuck him up and all that. I just reached behind me and closed the partition. I said, "Your conversation is disturbing my driving, so can I shut the partition?" I don't have to ask them, but I just wanted to be nice to them because I was starting to get scared.

If they are feeling uneasy with a customer, drivers will try to elicit more information from him, looking for signs of nervousness or evasiveness: "I will try and get to know somebody that I'm not sure about. I wouldn't use conversation like other people. I would just ask a few questions: 'Where are you from, where are you working?' And then I would notice if that person was nervous when he was picked up. . . . I can judge what the person is going to do to me" (driver Q6). When driver NM17 questions a suspicious passenger, he is both looking for clues as to the customer's intentions and signaling that he is not an easy target: "Every robber, the bottom line is to rob and get away with it. Nobody wants to rob and get caught. First of all, they want the right target. So if they know, they find out that you are the right person, then they rob you, yes? So if you are a driver and you ask too many questions, the robber don't like that. I mean, those people, they don't like that. They want you to be dumb, to be easy."

Location of Pickup and Destination

Drivers' reactions vary depending on the area in which they pick up the passenger or where he wants to be taken:

> If they tell me, "Take me to Soul Street," I know the neighborhood, and I know it's a bad neighborhood. I let my guards go up if I know it's a bad neighborhood. But when it's a good neighborhood, it's a different feeling. You know, your feelings changes from neighborhood to neighborhood. And then I also feel like, when you pick up somebody in a bad neighborhood, your guards go up again. See, it doesn't necessarily mean they're going to do you harm. But still, it goes up. (driver BX5)

Drivers' observation of the passenger becomes more intense under such circumstances, and they may engage in actions designed to probe for more information: "And so you get the person in the car, and then you start talking to the person. You know, I tell them, 'Good morning,' and, 'How's the weather,' and all about different things, whatever. Just to get the feeling of that person. I can't judge a book by its cover until I open it up, you know" (driver BX5).

Drivers' suspicions are also heightened if the passenger gives vague or inconsistent instructions about the final destination: "When you ask a person, 'Where you going?' and they don't want to tell you something or where they go, you know right there. They don't have a specific plan where to go, so they might be looking for trouble" (driver BX9). Drivers are also suspicious of the passenger who keeps changing his destination: "I knew, I was like, oh this person's not gonna pay" (driver Q3).

Brooklyn-based driver BR4 also looks for signs that the customer has some interest in the final destination and how much the fare is going to be: "When the person come into the car and don't say hi, I start discriminating. They didn't say good night, or they didn't say hello. Number two, if they don't at least say, 'How much is it?' It's like I give points to the customer."

If a passenger says at journey's end that he has to go and get money, that to drivers is a sign that he is not going to pay: "My sixth sense is when they start telling me—you know, after I pull away, maybe out half a mile away—they'll tell me, 'I have to go upstairs and get my money to pay you.' That tells me they're not going to pay me" (driver BX5). Rather than sixth sense, however, it may be that experience has taught him to make that inference.

Inquisitive Passengers

In Belfast the dominant convention is for a passenger to sit in the front seat. Unless the passengers are professionals or academics busily going over their papers or discussing matters among themselves, sitting in the back is perceived as an unfriendly gesture. In New York drivers do not expect that kind of easygoing attitude and, by contrast, prefer that passengers sit in the back. Driver BXF4 believed that, "whatever they decide to do, if they gonna do something, they do it no matter where they sitting." She would let only an older person sit in her front passenger seat: "I don't let no one, unless it's an elderly, sit in the front. No one sit in the front." Whereas driver Q9 would not let anyone at all sit in the front: "Personally, if it is three persons, they can all go in the back. . . . I don't like to have anybody in front."

As in Belfast, New York drivers are acutely aware of passengers who question them about how long their shift has been and how much money they are making. Such inquiries are interpreted as a negative sign: "Yes, yes . . . asking us, 'How much money you make a day? Is this your car? How you spending? How much daily for you?' And I said, I know that guy wants to give me a holdup. My intuition say, I say, 'Okay, you are the first passenger that I pick up. Now. I start right now.' Because if I say I was working during the day, they going to say, 'Oh, he has money' " (driver BX3).

Similarly, driver Q6 noted that when he suspects somebody, he complains about his work preemptively, saying, "Oh, I'm making no money. This is going really bad, and I'm not making anything out of it." He also always makes a point of telling nosy passengers that he is married, for he thinks a potential attacker will think that being married makes him less worth robbing:

And usually they ask me, "Are you from here or are you from another borough?" And that means that you make a trip from one borough to another, and it's a little bit longer, you have at least forty, sixty, or eighty dollars in your pocket . . . and that's the money that we have to carry sometimes. [If they ask,] "Do you live alone or do you have family?" if the driver says, "No, I have no family, I live in this country, and I work for myself," that means that that driver has money in his pocket, because usually people who live alone don't leave the money at home. And usually they don't have a can, so they keep all the money in their pocket. . . . [Then passengers] know that the driver has money in the pocket.

Driver YC1 is also wary of inquisitive passengers who *repeatedly* ask him the same question, since this shows that they are uninterested in the answer and are distracted by other, possibly malign thoughts:

Now, if during the way, for example, they ask you for your name three times, it means that the person did not pay attention, did not read your name on the license. It means that the person is nervous, is not thinking what he is saying. He's got a second intention. So if a person asks me the same question three or four times, I say, "C'mon, are you deaf or what?" It's not because he is deaf, but he has a second intention.

Although drivers are wary of passengers trying to elicit details from them, they are also suspicious of customers who offer too much information about themselves:

Another thing that makes me suspect that something is wrong is if people tell me what they're gonna do. You don't have to tell me what you're gonna do today or where you're going. When they start saying where they're going or what they're gonna do, then something's wrong. People who say, "Oh, I'm such a good person, I work," you don't have to tell me that. . . . When they try to make me feel comfortable, I say, something is wrong, because a normal person wouldn't do that. (driver BR4)

Driver BR4's inference has an ancestor in the Latin saying "Excusatio non petita, accusatio manifesta"—an unsolicited apology amounts to an admission of guilt.

Probing Impediments

Spanish-speaking drivers declare a preference for Spanish-speaking passengers. This bias does not reflect an affective disposition so much as the recognition that a greater familiarity with the passenger's ethnic background allows the driver both to perceive telling linguistic signs and cultural features and to read them with greater accuracy. This appreciation for Spanish-speaking passengers is particularly related to the fact that many drivers have poor English skills and value the importance of effective language communication to assess the passenger's true type. Driver Q6 explained: "Most taxi drivers, they just understand the addresses. If they don't speak English, they have to say to the passenger, 'Can you write down on this piece of paper the address where you are going?' So they can understand the directions, but they don't know what else. They don't know what they are speaking about . . . so that can make it hard for them."

Driver Q6 added that letting the passenger know that the driver does not speak English can be a severe impediment: "Sometimes when the driver doesn't speak English, they don't try to make conversations with them because they don't understand what he is talking about." This hampered rapport between driver and passenger can limit the tips that the driver receives. More seriously, this revelation makes the driver more vulnerable, since it makes him unable to perceive potentially relevant linguistic signs. Again, according to driver Q6, "they could be doing their plan right there behind you . . . and talking, and you hear them but you don't understand what they are saying so . . . what can you do about it? It is very difficult for people who don't speak good English, because they don't understand what they are saying . . . or what they're telling you, and you don't know how to respond, to give a reaction."

The inability to communicate effectively with the passenger also inhibits the driver's capacity to interpret the passenger's mood correctly. The misunderstandings and frustration that ensue can turn a bad passenger into a worse one:

> If you are driving the car, and some funny guy stop you, and you don't understand him, where he wanna be dropped or something like that, and the guy is a troublemaker, the guy is gonna give you a hard time, 'cause he can't understand what you're saying, and you can't understand what he tells you. (driver BR1)

> The worst kind of people in this city, on the street, were in jail before, and [although] they are out, they still have something pending with the law but they are still bad. Those people are really bad. You have to be careful with them, because if they do something bad to you, they will kill you. They will kill you because they don't want the police catching them because they have a record. They will kill you just 'cause you don't like them or you have arguments because you don't understand. So the driver has to be careful. The driver has to have sense, common sense, not to disturb a person like this. (driver BX10)

Ibrahim Diallo, a livery cab driver from Guinea, was killed in October 2001 during a robbery at a West African restaurant in Brooklyn. Mr. Diallo was taking a quick break during his night shift, and when he did not understand that the robbers were demanding his wallet, they shot him dead (Jones 2001).

Drivers with language difficulties have an even greater incentive to exploit nonverbal communication channels to acquire more information about a passenger's intentions.[2] Driver Q6, for instance, angles the rearview mirror in order to get a better look at the passenger's eyes:

> One thing I look for is in my rearview mirror. . . . I always try to have it so that the person in the back, I can see their eyes. And if a person tries to move away from that side and they don't want to be seen, then I know they are suspicious. If the person acts nervous and tries to step away from my sight, then I know. . . . I have stopped the car for police and said, "I have this person in my car. He's trying to avoid me."

Driver BX9 keeps the left-side door locked, forcing passengers to sit on the right side of the car, where he can see them better: "Yeah, I keep it locked, or even though they go to open it I say, 'It won't work.' So they sit on the right side of the car so I can see them. Because if they get behind you, then you going [to be] more nervous. . . . You cannot see them that well, and you do not know what they are doing behind you." Driver BX8 stressed that "most of the time we see people sit here on the right side. I don't like the people to sit behind me. I like to look through the mirror to see what they are doing. Anything I see wrong, I would go on my microphone. Like I tell you before . . . you got to be alert. Driving taxis in New York, you gotta be alert."

Belfast drivers are very particular about where passengers sit in the backseat. They particularly dislike having people sit directly behind the driver's seat because they cannot see what the passenger is doing. Because of the protection offered by the partition, the New York drivers were less generally concerned about this issue, though they did still pay attention to it if they felt suspicious.

Linguistic difficulties and cultural differences were not the only probing impediments we found. Among the drivers we interviewed, 38 percent avoid working at night because they consider it too dangerous and also because their absence from home at night is harder on their families. However, despite knowing that attacks are more likely to occur at night, 62 percent of them still choose to work then, since the decreased amount of traffic enables them to take more passengers and make more money. Fear of the dark and knowledge of attack statistics, however, are not the only reasons for drivers' reluctance to work at night: they also realize that the dark is a probing impediment. "You cannot see faces and eyes as well as during the day, and you cannot see faces very well through the partition," noted driver BX9.

Bona-Fide Customers with Negative Cues

Drivers probe their customers because they worry, first and foremost, about false positive mistakes—that is, picking up someone who looks like a normal passenger but is not. But they also probe because they want to avoid the reverse mistake—namely, not picking up passengers who cannot avoid displaying the "wrong" cues but who are bona-fide customers. In Belfast, for instance, drivers are wary of groups of two or three young working-class men: their gender, age, and style of dress cause drivers to mistrust them whatever their true intentions. False negative mistakes cause a loss of business for drivers and a loss of service for bona-fide customers. To reassure the driver and offset their negative traits, such passengers have an interest both in displaying signs that can offset the negative cues and in inviting drivers to probe their credentials.

As we know, in New York City drivers are most wary of young men, of men in a group, and of blacks, particularly if they are male, or worse, teenagers. We now consider what such individuals do in New York when all they want is a taxi ride. Just as mimics do, customers who want to be picked up for legitimate reasons adapt to drivers' thinking and try to act accordingly. As in Belfast, the strategies employed by disadvantaged good customers show that they understand drivers' concerns. Furthermore, some of their efforts to instill confidence in drivers mirror the attempts of mimics to persuade drivers that they are of a good sort when they are not.

Let us consider first those who are at a disadvantage because of their young age. Driver BXF4 felt that teenagers are not sophisticated enough to mask their true intentions: "If they are making a run, they act like that. If they do something bad, they act like that. Whereas, if they are decent, they want everybody to know that they are decent, especially in New York, you know. In New York, if you decent, you want people to know that you are." Honesty, in her view, shines through, and those who have it do not have to try hard. That is easier said than done, however. In fact, a lot of honest young people have trouble signaling their sincerity and often have to make an effort. Driver BXF4 herself believed that trustworthy teenagers should not even try to get a taxi as a group but should split up: "If they're honest, they don't come in groups. Never."

Yet even honest young people do move around in groups, and rather than split up, they may use the tricks we have already mentioned (see chapters 2 and 7). For instance, one member of the group, preferably a female, hails the taxi while the others stay hidden until the taxi stops. This strategy may amount, however, to taking a step forward—getting the taxi to stop—while taking two steps backward: the driver often becomes extremely alarmed because the strategy is identical to one used by mimics of the bad sort. "They have to let the base know how many people are traveling. If you tell the base the truth, then the driver knows that I'm going to pick up three guys, I'm going to pick up four guys. If you don't tell the truth, you know I'm an old-timer, if you lie about the number, that makes me think I'm not going to trust you" (driver NM17).

More reassuring is the presence of an adult. Driver BR5 is leery of passengers who are "anywhere from around [age] fourteen up to around eighteen. No, I don't pick them up if they're alone or with someone else—I don't pick them up. The only way I would pick them up [is] if I see them with adults. Then I would pick them up. But other than that, no you can't." Driver BR3 told us that sometimes teenagers, clearly aware of this propensity in drivers, get a grandparent to wait with them in order to win over the driver.

In Belfast passengers who display negative signs told us that once they succeed in getting a taxi to stop, they reassure the driver by displaying other signs of "goodness," such as offering to pay up front, a strategy that New York youth also resort to: "A lot of teenagers will show us that they got the money in their hand. He knows the taxi doesn't wanna pick him up, so he says, 'I give you the fare straight away.' Sometimes I will pick him up, sometimes I will leave him there anyway" (driver BR3).

Those who are at a disadvantage because of their skin color cannot even hope to grow out of the problem eventually, as other young people will do, and they cannot of course change their complexion. Although Mayor Rudolph Giuliani's team of officers disguised as passengers found few instances of discrimination (see chapter 7), the twenty black professionals (fifteen men and five women) we interviewed unanimously claimed that it is very difficult to get a yellow cab to stop for them. They all said that getting a cab is particularly difficult on weekends, when drivers have the most business and can afford to be choosy, and at night, when drivers feel less safe.

In New York there is also a close association between skin color and destination. Drivers assume that a black person's journey will end in an area that they do not want to go to, either because they feel unsafe in it or because they will lose out financially by being unable to get a fare returning to Manhattan. So skin color may lead to discrimination by being an observable proxy of other undesirable features rather than because it is menacing as such, or because drivers are racially prejudiced.

In Belfast, by improving their style of dress, young working-class men can improve somewhat their chances of getting a taxi. In New York, we were told, dressing well does not make much difference for blacks. Even David Dinkins, a former New York City mayor, has complained that he was refused a ride because of his skin color (Bumiller 1999), an experience that, as we know anecdotally, many black professional adults have had to endure in the United States.

In general, female customers are thought to be safer than male ones. One of our female customer respondents, BCF5, an accountant, believed that black women are more likely to be picked up than black men. However, even single females have to struggle to get a taxi. Another female accountant told us of her experience when she became ill at work in Manhattan and decided to go home in the middle of the afternoon. Even though she was smartly dressed for the office and it was daytime, ten yellow cabs passed her by before one stopped.

Dress becomes even more irrelevant when the driver's potential fare is made up of three or more men—worse still if they are young and black: "If there's more than one black male in the group, there's absolutely no way that we'll get a [yellow] cab. It's impossible even if we are all wearing suits and ties," said customer BC9.

A male and a female together are considered safer than two men, and most customers believed that a female presence would help a black man get a taxi. A distinguished middle-aged black professor of political science told us that when visiting New York, he has to send his wife to hail a cab or else he will not get one. However, as customer BC9, a black social worker, pointed out, femaleness is often not enough. Although his chances of getting a taxi improve if a female accompanies him, she must look at least semiprofessional or as well dressed as he is. Drivers are suspicious of a mismatch in a couple's clothing style.

All of the customers we interviewed agreed that it is easier to get a taxi during the day than at night. But what if one needs a taxi at night? They said that there are some locations, like churches, from which taxis are more likely to pick up, and several of them said that they move to a more reassuring location if they can find one. This expectation is borne out by what drivers say of their own reasoning: "Three or four teenagers, young boys? You got to look at them, or you see them coming out of the church or a nice place, they're probably nice. You see them in another place, you got to think about it" (driver BX8).

Despite their ingenuity, many disadvantaged bona-fide passengers in New York end up having to use other means of transport. Most New York passengers can exploit to only a limited degree a solution that is used by some Belfast passengers: deliberately becoming known to a taxi base and building up a relationship with its employees. In New York, where bases do have regular calling customers but service a much larger population, drivers do not get to know individuals in the same way as happens in Belfast. As in Belfast, the New York drivers who stop to pick up passengers with negative cues seem to be rewarded by larger tips— "Some people, they look really bad, but then they give you a tip" (driver BX10)—but the anticipation of a generous tip is not enough to allay their suspicions.

It is impossible to estimate how much good business is thus lost. The number of potential passengers who fail to secure a taxi or just give up trying must certainly be considerable. In many circumstances, they lack a cheap but hard-to-mimic persuasive sign. To overcome drivers' fears, they cannot age or change the color of their skin at will, nor can they

Table 10.1   Probing by Taxi Drivers in Belfast and New York

Probing Practices	Belfast (N = 45)	New York (N = 50)
Notice choice of seating	87% (39)	34% (17)
Consult gut feelings	40 (18)	34 (17)
Probe for local knowledge	31 (14)	N/A
Notice body posture or general demeanor	13 (6)	36 (18)
Probe passenger's eyes	11 (5)	14 (7)
Probe for the passenger's tone of voice	9 (4)	13 (6)
Probe location of pickup and destination	100 (45)	52 (26)
Notice facial expression	11 (5)	38 (19)
Test passenger's response to being told cost of journey	0 (0)	18 (9)
Is wary of inquisitive passengers	27 (12)	18 (9)

Source: Authors' compilation.
Note: N/A = not applicable.

change the time of day or their destination, which would of course defeat the purpose. An obliging granny or a reassuring female co-hailer is not always at hand, and a church whose holy halo they might exploit is not always nearby.

In conclusion, like their Belfast counterparts, New York's mostly immigrant livery drivers appear extremely adroit at negotiating and reflecting upon their world. Unlike Belfast, however, the New York metropolis is a much more unfamiliar environment for them, as reflected in the differences in their probing strategies (see table 10.1).

New York drivers have to face the additional challenges of a new language and culture, a much greater anonymity and diversity of customers, and a higher propensity of assailants to become violent. In seeking a better life for themselves and their families, these drivers end up taking serious risks and playing a complex series of daily trust games in which picking up the wrong passenger can be fatal. Making the right decision is not a luxury but is driven by necessity. It is the only way in which they can survive the perils of a job that supports their families while making sure that, as driver NM2 put it, "the incidents that have happened to me do not outweigh the good ones." In the concluding chapter, we dissect the exact nature of their reasoning and discuss the extent to which that reasoning is informed by an intuitive application of signaling theory.

PART III

CONCLUSION

Chapter 11

Street Wisdom Appraised

O UR FIELDWORK has provided a detailed account of how taxi drivers in two cities think and act to protect their safety. In spite of city and individual variations and idiosyncrasies, the overall results show that drivers possess a high level of reasoning sophistication in handling their daily risks that surpassed our expectations.

We cannot establish to what extent their skills are due to self-selection or to learning on the job, and most plausibly both mechanisms are present. Drivers who have been taxiing longer believe they get better at screening, and they were certainly more reflective about their practices. However, they may already be a self-selected group of "survivors." Our samples contained only a few of those who had left the job and none of those who had considered the profession and decided not to enter, so we do not have evidence on this issue. Still, we had several indications that those who do not have some street wisdom to start with, or at least the confidence and determination to try to learn it, leave the job. Furthermore, even though experience teaches drivers valuable information about the perils of taxiing in their city thus reducing the risks they run, some of their subtler screening skills, such as the *gut feelings* they heed, cannot be easily learned, suggesting self-selection.

That their street-level wisdom appears to be wide-ranging, level-headed, and often subtle is all the more striking given the reputation of taxi drivers for opinionated and stereotypical thinking, a reputation they may have gained through their penchant for expressing idle views. Yet when both income and safety are at stake, and especially when they pull in different directions, drivers' reasoning rises to the challenge. No matter how "incentive-compatible" its design, no laboratory experiment could replicate these real-life challenges, whose effects can be unveiled only by observing agents in the course of their natural interactions.

We now reexamine step by step how drivers reason in connection with our original hypotheses. In the process, we also illustrate what we learned that we neither expected nor theorized about. We first consider drivers' reasoning about risk and security generally, and then their reasoning as it applies to screening and probing specific passengers. At the same time, we reexamine our findings with regard to the other protagonists, the mimics and the genuine passengers, especially those who find it hard to be picked up.

Risk Versus Trust

Drivers unanimously said that to drive a taxi they *need to trust* that the vast majority of passengers are of a good sort. A driver has to be prepared to endure the risk of the job and remain steadfastly inclined to accept passengers rather than reject them. Worrying all the time about the possibility of being attacked and refusing to pick up passengers on the slightest suspicion would be unprofitable and make a driver's job a "living hell," as one of them put it. The only driver who said he has a generally distrusting attitude, driver P-CC12 from Belfast, was aware that this attitude is maladaptive. If he rejects too many passengers to start with, he is later forced, in order to make ends meet, to pick up other passengers who appear worse than some of those he previously avoided.[1]

On reflection, we think that drivers' positive if somewhat fatalistic prior expectation cannot be conceptualized as "trust" in any meaningful sense.[2] Drivers do not perceive their a priori expectations as part of a strategic situation—that is, as a basic trust game beset by mimics. If one reconsiders drivers' statements closely, their attitude does not seem to derive from a sense that their fellow citizens are for the most part trustworthy. Having more to do with the perception and mental management of risk, their attitude is better conceptualized as *a way to shut off the small-probability events when thinking about risk.* When asked to name his biggest concern driving a taxi, driver C-CC11 from Belfast, echoing many other drivers we have quoted, replied: "Apart from a bullet in the back of the head? As everyone knows, when something starts, the taxi drivers are usually the first people to get it, so that would be my main concern. But in saying that, *I try not to think of it too much,* because you wouldn't taxi-drive. You wouldn't go out of the house. You just try and get on—a job is a job." The proverb "fool me once shame on you, fool me twice shame on me," expresses a disposition that most of us manifest in our daily dealings: we are inclined to give others the benefit of the doubt and become alert to their untrustworthiness only after being cheated. That proverb also captures something of how drivers manage risk: they do not think all the time about being taken in, even though they know that occasionally they will be.

Most of us also have the capacity to refrain from thinking about small-probability events, and in all likelihood it is a capacity that is not intentionally governed. Even if we "need to trust" and describe the ability to do so as a response to that need (else "we wouldn't go out of the house"), we cannot decide to forget and relax at will. The need to trust may bring about hope or a sense of resignation rather than trust.

Whatever its source, we can be sure that the greater (or more salient) the risk we believe we are facing, the more that "shutting-off" capacity will be taxed. It is thus relatively easy for us not to think about the insignificant risks we run in our daily lives—the risk that a car will career off the road and run us over, for instance, or that the proverbial lightning will strike us—but it must be harder for taxi drivers. Even if the probabilities of being attacked are small, they are on the large side of small compared with any other modern-day occupation. Let us not forget that driving a taxi is a dangerous profession in the United States—the most dangerous in terms of the probability of being killed and the second most dangerous (after police work) in terms of the likelihood of being violently attacked. In the drivers' replies we have quoted here (see especially chapters 4 and 9), we can detect that not thinking about small-probability events requires some effort. The drivers said that they *try* not to think about the risks they face. In northern Manhattan, where the dangers are greater than in Belfast, the effort of not thinking about the risks is too much for some drivers, and so they call upon a higher power for protection. This fatalistic belief that God will keep them safe is the best way for them to manage their fear even as it reveals how little they think they can do to help themselves.

This reflects a difference in attitudes toward risk we detected between drivers in the two cities. The drivers of New York frame their disposition more as one of unavoidable risk-taking than of generalized trust in their fellow citizens. This attitude is a response, we can surmise, to the higher likelihood of being attacked in New York and to the somewhat more irrational kind of attackers these drivers expect to encounter. They seem more fatalistic than Belfast drivers and feel generally that they have little control over events. Although plagued by deep sectarian divisions, the denizens of Belfast feel a greater sense of community within the boundaries of their religions. Unlike their New York counterparts, drivers in Northern Ireland are not immigrants; they perceive the city as their own turf and feel their presence as natural and legitimate. They contend with a smaller-scale world in which the anonymity of people and places is contained and the sources of risk are believed to be more readily knowable, albeit imperfectly.

The theory of cognitive dissonance reduction could explain why drivers caught in the tension between the risk of taxiing and the need to make money manage to rearrange their beliefs and minimize their perception of risk (see Akerlof and Dickens 1982). The theory would predict that drivers try to avoid the perception of negative signs and search instead for signs that reinforce their perception of basic safety. This, however, does not happen. Although the pressure to make money is strong, the pressure to avoid danger is equally strong and never dormant. Drivers in both cities do not sit back and forget about risk altogether. Rather than shutting off their mental door, they leave it ajar. As their accounts uniformly reveal, they remain vigilant, and their worries quickly resurface into full consciousness if something makes the alarm bells in their heads go off. When asked whether he would be more concerned about a sectarian attack or a mugging, driver C-WB3 from Belfast replied: "You don't think of these things *until they approach you.*" And driver C-CC11 said: "You try not to think about it—*until someone gets in and says something or somebody is a bit nervous getting into the car.* Say they want you to go one place, and then you are asked to head up another place."

Once "something happens," drivers enter into a different domain in which the potential risk is no longer generically perceived but is incarnated in a particular person. At that point the passenger's trustworthiness becomes an issue, and the driver's dilemma evolves into a basic trust game. Deciding which type of passenger he is dealing with becomes an issue. Before delving into that game, we need to focus on other actions that drivers take regardless of the trust game.

Precautions

Drivers do not push the perils of driving a taxi to the back of their minds merely by mental gymnastics. Drivers manage the risk they face prior to, and regardless of, their attempts to establish the trustworthiness of specific passengers. They all take precautions and think of ways to get out of dangerous situations should any occur.

A host of precautions have the purpose of *deterring* an attack by increasing the cost or the risk for an attacker. Cameras make it easier for an attacker to be identified later. Partitions, which inhibit an attacker's ability to act from within the car, make particularly good sense since we know that most violent attacks on drivers occur inside the vehicle. In cities where the attacks are more likely to be random and the threats are harder to ascertain from observable features, these fixed, blanket devices are more likely to be used. Drivers in New York employ them much more than do drivers in Belfast.[3] Even so, until recently New York drivers did not voluntarily install partitions or cameras, neither individually nor at the firm level. The Taxi and Limousine Commission made the installation of at least one of them a legal requirement in 2000. This reluctance to act independently may have been partly a matter of cost. (The TLC provided some funds to help drivers to purchase these devices.) It may also have been partly a coordination problem: no one wanted to be the first to introduce devices that could make passengers uncomfortable and decrease competitiveness. Just as in the case of ice-hockey helmets, which players refused to wear until they were forced to do so (Schelling 1978, 213–14), the problem in the drivers' case was solved by making the devices compulsory.[4]

Other precautions are specifically designed *to respond to actual attacks* (though their existence may also have a concomitant deterrent effect). Alarm buttons, special phone lines, flashing lights, and the like increase the chances that the victim will be able to ask for, and receive, help from colleagues or the police. Not wearing a seat belt allows a driver more room for maneuver and gives him the freedom to run away. Automatic door locks can be used to keep passengers from running off or getting in.

A different set of measures that are designed to *reduce the risk* of encountering villains posing as passengers follow from inductive generalizations as to the relative risk of being in certain places at certain times. Drivers have a sort of homemade actuarial map in mind and expect that statistically they are more likely to meet undesirable passengers in deprived areas or during boisterous nights. Choosing to drive to and from "safe" areas only and avoiding night shifts and weekends are some such precautions. Drivers who are more risk-averse take precautions of this kind.

No-go areas are selected on the basis of a finer grid. Drivers stay away from government project housing and notorious public places in New York, and they avoid the crowds at football matches or religious marches in Belfast. Risk-limiting choices depend also on how detailed a knowledge a driver has of certain areas. The greater this knowledge, the finer the selectivity applied. Drivers' precautions further depend on the type of predators they fear: the more specific the threat, the more specific the response. In Belfast the fear of blind sectarian attacks leads some drivers, especially Catholics, to avoid areas whose inhabitants are members of the opposite side. They also avoid areas, such as North Belfast, in which the two communities are in such close proximity that one cannot easily tell who is who, or at least not quickly enough. They also stay away from other locations that have religious associations, such as hospitals, pubs, or clubs.

Strategic Precautions

Many drivers do not simply take precautions derived from inductive reasoning and knowledge of differential risks. They see themselves as potential prey in a prey-predator game and take *strategic* precautions; some of these are kept in place all the time, while others are turned on and off in response to specific situations. Strategic precautions are not supposed to reduce the chances of a bad encounter generically but to reduce the chances of *attracting* predators of a certain kind. These precautions reflect the drivers' understanding of potential attackers' motivations and psychology.

Camouflaging the features that may trigger predators' interest in attacking them is one such precaution. In New York, where the main threat is violent robbery, drivers limit their display of wealth by removing their jewelry and by preemptively and obliquely informing passengers that they have little money on them. In Belfast, where the most dangerous predators are driven by sectarian motives, drivers mask the signs of their religious affiliation by choosing to work for larger and religiously nondescript firms and by removing the cards that display their name and address or the insignias that identify their firm and thus reveal religious affiliation. They are also careful not to disclose to bystanders or passengers they suspect are on the other side which football team they support (Catholics are fans of Celtic and Protestants follow Rangers) or their unfamiliarity with the opposite side's neighborhoods.

Camouflage, however, is not an effective option for the drivers who are more at risk of a sectarian attack. Those with a paramilitary past are targeted because of who they are rather than because they are members of either religious group, and this risk demands draconian precautions. Many wear baseball caps that help to mask their features, and they dress in a uniformly casual way. However, short of masking their faces completely, which would look menacingly odd and make matters worse, no amount of innocent-looking camouflaging of signs would ensure that they are not identified for who they are. Thus, another strategy for these drivers is to work only in their local area and mostly with people they know.

A different strategy we found in the prey-predator game is *deterrence* achieved by inducing the belief in the potential predators that the cost of an attack would be high. In Belfast the bolder drivers talk tough, adopt a "tough guy" demeanor, or drop the names of men of violence with whom they are connected. They convey the message that they are prepared to play "hawk" rather than take an attack lying down. At least, they do so when the threat is from nonsectarian attackers against whom they may stand a chance.

In New York drivers do not engage in anything of the sort. They go out of their way to signal that they want to play "dove" and try *to appease* their predators, both before they know for sure whether they are predators and in the course of an attack, in order to reduce the risk of a violent escalation. They do not carry weapons, shy away from confrontations, and keep enough money on them to pacify attackers. They do not think of themselves as having a fighting chance. Partly they try to persuade attackers that using violence would not be worthwhile, since they can get anything they want anyway. Partly they treat attackers as individuals who can very easily lose control at the slightest problem and need to be handled with the utmost care.

The different approaches taken by drivers in the two cities depend partially on predator properties we have already mentioned and partly on those of the prey. The New York drivers feel like fish in foreign waters, and for the most part that is what they are. In contrast, Belfast drivers operate mostly in familiar straits, and those who display a pugnacious attitude do not often fake it. For the most part they *are* tough. We know that around 10 percent of them have a paramilitary past, many more have contacts with paramilitary groups, and the rest bask in the collective reputation for toughness. Would-be attackers must surely take these associations into account.

Trust-Warranting Properties

The primary problem of trust lies in the truster's uncertainty as to the trustee's payoffs: is he governed by "raw" payoffs—that is, by the payoffs that would be his were he motivated by the most unbridled form of self-interest—or by the payoffs induced by trust-warranting qualities that temper his self-interest? The truster, in short, needs to find out whether the trustee is a good or a bad type. He needs to do so not in universal terms but more modestly with respect to the actions about which he should or should not be trusted. We do not rely on an all-encompassing notion of trustworthiness, but on one linked to doing something specific—in this case, simply being a "good enough" taxi customer.

The first step we need to take to understand how the drivers solve their primary trust dilemma is to describe which trust-warranting properties drivers bring to bear on their screening criteria and then unpack the knowledge and reasoning that lie behind their choice of these properties.

Trust-Warranting Properties Sought by Taxi Drivers

We identified twelve properties that drivers prefer because they believe these properties are related to trustworthiness in this game; some are continuous variables, while others are dichotomous. In a different trust game, trusters may look for different categories, but some of the categories that drivers look for—such as candid manners rather than shifty ones—are relevant in many trust games.

1. Older over younger
2. Women over men
3. "White" over "black"
4. Spanish over other ethnic groups (if the driver is Spanish)
5. Individuals over multiple passengers
6. Wealthier over poorer
7. Known passengers over strangers
8. Callers over hailers
9. Catholic over Protestant if driver is Catholic (and vice versa)
10. Self-absorbed over inquisitive
11. Candid over shifty
12. Friendly and calm over aggressive or agitated

The properties that drivers do *not* prefer, or prefer less, can be either distrust-warranting (for example, "aggressive" and "teenage") or simply uninformative ("male" and "stranger," for instance, are properties that reveal little either way).

The properties are related to being a good (or bad) passenger in a probabilistic way. Drivers, in other words, do not assign certain trust-worthiness to them. Women, for instance, are thought to be safer, though not invariably so. Agitated passengers are thought to spell trouble, though their state may be due to circumstances unrelated to the taxi ride. Often the final verdict on trustworthiness or untrustworthiness is the result of assessing a cluster of these qualities.

If we put all the undesirable and uninformative properties together, we obtain the profile of the least preferred customer (the features that are relevant only to one city are in brackets):

> Male, teenager, [black], [different ethnic group], with other teenagers, not wealthy, stranger, hailer [of a different religious group], inquisitive, shifty, and aggressive[5]

And if we put together all the preferred properties, we obtain the profile of the most preferred type:

> Woman, adult, [white], [same ethnic group], alone, wealthy/professional, known, caller [of the same religious group], self-absorbed, candid, and friendly

What is important to stress at this point is that there are several other properties that drivers do *not* consider. For instance, piety, honesty, cred-itworthiness, and generosity would in principle be informative of trust-worthiness, even more so than those to which drivers attend. In other trust games where the opportunities for probing are greater, trusters do look for signs of them and trustees display evidence of them. In the taxi game, however, the constraints are such that a driver cannot observe the signs of more covert properties and would look for them in vain. A driver's selection of the properties to look for is influenced by the opportunities he has to observe signs of them. He cannot seek properties in the void. Although logically properties come before signs, it is very likely that trusters observe signs first and ask themselves whether these reveal anything interesting about trustworthiness. At the same time, however, drivers avoid the first mistake they could make and do not entertain extravagant beliefs about properties clearly unrelated to trustworthiness. Their whole approach is permeated with common sense.

Sources of Knowledge Used to Establish Trust-Warranting Properties

Now we need to establish how taxi drivers arrive at considering these properties important for establishing trustworthiness. From what we can evince from the interviews, drivers use the three basic sources of knowledge that we all use to form a view of other people—statistical, experiential, and causal inferences, and combinations thereof. From their accounts, it is not often possible to disentangle which particular source of knowledge they use. Still, it is worth reviewing each of them separately.

Statistical Discrimination

Some of what drivers do when deciding whether to pick up passengers approximates "statistical discrimination" (see Arrow 1998). This concept has been studied mostly by economists and applied to investigations of firms' hiring practices (for example, Phillips and Phillips 1993). If firms have limited information on the features of new workers, they may choose to use "easily observable characteristics," such as years of education or gender or race, to "statistically discriminate" among workers. Statistical discrimination "occurs when employers resist hiring any specific group of workers—be they women, racial or ethnic minority, young people, etcetera—for a job because they believe that members of that group are more likely to have certain behavioral characteristics that reduce their long-term economic benefit to the employer" (Phillips and Phillips 1993, 64).

The concept has also been applied to stop-and-search decisions by law enforcers. "Some people are more likely to be convicted of a crime than others. . . . Group characteristics, such as race or age, might influence individual probabilities of conviction." Since it is prohibitively costly to investigate every crime, "police and other enforcement agencies may rationally use 'statistical discrimination' to minimize search costs" (Leung et al. 2002).[6]

Taxi drivers reason in the same way and act according to the instructions that logically follow from their reasoning: "younger people are more dangerous—be careful"; "dark-skinned people are more dangerous—be careful"; "one individual is less likely to be trouble than multiple passengers—pick up." Being a member of a category that is statistically more or less dangerous is a type of trust- or distrust-warranting quality, and drivers look for the signs of membership in those categories. Statistical discrimination revolves around the usual suspects—age, gender, ethnicity—and the signs thereof, which we consider more closely later in the chapter.

Table 11.1 sets out the main properties of passengers that drivers have identified as being high-risk, and in it we show, as best we can, whether these properties truly are associated with dangerousness.[7]

In most cases, we found a clear match between the properties that drivers considered to be risky and those that the evidence on attacks on drivers highlights as being actually risky. In terms of the underlying cognitive operations, statistical discrimination is identical to the general precautions aimed at risk avoidance. The only difference is that the

Table 11.1   Taxi Drivers' Perceived Risk Versus Actual Risk, by Passengers' Properties

Perceived Higher-Risk Properties	Actual Risk: Belfast	Actual Risk: New York
Younger versus older person	No data on age of attackers of taxi drivers, but in 1997 the rate of conviction was highest for males age nineteen and females age eighteen (O'Mahoney and Deazley 2000, 10). In 2001, 52 percent of the average immediate custody population in prison was between the ages of seventeen and twenty-nine (Northern Ireland Statistics and Research Agency 2001, 77).	Forty-six percent of those accused of attacking drivers in the sample were teenagers. Eighteen- to twenty-four-year-olds between 1976 and 2000 had the highest homicide rate in the United States (U.S. Department of Justice 2004a).
Male versus female	In all forty-nine cases of drivers being attacked in the sample from 1972 to 2002, the attackers were men. In only three of these cases was a female an accomplice. In 1997 the conviction rate for juvenile males was 400 per 10,000, while that of juvenile females was 48 per 10,000 (O'Mahoney and Deazley 2000, 10). In each year between 1992 and 2001, the average total prison population was 98 percent male (Northern Ireland Statistics and Research Agency 2001, 76–77).	Eighty-six percent of those accused of attacking drivers in the sample were male. In 2000 in the United States males were ten times more likely than females to commit murder (U.S. Department of Justice 2004a).
Black versus white	Irrelevant—nearly every one is white.	In 2000 in the United States blacks were seven times more likely to commit murder than whites (U.S. Department of Justice 2004a).

(*Table continues on p. 197.*)

Table 11.1   *Continued*

Perceived Higher-Risk Properties	Actual Risk: Belfast	Actual Risk: New York
Different versus same ethnic group	Irrelevant—there is very little ethnic difference.	No specific data on taxi drivers, but most murders in the United States are intraracial. From 1976 to 2000, 86 percent of white victims were killed by whites, and 94 percent of black victims were killed by blacks (U.S. Department of Justice 2004a).
Multiple versus single customers	Twenty-six percent of the attacks we reviewed in our study involved more than one attacker.	Fifty-five percent of livery robberies between January and April 2000 in northern Brooklyn neighborhoods occurred in taxis carrying multiple passengers. Of all homicides between 1976 and 2000, 46.1 percent committed by whites and 51.6 percent committed by blacks involved multiple offenders (U.S. Department of Justice 2004a).
Poorer or lower-status versus wealthier or higher-status	Ninety-one percent of the attacks in our sample took place in poorer working-class areas.	Sixty-five percent of the attacks on drivers took place in the poorer neighborhoods of the Bronx and Brooklyn, implying that the customers were also poor. In 2002 persons in households with an annual income under $75,000 were robbed at a significantly higher rate than persons in households earning more (U.S. Department of Justice 2004b).
Stranger versus known customer	Eighteen percent of sectarian attacks involved	Drivers make efforts to get regular known fares.

(*Table continues on p. 198.*)

Table 11.1   *Continued*

Perceived Higher-Risk Properties	Actual Risk: Belfast	Actual Risk: New York
	Loyalists passing off as known customers in order to appear bona-fide. There is no evidence of known passengers attacking drivers.	There is no evidence of known passengers attacking drivers. New York drivers meet many more strangers than Belfast drivers do. However, homicide victims are more likely to know the offender. (Young victims were more likely to know the offender than older victims.) (U.S. Department of Justice 2004b)
Hailer versus caller	In both cities, callers out-number hailers for this type of taxi, yet 26 percent of the attacks were from hailers, and 19 percent were from callers.[a]	Eighty-two percent of the livery cab robberies and at least six out of seven of the homicides between January and April 2000 were street-hails.
Opposite versus same religious affiliation	Sixty-one percent of the attacks we reviewed in our study were sectarian.	Irrelevant—sectarian divide does not exist.

Source: Authors' compilation.
[a]The rest of the attacks were ambushes when a driver was on a regular route (9 percent), drive-by attacks (15 percent), attacks on depots (11 percent), and car bombs (4 percent). In the remainder, the driver was attacked at home.

inductive reasoning is applied to observable features of people rather than to locations or times of the day or week.

Statistical discrimination warrants a short ethical digression. One can fault drivers (or anyone else) for adopting it on two counts: for *wrongly* attributing probabilities to the categories they discriminate for or against; and for engaging in category-based discrimination at all, namely, assigning positive or negative values to individuals on the basis of the true probabilistic properties of the group to which they belong. Considering first the second reason for finding fault, suppose beliefs are well founded; then, in the case of both police and employers, the stereotyping can be deemed to be "rational," and it has in fact been so defined by economists. However, the fact that it is rational does not make it fair.

Still, it is hard to see why drivers should be subject to more stringent demands, such as those imposed by the TLC, which is fearful of litigation and bad press. If anything, drivers already work in stricter predicaments than either police or employers, since they have very little to go by in assessing passengers and no time to gather a dossier on and investigate every passenger. In addition, as we have repeatedly seen, the costs of an incorrect assessment based on ethnic, gender, or age markers can be very high, even fatal for them.

Not just New York taxi drivers make such calculations. In Israel, where suicide attackers target buses, Moti Shaman, a Jerusalem bus driver, described the dilemma he faces in quickly assessing his passengers. He has no authority to check people's bags as they enter his bus and very limited opportunity to probe suspicious-looking passengers because, "once he's on . . . it's too late." Yet, "if I have to screen everyone looking suspicious, every third person is ruled out . . . and here enters racism" (Bennet 2002). So one may not like it, and one can see the unfair consequences of discrimination in terms of bona-fide passengers with negative cues being rejected or having to bear a greater cost of persuasion. However, the question as to whether the sum-total of the burdens the drivers impose on those unfairly discriminated against outweighs the security benefits they gain is hard to answer. As Jon Elster pointed out to us (private communication), "In an extreme case, suppose that if they ignored ethnic markers they would be virtually certain to be killed on the job at some point. Would it still be unacceptably unfair to take them into account?" How high should the likelihood of being attacked be before discriminating against those carrying an ethnic marker stops being unfair?

In cases in which discrimination is not well founded, it does follow that discrimination is both inefficient and not even minimally justifiable. As far as we can tell from our data, drivers tend to apply negative statistical discrimination with considerable care. They do so in three ways. First, even though they may not use proper statistics to establish the facts, they discriminate against categories that seem truly more of a risk (see table 11.1). Next, they are not draconian in applying statistical discrimination; with a few exceptions, they pick up members of the discriminated group, albeit with caution and probing. Third, if they decide not to pick up, they do so having simultaneously observed other negative signs. Drivers are not systematically averse to weaker categories: they are no more "racist" than they are "ageist," "sexist" in reverse (fearing men and younger people more than older people and women), or "groupist" (fearing groups more than individuals). They simply select categories that they believe are more likely to be harmful to them.

Drivers are under strong economic pressure to get their selection criteria right, for even without fairness considerations, they suffer an income loss from any failed pickup. It does not follow, however, that they do not make false negative mistakes, as bona-fide passengers with negative cues know only too well. Drivers view these as genuine mistakes that the availability of better information would have enabled them to avoid. Self-interest works in favor of greater fairness in this case.

Experience

An intuitive form of statistical induction governs the driver's choice of locations, times, or categories of people to exclude from his routes, and so do the corresponding positive choices of areas or type of passengers to include. These choices, however, especially those connected to passenger type, may also rest on different sorts of wisdom, one of which is the experience, direct or vicarious, of certain passengers or of certain types of passengers. We confer the reputation for being good (or bad) on those individuals we encounter who in some way demonstrate this quality to us. Provided that these individuals are reidentifiable in future encounters, over time we tend, because of the existence of "trait laws," to attribute constancy to that quality we have experienced.

> Common-sense belief systems contain trait laws. These are laws of constancy, of two kinds: individual trait laws, of the form "once a k always a k"; and categorical trait laws, of the form "one X a k, all Xs k's." A categorical trait law is a schema in which both 'k' and 'X' are variables. It is not of the form "all Swedes are fair-haired" (a specific reputation of Swedes), but rather "all people of a given nationality have the same hair color" or "hair color is a national characteristic." Similarly, an individual law is not of the form "Alderman Brown is a stuffy so-and-so" but rather "someone's degree of stuffiness is the sort of thing that doesn't change." (Bacharach and Gambetta 2001, 163)

Trait laws are invoked when we deal directly with someone or when we are reliably informed about someone. These laws underscore the existence of a good or bad reputation. Once we know someone has a property, we believe he always will, regardless of whether we know why he has it in the first place.[8] This is epitomized by sayings such as "A leopard never changes its spots," or, as one of Raymond Chandler's gangsters says, "Once a patsy always a patsy." Our drivers and dispatchers make ample use of reputation and of the individual trait law. They look for passengers they already know, readily picking up those who, in previous encounters, proved to be trustworthy and avoiding those who proved to be troublesome.

There is some indication that drivers use the categorical trait law too. For instance, driver P-PH5 said that, unlike football fans, "rugby fans are no problem. I would say that rugby fans are noisier, more boisterous, and they would drink more, but there's no trouble with them." (The categorical reputation is the obverse of statistical discrimination: while the latter attributes to an individual the same property of the group, the former attributes to all members of a group the properties we experience of some individuals in that group.)

Causal Knowledge

Another source of knowledge that sustains screening is derived from folk behavioral theories and has to do with causality. Causal theories can be applied even if nothing is known of the statistical risk associated with certain types of people and even without previous experience of them. For instance, a distrust-making quality is "to be shifty," for why would anyone be less than candid and transparent with a taxi driver if he did not have something to hide from him?

Sometimes the same screening criterion is identified by more than one form of reasoning. For instance, younger people are believed to be more dangerous not just because statistics say so, but also because "they have nothing to lose" or they are more likely to be on drugs. The belief that a Catholic will not harm another Catholic can be governed by having experienced that this is the case (reputation cum trait law), by believing that affinity tames aggressive impulses (causal), or by knowing that this rarely happens (statistical).

Signs

Regardless of whether the trust-warranting qualities that underlie screening criteria are sustained by statistical, experiential, or causal reasoning, these qualities are typically not directly *observable*. To find out about them one relies on observable features of them—that is, on *signs that manifest those properties.* In virtually all trust games that occur naturally—and without doubt in the taxi trust game—"the truster sees or otherwise observes the trustee before deciding. She therefore can, and should, use these observations as evidence for the trustee's having, or lacking, trustworthy-making qualities" (Bacharach and Gambetta 2001, 148).

As we pointed out in the introduction, there is nothing in current theories of trust to say that trusters pay attention to signs when deciding about trustees' trustworthiness. In general, theories of statistical screening, just like theories of trust, are also virtually silent about signs. The only thing they predict is that, for instance, statistical discrimination will be applied rationally to characteristics that are truly discriminating, the more so the better. They completely bypass the sign-reading operation and take the perception and assessment of signs as unproblematic. In addition, theories of reputation, for instance, take the reidentification of the reputation bearer—whose success is crucial for reputation to travel, for if it were impossible, reputations would be stillborn—as an uncomplicated operation not even worth mentioning.[9]

Our theory takes a new line, and our study vindicates our basic claim. It clearly establishes not only that taxi drivers do indeed look for signs of trust-warranting properties, but that "sign-reading" informs their decisions. Our study thus makes a strong case for the central importance of explicitly addressing the issue in theories of trust. Our theory also goes further and develops an understanding of *which signs* trusters disregard, to which signs they attend, and under what conditions they probe for more signs.

We shall now discuss which signs drivers use to establish whether passengers have the properties they are interested in, how hard it is to fake these signs, and whether the difficulty of faking signs affects the weight the signs are given by drivers as predicted by our hypotheses. At the same time, we consider whether customers who possess negative signs—both mimics and bona-fide passengers—manipulate positive signals to persuade drivers.

The first indication that drivers, as we predict, are not satisfied by *cheap* signals with regard to the trustworthiness of prospective passengers is their belief that just hailing or calling for a taxi does not truly mean a customer wants a ride and is prepared to pay for it. They do not necessarily take the most elementary sign in this game at face value. To be reassured they look for more signs over a wide range of possible properties of passengers.

Older over Younger

Drivers in general prefer older customers to teenagers, whose troublesome behavior ranges from being disrespectful to murder. (The exception to the rule of "the younger the deadlier" is in Belfast, where drivers believe the most dangerous mimics—sectarian attackers—are age twenty-five to forty-five.) In New York in particular, youth is the most worrisome of the features that drivers consider, and statistically they are justified in this perception. Lots of young people are well behaved, of course, but the probability of good behavior is strongly in favor of older people. This criterion is crude, but probabilistically accurate.

Above all, age has two clear advantages that compensate for its imperfect discriminatory accuracy: it is easy to observe and hard to fake. The age of an individual is visible in his facial features and observable in personal encounters. A person's voice also reveals something about his age group, though only for the very young or the very old. Yet even if a teenager manages to persuade the dispatcher on the phone that he is older than he is, the ploy will be short-lived, for his true age is revealed in the inevitable face-to-face encounter with the driver. Thus, insofar as age is inversely related to trustworthiness, the signs of it are robust. It is very hard to look older at will. One cannot even rely on cosmetics, since the industry does not design its products to make people look older! Signs of age are not only hard to fake but also counterproductive to hide. If youngsters veil their faces by using hats, hoods, or scarves this would simply increase drivers' prudence by giving signs of nontransparency.

Unable to disguise their youth, bona-fide teenage passengers pay the cost for the reputation of their age group and often find it hard to get picked up by drivers. Some try to compensate by improving on soft signs, such as politeness and better apparel, or, more convincingly, by recruiting an adult when hailing the taxi. Given the positive connotation of femaleness, younger women also compensate for age when calling a taxi company by, as one of our customers (P-CustF1) told us, raising the tone of their voices to make them sound more "girly."

Women over Men

Drivers view femaleness, especially in an adult, as a positive trait. Cues of gender are visible in the face and body shape. Other signs of femaleness are also readily visible in hairstyle, posture, dress, and accessories such as a shoulder bag. The physical signs of femaleness are so manifest and easily observed that in normal visibility conditions other signs are not necessary to persuade the driver that the customer is indeed a female. Natural cues of gender are also extremely difficult to mimic successfully in face-to-face encounters, and men find it very hard to pass off convincingly as a woman. As with age, insofar as being a woman is a property related to being a trustworthy passenger—as it is statistically— taxi drivers are able to trust the signs of it.

Drivers occasionally make incorrect assessments with respect to this sign owing to the probabilistic nature of the relationship between being a woman and being trustworthy, not to the ability of men to fool them by passing off as women. (Men who mimic female signs often do so in a transparent way. Even a cursory look reveals that they are men who are posing, revealing their sexual preferences rather than making any attempt to deceive drivers. Transvestites and gays are thought not to be a threat, for they display a "feminine" disposition.)

There are ways, however, in which femaleness can be mimicked, especially over the telephone. First, the voice reveals gender, but not as safely as visible signs do. A man can imitate a woman's voice more easily than he can look like one. Still, the mimicry acts we recorded did not include this trick. The driver would easily detect the ploy as soon as the real caller appeared in person, making it a counterproductive manipulation. If a man appears instead of the expected woman, the driver would respond accordingly. Mimics resorted to a different ploy: they used a real female as a decoy to call a taxi. In this case the female does not pretend to be anything other than female; instead, she feigns looking for a taxi when the real customers are one or more men. Enlisting a female for this fraudulent task is not so difficult, yet its use in our research was limited to nasty sectarian ambushes: the drivers were lured by the female decoy and attacked *before* they had a chance to work out the mismatch.

White over Black

Drawing from a combination of folk statistical knowledge and negative experiences, drivers in New York are more wary of black customers, especially black men. Crude and marred by unpleasant racist undertones as this criterion is, it shares with age and gender the same advantages. Insofar as skin color is correlated with dangerousness, it is a good sign of it, for skin color is easy to observe and hard to fake. Cosmetics have a limited effect, and vitiligo, the skin-lightening disease that the singer Michael Jackson suffers from, is rare. The signs of race are so discernible and strong that no other signs are necessary, and drivers view any attempt at veiling skin color with scarves, hats, or gloves with even greater suspicion.

For Spanish-Speaking Drivers, Spanish over Other Ethnic Groups

There is some indication that in New York Spanish-speaking drivers feel safer with Spanish-speaking customers. Statistically we have no evidence that members of the Spanish-speaking community are *less* likely to attack Spanish taxi drivers; in fact, many drivers fear teenagers of *any* ethnicity. Rather, drivers trust Spanish customers only partly because of ethnic affinity and more perhaps because sharing a language and culture puts them in a better position to read a customer's dispositions and mood accurately. Thus, "Spanishness"—or more generally, "ethnic sameness"—is not so much a property related to trustworthiness as one that allows a clearer observation of other trust-related properties.

The signs of Spanishness lie only partly and approximately in looks. Sometimes, for instance, they cross over with blackness, since some Hispanics have a dark complexion. More definitive signs are in Spanish language fluency and in names. These signs are usually quite robust, for while one can easily adopt a Spanish name, only the very linguistically talented and diligent can speak a second language like a native with an authentic-sounding accent and intonation. Unlike signs of age, gender, and race, ethnic signs have the disadvantage of not being always discernible at first sight; a closer contact, such as a verbal exchange, is often necessary to establish their presence.

All these signs of age, gender, race, and ethnicity may be called *cues* to distinguish them from other signs. Cues, as we explained in the introduction, have an important quality in terms of our hypotheses: they are costless for those who truly possess them.[10] An example of a cue "is an honest look, or, in identity signaling, one's handwriting or voice. There is no guarantee that cues satisfy the cannot condition: if assuming an honest look were easy enough, the cannot condition would fail and honesty would be mimickable through an honest look. However, cues usually have at least some positive cost for [mimics]" (Bacharach and Gambetta 2001, 168).

Cues of age, gender, and ethnicity are in fact very costly for mimics to display (even if the payoffs are much higher for a mimic than they are in the taxi trust game). So they almost perfectly reflect the separating equilibrium condition of signaling theory, which guarantees that truth is transmitted even when there is an interest to mimic. If mistakes are made in assessing trustworthiness using these signs, they are not made because of the trustworthiness or untrustworthiness of the signs, but because the properties crudely discriminate between trustworthy and untrustworthy customers.

Often, though not always, cues have another interesting property: they are "there anyway," and true possessors of the property need take no action to manifest them. These are "automatic cues." When cues are automatic, an honest signaler can take it easy. Indeed, he need hardly be aware of the cue's effect to benefit from it. Those who truly are of a particular age, gender, race, or ethnic type do not have to do anything to signal that other than show themselves, as they have to anyway. They do not even need to be conscious that their natural cues convey trustworthiness; only the drivers need to be aware of this.

Passengers tend to become aware of cues only if their cues are negative. If this is the case, they could veil or alter their cues somehow when the consequences are punishing for them. But precisely because such modification is hard to achieve, drivers can trust those cues insofar as they are cues that yield information about trust-warranting qualities. Just as the signs of certain emotions become manifest regardless of intentions and are therefore reliable indicators of those emotions, the cues of membership in these basic human categories are hard both to fake *and* to suppress at will. Thus, assuming that the qualities they manifest warrant more or less trustworthiness, one can rely on those *cues*, for they are both easy to observe and hard to mimic.

We can therefore expect that taxi drivers will use cues—and indeed they do. Even if they are far from perfect, as drivers know, they are very convenient when more in-depth probing is hard to accomplish. By contrast, while a property like religiosity may be more accurate at revealing trustworthiness, its signs are not as easy to observe at a glance and its symbolic manifestations are easier to fake. We found no indication that these signs are used, except in the rare instances in which a passenger is seen coming out of a church, a sign mentioned by New York drivers as well as by black bona-fide passengers.

Individuals over Multiple Passengers

There are several other cues linked to trust-warranting properties that drivers look for. Drivers feel safer with individual customers than with multiple passengers, especially, though not exclusively, if they are men. Again, this preference is statistically justified: it reflects the much higher likelihood of an attack by multiple passengers than by individuals. Being able to count is enough to enable a driver to perceive whether there is one hailer or more, and for the single hailer, showing himself is enough to signal that he is alone. Visual display of this property is a cue—that is, costless to genuine passengers.

Yet unlike the cues previously mentioned, this one can be manipulated. Even though it is physically impossible to change three individuals into one, a hailer, by standing alone, may be deliberately signaling that there are *not* more passengers waiting in the wings. A caller may lie to the dispatcher about how many passengers are to be picked up. One can easily pretend at little cost to be a singleton, and this strategy is employed by both bad mimics and bona-fide passengers who fear being unable to persuade a driver to stop.

As a cue, passenger number thus appears less resilient to mimicry. Yet, as with using a female decoy, the deception is short-lived and exposed as soon as the other passengers emerge from the shadows. Because mimicry is easily detected, the cue thus retains some strength. However, it still makes sense for passengers to use it, for while hiding a group behind a singleton may scare the driver off even more than if the group had stood together, the ploy can still be useful to get him to stop. At that point, the passengers may be able to convey other information to the driver that persuades him to pick up all of them (or sometimes they may bully him into picking up all of them). It makes particular sense for hailers to use this strategy, for it is never clear whether it was a ploy, and thus a lie, or it just happened that one hailed while the others were accidentally left behind. By contrast, when one lies about gender or age or number of passengers over the telephone, once the person is directly observed the lie is exposed and drivers become very suspicious.

Consistent with their preference for women, drivers also believe that a group of customers that includes at least one female is safer. Drivers consider two men with a female safer than three men or even two men. This sign, however, is not as reliable as mere femaleness, for it is not so difficult for a group of ill-intentioned men to recruit a female, and villains in several instances have done precisely that.

Wealthier over Poorer

Drivers also look for properties related to the professional and financial status of prospective passengers. The idea is simply that the wealthier and more established the customers are, the lower the chances that they will have a motive to attack drivers. Although some indication of status can be evinced from a passenger's accent and linguistic competence, several signs of that property are even more visible. To some extent, a higher financial and professional status is conveyed naturally through cues that require no conscious attempt or extra cost on the part of the signaler. Rich people often wear expensive clothes with no thought of conveying anything about their wealth, but merely to make a bella figura; as an unintended by-product, however, what they wear gives evidence of their wealth. In such cases their apparel works as a cue of their wealth because, even though it is costly to produce, it is not a costly input into the activity of inducing a belief in their wealth (Bacharach and Gambetta 2001, n. 24).

The persuasive force of expensive clothes, however, works well only at a high level of quality, for this sign is expensive for mimics, at least given the low payoffs of cheating in a taxi trust game. Drivers avoid manifestly disheveled hailers and pick up elegantly attired ones, yet the vast majority of customers dress in between these extremes and over the wide variety of styles typical of modern societies; the quality of their dress is thus not something from which drivers can infer very much. In keeping with our expectations, drivers gave clear indications that the cost of looking reasonably well dressed is too easily afforded to place any trust in it as a sign of wealth and professional status, and conversely, that looking shabbily dressed is not a sign of dangerousness.

Interestingly, drivers also look for *mismatches* between sartorial and other signs: someone who is well dressed and hailing from a deprived neighborhood, or whose accent or speech are of a low quality and dissonant with his attire, raises more suspicions than someone who is dressed to match his other signs. The cost of mimicking more than one sign may be unaffordable for the mimic in this game, and ironically, mimicking only one sign out of a range can backfire by creating salient anomalies.

There are other signs of status that drivers look for. Carrying working tools or equipment are strong indications that the passengers are truly engaged in a professional activity. Drivers also take into account the location of the pickup and the destination; drivers in both Belfast and New York are less willing to venture into poorer neighborhoods or to drive to notorious venues to pick up or drop off passengers. However, these locations are easily faked: mimics have duped drivers by moving to a safe pickup point and at first requesting a destination to a wealthier or safer area, only to change their itinerary later. But such a change, as Heather Hamill found out, causes problems and requires an energetic effort to persuade a driver that the change is in good faith.

An ancillary property related to having a higher status, and thus in turn to trustworthiness, is being an air traveler. The belief that passengers going to and from airports are safe is not statistically inferred but relies on causal reasoning: being an air traveler implies being wealthier and better established professionally than average. This works as a trust-warranting quality, and those who have it are also believed to be bona-fide taxi passengers, for they have better things to do than harming drivers. (This reasoning, of course, does not imply that they would be trustworthy in other trust games.) The older drivers in Belfast who choose to work from Belfast City Airport only effectively adopt a draconian way of ensuring that all their passengers are air travelers. Unlike dress style, the signs of being an air traveler are not easily faked—not for the small benefit one can derive from harming drivers. A mimic would have to go to the airport, dress up to match, carry luggage, and schedule his movements to coincide with incoming flights. One can easily justify carrying off these ploys for higher stakes, but not for the sake of robbing a cabby or doing a runner on him.

Known Passengers over Strangers

The signs we have considered so far are, for the most part, easily observable and require little probing, and most are also hard to mimic or camouflage. Now we consider more complex signs that require either a closer scrutiny to be detected or a richer sequence of interactions between drivers and customers.

Nothing reassures a driver more than encountering customers whom he knows from previous experience. Having been a good customer in the past is a trustworthiness-making quality, a reputation that discriminates well. Identity is itself not a directly observable quality; signs of it can evince it. The person must be reidentified as the person who was previously encountered, a quality that is observable through the passenger's signs of identity. Identity signaling is a strategy for signaling an unobservable quality that works by giving evidence of another unobservable quality, that of being the reputation bearer. Signs of identity tend to be good signs of it because they are cheap for the person with that identity and many are hard to fake. People are primarily reidentified by a cluster of cues—their face, their bodily features, and their voices, none of which can be easily manipulated.

The problem with using identity signs is that the driver needs to have had at least one previous encounter to experience the passenger and memorize his identifiers. In the first encounter, identity cum reputation cannot of course play a part, so there has to be some other condition to induce a driver to pick up. Next, there must be future encounters with the same person, and that condition requires other special conditions, such as a lively local demand—which we found only in West Belfast in our fieldwork—or an effort on the part of customers to re-call the same taxi drivers or company. Becoming a regular sometimes make sense for passengers too, especially if they expect problems in being picked up, like customer P-Cust5 in Belfast, who sought to gain a reputation for being a good customer with a taxi company with the intent of using that company in future instances. But the fleeting and sparse types of transactions that make the taxi service useful prevent identity signaling from becoming as widely used as it is in other markets.

However, mimics have exploited the property of being a regular customer. In Belfast sectarian attackers have studied the movements of regular fares; by calling from the same pickup location and time and using the name of a regular caller, they have successfully passed themselves off as that person. Once again, this was done with the intent of ambushing a driver before he had a chance to detect that the caller was not the regular one.

Callers over Hailers

Drivers believe that callers, by the simple fact of ordering a taxi over the telephone, are more likely to be trustworthy than those who hail a taxi from the street. The statistical evidence suggests that this assumption is correct and that hailers are indeed responsible for most of the attacks, even though the majority of customers for our type of drivers are callers. Several drivers stick to picking up callers only, and not just because they abide by the laws in both cities that prevent them from picking up in the street.

Drivers are aware that by calling, customers, while avoiding exposure in person, also give information about themselves that is not as easily available or collectable from hailers. They unavoidably reveal their gender, accent, and linguistic competence to the dispatcher before any close contact is made. In addition, customers are asked to supply (or the dispatcher's switchboard automatically records) their name and phone number, and they also must provide the location of pickup and the destination. Although there is always the possibility that any of these details may be false, their disclosure establishes a general trust-warranting property—the willingness to make oneself identifiable.

The fact that this information is given verbally without a concomitant display of visible features does weaken these signs somewhat, for "words are cheap," and drivers showed a keen awareness of this. They uniformly said that they reserve the option of rejecting a fare if the further information they gather by meeting the fare raises their suspicions.

Still, calling retains much persuasive force, along with the information that goes with it. Obtaining information over the telephone offers a later opportunity to observe the caller and detect mismatches. The mismatch is an additional sign in its own right that results from coupling two signs to check whether they are at odds with one another. Drivers reason that inconsistencies between observed signs and information given to the dispatcher, such as gender, age, number of passengers, or destination, are themselves a worrying clue from which they can infer a higher probability of malevolent intent.

Moreover, even though it may be easier to mimic signs that are verbally transmitted than signs that are displayed when a person shows herself, the costs of mimicry increase with the amount of information the customer is required to reveal. Each property must be credible and consistent with other properties. Drivers place their confidence more in a sequence of signs than in any one of them, and calling adds to that sequence significantly.

For Catholic Drivers, Catholic over Protestant—and Vice Versa

In Belfast the fear of a sectarian attack makes drivers prefer customers who share their religion. There are no inherent physical cues of religion: Protestants and Catholics share the same skin color and have no facial or other physical differences. Styles of dress have no religious connotations, so by observing a person one cannot normally infer their religion. Drivers therefore look for less overt signs.

Because Belfast is highly segregated religiously, the pickup location or the destination is a fairly robust sign of religion, and drivers often refuse fares on that basis alone. Those in the west of the city are likely to be Catholic, and those in the east to be Protestant. Although it costs a Catholic nothing to be in a Catholic area, the costs for a paramilitary to be in an area dominated by members of the other religion can be high, even fatally so. Although drivers rely on the costliness of this risk to an extent, they are not totally reassured because they also know that paramilitaries intent on murder have taken such high risks. Because of the tragic consequences when Protestant mimics have been this audacious, Catholic drivers either make the draconian decision to pick up only known local customers or choose not to rely on any one sign alone. In the latter case, they seek assurance from a series of signs, probing to see whether additional signs match those acquired already.

Drivers do not rely too much on first names. Even though these are often religiously connoted, they are easily fakeable for the duration of the taxi journey. The pronunciation of the letter h (Catholics pronounce it haitch, while Protestants say aitch) can also be modified, and tattoos

displaying paramilitary insignia can be covered up. Sporting preferences also signal religion. Catholics support Gaelic football and hurling
and certain local and Scottish soccer teams. Protestants, on the other hand,
support rugby and different local and Scottish soccer teams. Therefore,
passengers talking about the All-Ireland Gaelic football final, for instance,
are likely to be Catholic. For a Catholic fan of the sport, such a conversation is easy and natural, but a Protestant mimic must exert some effort
to be primed to answer the question "What did you think of the match
last night?" as convincingly as if he were a true fan.

Reliable evidence can also be evinced by probing the extent of the
passenger's local knowledge. Every native is familiar with such information and gains it with little effort in the natural course of his life, but
a stranger of the opposing religion finds it much harder to acquire. Nevertheless, the costs of being in "enemy" territory and gathering information about it have not deterred some Protestant killers who have
successfully deceived drivers by, for example, displaying just that kind
of knowledge of bars and clubs. They have developed such knowledge
by going to considerable lengths to acquire the information a Catholic
would naturally have.

Self-Absorbed over Inquisitive

Drivers also look for signs that manifest passengers' mental and emotional states. Signs of these are gathered by making contact with passengers and observing them closely, often after they are in the car.

Drivers feel more comfortable with customers who appear to be
absorbed by their own interests and are paying little attention to the
driver, the car, or the journey, either overtly by asking questions or
covertly by the way they behave and in what they observe. Benign passengers are concerned with getting to their destination, while malevolent ones may display an undue interest in how much money the driver
is making or what religion he is. Cues of self-absorption are reading,
absentmindedly looking at the landscape, talking on a cell phone, being
moderately drunk, sleeping, carrying on a previous conversation with
fellow passengers, kissing or flirting with a fellow passenger, or maintaining a happy mood from a good night out. These signs can be faked,
but to keep them up consistently, making sure lapses do not occur or
that they escape the driver's notice if they do, the mimic must be very
skilled. Drivers pay attention to the conversation and observe passengers through the rearview mirror in order to search for undue signs of
behavioral nosiness, such as watching the driver closely, looking around
the car, fidgeting, and constantly glancing out the window.

Drivers are also suspicious if they feel that a passenger is trying to
persuade them of how nice he is. Why should a passenger care about a

taxi driver's opinion, in whose company he will be for ten minutes and whom he may never see again? This kind of concern indirectly signals an interest in the driver that is excessively friendly, thus potentially unfriendly. Another sign that a passenger may be excessively alert is any violation in the patterns of "normal" behavior. For example, in Belfast drivers are suspicious of men who are *not* drunk on a Saturday night.

Candid over Shifty

Drivers' prudence increases if they detect signs that a passenger may be trying to hide an object or some of his features from view. A woman's handbag, if she is with a group of men, or a coat, especially if worn in summer, may hide a gun. No one knows for sure whether people who wear coats in the summer are likely to be dangerous rather than just innocuously odd or ill. Still, the chances that they are hiding something increase, and drivers raise their guard. Those who have nothing to hide have no cost in *not* wearing a coat in warm seasons.

Analogously, wearing a baseball cap or other garments that veil facial features is regarded with suspicion, as is sitting behind the driver, since this prevents him from seeing what the passenger is doing. Passengers who talk with each other in a guarded or whispering way that excludes the driver are also monitored closely. Many of these signs require that the driver be alert and observant, since, for example, slight glances between passengers or at the driver can easily be missed. But as driver C-WB5 astutely pointed out, "If you catch the first one of them, then you see the second, and the third."

Friendly and Calm over Aggressive and Agitated

Passengers who appear friendly and relaxed are believed to be safer than those who are aggressive or agitated. Signs of friendliness are found in the passenger's manner as he gives instructions, in whether he is polite, and in how he dictates the route or haggles over the fare. Someone intent on getting a taxi, however, can easily fake these signs at little cost. So drivers look for signs that are harder to fake, such as sweating, speed of eye movements, lack of eye contact, or excessive formality, which are all viewed as signs of nervousness heralding danger. The exact source of these signs, however, can be easily misinterpreted. Paul Ekman (2001, 96) warns against interpreting behavior without having first established a baseline of normal conduct, so that "the lie catcher is vulnerable to errors unless he knows what the suspect's usual behavior is." For one thing, as driver C-NB1 pointed out, a passenger's mood may be related not to the taxi journey but rather to some other event that he has either experienced or is expecting.

Next, several gestures connected to mental and emotional states are difficult to decipher because they point in opposite directions depending on whether they are sincere or strategic. Passengers who do not talk could be either thinking about their business or silently plotting an attack. Those who offer money up front could be candid, wishing only to persuade the driver that they are willing to pay. Or those who inform the driver up front that they have no money and will have to get it either from a cash machine or from home may again be revealing their candor and hence trustworthiness. Yet both gestures could be duplicitous: a strategy typical of con-men is to relax the victim by making him feel comfortable and very well treated before hitting him later. We recorded a few episodes in which runners resorted to these artful ploys.[11]

How Effective Is Screening?

The results of our fieldwork are most encouraging for the hypotheses we started from and more generally for the theory of "trust in signs" that we set out to test. Still, there are two important questions that need to be addressed. How effective is drivers' sign-screening in increasing their safety? And can we generalize our results to trust decisions in other contexts?

The first question must be put more precisely: we cannot expect drivers, even rational and prudent ones, to be able to screen out *all* dangerous fares and to let in *all* the bona-fide ones. Drivers make mistakes both ways, of course: they not only suffer from various forms of aggression but also lose business by excluding perfectly good passengers when they make wrong inferences from the cues displayed. We gave accounts in chapter 5 of a number of false negatives that Belfast drivers reported to us, many of which they laughed about. So the efficacy of their screening cannot reasonably be measured against the claim that they always get it right. The question must be: do they get their screening right a sufficient number of times so as not to make it a futile exercise or one that goes against their financial interests? Do they, in other words, do better than chance at screening out truly untrustworthy passengers, or are they just the victims of a delusion of control?

We have no definitive evidence to help us answer this question. When passengers are screened out, evidence as to whether they truly were dangerous is not often available. But sometimes we did get just that evidence. For instance:

- A driver or dispatcher decides not to take a passenger. Then his fears are justified when another driver, paying no attention to his advice, picks up that passenger and is robbed or attacked.

- As a result of probing, a driver decides to evict a passenger or stop at a police station, and in some way it becomes clear that his fears were justified.

- A dispatcher doubts the good faith of a caller and suggests that he call back, using as an excuse the claim that all the drivers are busy. If the individual calls back, this is taken as a positive sign, but sometimes the screened-out caller works out that he was suspected and, irrationally, calls back to threaten the dispatcher.

- A driver decides to drive on, for he suspects a hailer of being dangerous. The hailer somehow manages to attack him anyway from the street (and not just because he was passed by!).

- A driver feels uneasy about picking someone up, reads all the signs that should make him prudent, but disregards his gut feelings and picks up. If he lives, he then learns that he should have heeded his intuition.

We also have ample evidence that drivers' screening is highly realistic and that the signs they worry about reflect the signs that mimics try to manipulate. There is a remarkable matching between the reasoning of drivers and that of mimics. Drivers do not live in an insulated mental state, dreaming up perils or worries attached to stereotypes that have no existence outside their heads. Mimics try to think as drivers do to outwit them, and drivers try to think as mimics do to stay one step ahead.

(We should note that mimicry can fail because it is of poor quality and not because the driver spots an intention to deceive him. For example, a passenger may wear fake jewels with the intention of fooling a driver into thinking she is rich, but the driver can see clearly from other signs that she is not wealthy and may think that she just likes to wear fake jewelry, perhaps to impress others rather than him. So he may not pick her up because he is not fooled into thinking she is rich, but he may also not understand that wearing such jewelry was *intended* as an act of deceitful mimicry. In this case, he perceives a bad customer without perceiving that she is also a mimicking one. We cannot measure how many incompetent mimics there are because their encounters with drivers leave the latter feeling as though nothing happened.)

The fact that drivers are good at screening can also be argued on theoretical grounds. There is an asymmetry between prey and predator that is commonly recognized in biology. Under natural selection pressure, the former becomes "smarter" than the latter, the reason being that a predator's mistake is "a missed dinner," while a prey's mistake can be fatal. A predator needs to get it right only some of the time, while a prey needs to get it right all the time. (An awareness of this asymmetry is reflected in a statement released by the Irish Republican Army

[IRA] after it unsuccessfully tried to assassinate British prime minister Margaret Thatcher in 1984: "We just need to be lucky once, she needs to be lucky every time.")[12] In the course of a night a driver needs to make the right decision every time he picks up. A sectarian attacker or a violent robber can afford to fail to fool all drivers except one to reach his goal.[13] In economic terms, the prey's constraints are more stringent than those of the predator. It does not automatically follow that drivers will become smarter, but the pressure is undoubtedly there. As we saw from the dynamic of attacks in New York (see chapter 7), a peak in the number of attacks is followed by a trough, an indication that as the pressure from attackers grows and becomes salient, the screening efforts improve too. The drivers murdered in New York were either inexperienced or had relaxed their guard under the countervailing pressure to make money.

"Bent on Fooling" a Driver

Most drivers do acknowledge that if a villain is really "bent on fooling" them, there is little they can do to prevent it. By saying this, they do not so much show skepticism over the value of their screening efforts as realistically admit that if a mimic is prepared to pay *any* cost for getting them, then no amount of sign-reading will spare them from being taken in. They recognize that one can seldom count on signs that give rise to a perfect separating equilibrium. Applying the principle of signaling theory does not protect one against irrational actors who are prepared to pay costs that are higher than the value of what they may get in return.

More importantly, it is not always easy to assess what kind of rational mimics one is playing against, what benefits they are seeking, and what costs and risks they are thus prepared to sustain. If a terrorist, with no prior criminal record, is clean-shaven, wearing a suit, carrying a valid passport, and behaving normally, there is no sign-reading or probing that can reveal his intention to hijack an airplane barehanded, and thus he cannot be prevented from boarding. The drivers who were the victims of vicious attacks in Belfast were caught in this trap: they sought signs that were costly enough to screen out runners and robbers but not costly enough to deter sectarian attackers, whose sick rewards from harming Catholics exceeded even high mimicry costs. The mistake these drivers made—if it is a mistake—was to think that they were playing a game against a "cheaper" mimic.

In the course of this study, the most successful mimics we found were not the villainous types but the DOE agents in Belfast who were intent on catching drivers for illegally picking up street-hailing passengers. In just over two years they gained over one hundred convictions. Therefore, they had successfully persuaded at least that number of drivers that they were bona-fide passengers. There were a number of reasons for their success. Initially, Belfast drivers assumed that they were only up against runners, robbers, hijackers, and murderers. They were unaware of this new breed of mimics. As drivers grew to realize their existence, they initially underestimated the amount of time and resources the DOE was willing to invest in acquiring and displaying the exact signs of trust-warranting properties for which drivers screen. Individual officers devoted five or six weeks of preparatory work before a sting operation, monitoring drivers and firms, becoming known to them by getting mock rides, and gaining local knowledge. They astutely operated in mixed-gender adult groups, hailed taxis pretending to be leaving popular venues on weekend nights along with many normal customers, and gave safe destinations to the drivers. They ensured there were no mismatches and timed their departure from a cinema with the end of a film or their appearance at an airport with the arrival of a flight. They dressed in a casual but respectable style, as would befit a social occasion. They appeared friendly, relaxed, and self-absorbed while in the cab, carrying on rehearsed conversations with one another about jobs or the evening they had just enjoyed. They maintained their mimicry act right to the very end of the journey, for they needed the driver to charge them for the fare before they could catch him doing something illegal. They acted for the public benefit and could draw from the public purse to perfect their ploy.

Drivers were fooled—we recorded only one occasion on which a driver suspected that something was wrong and refused to charge passengers who turned out to be DOE agents. But drivers were not fooled because of carelessness but rather because there was no way they could rationally afford to probe the real identity of the agents. Only stopping their practice of picking up hailers altogether could have saved them from being caught. Eventually the DOE began to run up against a cost constraint: the pool of mimic officers was relatively small, and the DOE feared that after a number of operations their cover would be blown as their identities became known to the drivers.

Gut Feelings

The most remarkable evidence of the effectiveness of sign-reading, as well as of the clear potential for generalizing our results, comes from a link that we did not expect to find between our findings and the findings of psychological research on deception. Several drivers claimed that what ultimately shapes their verdict as to a passenger's trustworthiness are their "gut feelings." In particular, the more experienced drivers in both cities claimed that they rely on their "instinct" and even studiously try to learn to trust their instincts more. Facial expressions, looks in the eyes, and tone of voice were mentioned as properties that, in their experience, betray a passenger's true mood and intent. Several drivers claimed that they could detect the tension in a customer by how supple or rigid his body movements are when entering the car. One driver claimed he can even feel the lowering of the temperature or the "energy level" inside the car when his passengers are up to no good, echoing, literally rather than metaphorically, the common saying that people who sense danger feel "chills run up and down their spine."

These veteran drivers were not always able to unpack their reasoning and pinpoint which signs prompted their verdicts about customers' trustworthiness, and why. This elusiveness could be interpreted as an indication that drivers are simply prey to some delusion about their real ability. Yet their unawareness of the exact stimula could simply reflect the fact that some individuals are very good at detecting deception in what are called "micro-expressions" without necessarily also being able to explain it to others. The evidence from psychological research on interpersonal deception strongly encourages us to take drivers' accounts in this regard very seriously.

From the work of Paul Ekman and his associates we know that a small number of people have an uncanny ability to "read" deception in a complex combination of facial features with a much higher than chance rate of success. Conversely, there are a few gifted deceivers who know how to control the many facial muscles that would otherwise give their lies away. This is a rare natural gift, which only extremely costly acting training could bring about intentionally. The best lie spotters are not aware of the many facial features they process—we do not even have the vocabulary to identify these micro-expressions—but nonetheless they have the cognitive ability to do so (Ekman 2001).[14] There is also evidence that aphasics—those who, like some stroke victims, have lost their ability to understand language—are particularly good at reading faces. This is an indication that a subject's greater reliance on nonverbal cues—on "gut feeling" and a "sixth sense"—may be precisely what makes them successful sign readers. There is also evidence that youngsters who have been victims of abuse are good at detecting nonverbal cues. This suggests that being under great pressure to identify the onset of aggressive behavior may foster the same ability that some drivers could develop.

The psychological literature does not offer an explicit theoretical insight on the mechanisms that could explain why those cues should rationally be interpreted as evidence of deception.[15] But it does not take much to see that the way these cues are produced is entirely consistent with the key principle of signaling theory: the facial alterations associated to the emotions that are triggered by lying are costly to suppress.

"Microexpressions have the potentiality of displaying a multitude of affective states, while at the same time are difficult to self-monitor and *nearly, if not impossible, to inhibit*" (Decaire 2000, emphasis added).[16] This makes the unperturbed facial expression associated with telling the truth entirely natural and costless for the truth teller but costly to fake for the mimic. Thus paying attention to the signaler's microexpressions provides a more reliable source of information than relying on language, which is hazardous since a mimic can more easily lie with it too nimbly.

In a similar vein, psychological research offers evidence concerning other nonverbal cues. Looking people in the eyes is not by itself a sign that one is telling the truth. But it is a sign nonetheless that one does not protect oneself from the other person's scrutinizing gaze. Looking in the eyes of a person bent on deception thus increases his cost of deception insofar as the emotions associated with deception tend to show up in the eyes, even if only for milliseconds, whether the deceiver likes it or not. An honest signaler can thus afford such exposure much more than a dishonest one. Much research appears to be consistent with the folk belief that "the eyes are the windows of the soul" and supports "the conclusion that eye contact variations occur concurrently with the stress related arousal present during deception" (Decaire 2000). We further know that one of the consistent signs of deception is associated with an increase in the pitch frequency of speech, which is "thought to be the result of heightened physiological tension brought forth by the arousal of the sympathetic arousal-deception reaction" (Decaire 2000). And finally, we even know that deception has been consistently found to be associated with "a rigid and frozen nature of postural shifts and body movements" (Decaire 2000). As we mention in chapter 5, this is something driver C-NB1 pays attention to: "There's a way of getting in and out of a car. You can't have a rigid upper body structure if you're getting into a car, you have to relax to get into a car and then to get yourself into the bucket seat of a car you have to relax and if a person's not relaxed then they're up to something and then the body posture is instinctively wrong."

In conclusion, there is an uncanny degree of coincidence between the nonverbal cues that subjects display in experimental deception conditions and those that our drivers said they observe. In fact, we have come to view their statements on "gut feelings" as some of the most interesting material we collected. This has provided us with evidence both that drivers outside experimental conditions use subtle cues to identify deceivers and that the common thread running through all these cues, crude and subtle alike, is their costlessness or cheapness for the honest signaler and their costliness for the untrustworthy one. If we compare the two cities, this evidence strengthens our expectation that, despite local variations, there is a universal logic governing trust-related decisions.

A Microcosm of Trust Decisions

Taxi drivers' dilemmas and the ways they tackle them epitomize the real-life trust decisions faced by all those who work in occupations in which identifying cheaters or attackers who mimic being of a good sort either is part of the job—as it is for bouncers, custom officers, and police officers—or is indispensable in safeguarding their property and safety when dealing with new customers, as with retail jewelers and prostitutes.

Taxi drivers' trust decisions are indicative also of what we all do when dealing with strangers in situations we perceive as dangerous, either because there is a high probability of being attacked or cheated or because we would expect the consequences of being attacked or cheated to be dire. Let us take an extreme yet all too real example. Before 9/11, very few air travelers looked at their fellow passengers with a scrutinizing and suspicious eye. We did not think we were playing *that* trust game with them, and we assumed that other passengers, by simply boarding a plane with us, gave a good enough sign that they were not intent on causing it to crash. Yet now the terrorist threat has become as salient as the threat of being attacked is for taxi drivers in dangerous cities. We now know that there are people who are prepared to drink, as it were, from the poisoned chalice. We know that boarding a plane is not invariably a discriminating sign of wanting to land safely at the destination. We also know that to avoid detection the terrorists, like all deceiving mimics, take deliberate steps to look like normal passengers—shaving their beards, carrying presents, and wearing business suits and apparel. Suddenly all those signs we previously did not even think about have become worth probing. We now quietly accept the extra time it takes the authorities to screen bona-fide air travelers by increasing precautions and gathering more information about them and their luggage before boarding. And as passengers, we remain alert to the dangers just as taxi drivers do when they feel suspicious about a customer they have picked up. In December 2001, Richard Reid, a would-be suicide attacker who packed explosives into his shoes, was stopped by fellow passengers from lighting the fuse after they noticed him fumbling with matches—a gesture that with a pre-9/11 mind-set they might have put down to weirdness rather than to an intention to bring down the plane on which he was traveling.

The parallels that we can draw from the taxi world are not limited to the actions of trusters and mimics but extend to the innocent persons who carry negative cues and try to offset them. Usama Darawashe, a twenty-two-year-old Israeli Arab, travels by bus and deliberately masks signs of his "Arabness" by dressing like a modern young Jewish man with "cropped, spiky black hair and wispy goatee," reading a Hebrew newspaper, carrying a cell phone with the digital readout in Hebrew, and not speaking any Arabic into his phone when it rings. While passing himself off as a "good Jewish" passenger in order to avoid raising suspicions when boarding a bus, he, like all the other passengers, simultaneously scans his fellow passengers looking for any signs that might betray them as a Palestinian suicide bomber (Bennet 2002).

Thankfully, we do not all face such perilous journeys on a regular basis. Still, we are faced with many less extreme trust decisions—whether to accept a date with someone about whom we know little, whether to transact with someone whose identity we are not sure about—whose logic can be understood thanks to our knowledge of the taxi drivers' microcosm. We look for signs of bona-fide intentions in our trustees that, while not necessarily the same as the signs taxi drivers look for, nonetheless follow the same principles.

There is, of course, a huge variety in the signs of trustworthiness that we use. Some signs of trustworthiness can travel from one trust game to another, such as the face of a known and reputable person. Other signs of trustworthiness vary and are specific to the requirements of a particular game—a nervous person, for instance, is not the best partner for a mountaineering expedition. Some signs are multipurpose: a fat bank account can persuade many a truster of one's ability to make and keep one's money. Other signs are bound by convention to special occasions—an engagement ring is appropriate reassurance only for one's fiancé.

Sometimes we can depend on signs that are created, from both private and public resources, precisely for the purpose of checking for trustworthiness, such as identity cards or private passwords stored with our bank in order to facilitate accurate reidentification. At other times, to persuade the truster, we must invent new signs. Cervantes' Don Quixote provides us with an example of our inexhaustible creativity in this department. He asks a friend to write a poem, which he plans to give to Dulcinea, the woman of his dreams. He instructs his friend to write it so as to make the first letters of each verse form her name when read vertically: D-U-L-C-I-N-E-A D-E-L T-O-B-O-S-O. Otherwise, Don Quixote explains, without this "signature," she would believe the poem was recycled rather than written for her—cheap words rather than words of true love.[17]

Signs also vary, of course, depending on the medium of communication we use. Some signs are good for one type of medium but unavailable in another. Over the telephone one cannot see the face or the handwriting, but one can hear the voice, the accent, the tone, and the spoken language that one cannot see in a letter. New transacting media generate new signs, and the knowledge of them spreads and refines over time. When we check the genuineness of an email from a stranger, we now look at the suffix of the sender's address to see if it comes from a reputable institution that gives out email addresses only to its bona-fide members; we "Google" the sender to see if he has a web page with meaningful information in it; we check whether his vocabulary is reveal-ing of oddities; and we make use of new technologies that inform us about the source of a message or website (Donath 1998).

Effective signs of trustworthiness also vary crucially in terms of cost-liness, depending on the payoffs. The more there is to gain from trusting someone in a particular situation, the more tempted we are to trust him. Con-men lure their victims by making exceptionally attractive proposi-tions (Frankel, forthcoming)—so attractive, in fact, that rather than look-ing more suspicious, they cloud the judgment of gullible people. Instead of seeing the proposition as "too good to be true," they think of it as "too good to miss." But the more there is to lose from being wrong in judging someone's trustworthiness in a given trust game, the more vigorously the rational trusters probe the credentials of the trustees. What are the signs that a deceiving mimic could not afford given what he expects to gain from taking us in? Those who are cheated do not take this question seri-ously enough. According to a March 6, 2001, report in the *Express*, Lon-don, "college dropout Saqib Mumtaz masterminded a GBP 1.5 million diamond heist by ordering a Lear jet, limousines and Rolex watches on the [stolen] cards of billionaire bankers, celebrities and Arab princes. In April 1999, Kingston Crown Court jailed him for three-and-a-half years for his role in the plot, which involved impersonating the brother of the Sultan of Brunei to con the exclusive Beverly Hills jeweller Bijan." The more the mimic stands to gain from leading someone to trust him, the more he can afford to invest on mimicking the signs of a genuine trustee. Thus, the discriminating signs that the truster demands of the trustee to probe his trustworthiness before being persuaded should be that much more costly. Signs that can reassure a taxi driver can hardly reassure a cautious jeweler.

Yet, despite the variety in signs, the logic is the same: we look for or try to display signs of trustworthiness that are hard for a mimic to fake, while being affordable to the trustworthy. Before we can trust anyone, we need to trust their signs.

Notes

Acknowledgments

1. This conference, "Vertraven in Organizazionen," was held in Tutzing, Germany, at the Evangelische Akademie, May 19 to 21, 2000.

Introduction

1. This occupational classification also includes drivers on regular routes, such as drivers making airport-to-airport transfers and drivers for limousine-style services. However, because of the clientele served, the regularity of the drivers' routine, and the noncash payment methods, these drivers have a low relative risk of being the victims of homicide.

2. In the United States between 1993 and 1999, almost four of every ten robberies that occurred while the victim was at work or on duty were committed against persons in retail sales or transportation (U.S. Department of Justice 2001).

3. A profession that poses some of the same hurdles is street prostitution, but prostitutes do not have as many encounters with strangers as drivers do (Sanders 2004).

4. There is a small scholarly literature on taxi drivers; see, for instance, Mayhew (2000) and Haines (1997). We found nothing, however, on the trust dilemmas faced by taxi drivers that we investigate in this study. There have also been several TV documentaries on taxi drivers—for instance, the PBS production *Taxi Dreams*—but again, not much has been broadcast on the particular problem that concerns us.

5. These two conditions are posited also by James Coleman (1990, 98) as essential to a trust situation.

6. One could only imagine an untrustworthy trustee as someone who is unable to see his self-interest, so untrustworthiness would become synonymous with some kind of irrationality.

7. Rather than offering an abstract discussion of how trusters learn about trust-warranting properties, we proceed assuming that they do learn something and postpone the problem to the conclusion.

8. A recent exception concerns only facial expressions; see Eckel and Wilson (2003).

9. "Ian Wright [black], Paul Ince [black] and Ryan Giggs [white] left the . . . BBC Sports Personality of the Year award and were in the street trying to hail a taxi. Up went Wright's arm three or four times, but no cab would stop. So Wright and Ince hid while Giggs hailed. Sure enough the first cab to come by stopped" (Thorpe 1994).

10. A faculty member at Fordham University as well as a Princeton University and Harvard Law School graduate, Graham wrote a widely discussed account of the clever behavioral strategies he employs as a black American to "reassure" the whites he encounters in various social situations that he is a nonthreatening individual. His book *Member of the Club: Reflections on Life in a Racially Polarized World* (1995) was viewed as very controversial. From the standpoint of our research, however, it illustrates the sort of resourceful behavior that an individual who carries a negative cue feels compelled to use when trying to hail a cab or get assistance from someone on the street.

11. See London Metropolitan Police website, "Sapphire: Improving Rape Investigation and Victim Care: Mini-cab Rape," available at: http://www.met.police.uk/sapphire/sapphire_minicabrape.htm (accessed March 5, 2005).

12. We did not collect institutional data such as training manuals or internal reports. In Belfast it was unavailable because of the small size of firms and the unregulated nature of the taxi industry. In New York these data exist only within the yellow cab industry and not in the livery industry; in the latter, drivers informally train each other and share information.

13. Table 1.1 shows the religious and gender breakdown of the forty-five drivers we interviewed, as well as the type of firms they worked for. We paid drivers £15 for their time. This is the average amount drivers could hope to earn in an hour.

14. Our "bad-looking" customers, runners, and robbers were all contacted with the support of People's Alternative to Drugs and Alcohol (PANDA), a charity that works with addicts and recovering addicts.

15. The 9/11 terrorist attack on New York affected our research only in a minor way by delaying the start by over a month. We commenced on October 10, 2001, and finished in May 2002.

16. We paid the drivers $20, which is the average amount they could hope to earn in an hour.

17. In addition, in Belfast most of these people had pleaded not guilty, and it would have been pointless to ask them about what they claimed they did not do.

Chapter 1

1. The population of Northern Ireland is 1,685,267, and the population of Belfast is 277,391 (Northern Ireland Statistics and Research Agency 2002, 8).

2. See Police Service for Northern Ireland website, "Security Statistics (2002)," available at: http://www.psni.police.uk/stats/securitysit.shtml. The apparent discrepancy between the high proportion of Catholics killed and the high proportion killed by Republican paramilitaries is due to Republicans killing people in their own camp, often as a punishment for some form of disloyalty.

3. "Fears are growing that more people will be killed before the feud is brought to an end. And last night black taxi drivers were taking no chances. Shortly after being targeted in broad daylight in the UDA stronghold of the lower Shankill Road, they crossed the peaceline on the nationalist Falls" (*Irish News* 2000b).

4. The airport drivers have formed a separate organization and now regulate themselves.

5. This alternative transport system is similar to the Jeepney system in the Philippines, which began after World War II when the American forces left thousands of jeeps on the beaches after landing. The Filipinos customized the vehicles and turned them into elaborate elongated buses.

6. Ex-prisoners convicted of paramilitary offenses and released under the prisoner early-release provision of the Belfast Agreement (1999) are categorized with those convicted of "ordinary" offenses, but their case is currently being reviewed by the DVLNI.

7. "The game they play is to drive at high speed and then brake as they knock into them to try and scare the taxi driver" (*Irish News* 1999b). "A taxi driver said that the Shaws Road, the Stewartstown Road and Finaghy Road were particularly bad, causing panic amongst drivers who feared for their safety. He added that taxi drivers were calling in warnings to other drivers" (*Irish News* 1999a).

8. One driver was Scottish but had lived in Belfast for twenty years.

Chapter 2

1. In Northern Ireland, Protestants are said to "kick with their right foot" and Catholics to "kick with their left foot."

Chapter 3

1. Also, passengers sometimes wish to keep their religion secret from the driver. For instance, although there are many similarities between the Catholic and Protestant black taxis that operate shuttle services in parts of Belfast, there are subtle differences in protocol. By getting these wrong, the passenger may unwittingly advertise his religion. A passenger in a Catholic black taxi who wants to be dropped off taps the separating panel with his money and the driver stops the car. The passenger then gets out of the taxi and pays the driver through the front passenger's side window. Protestant black taxis are stopped when a passenger calls out, "Next stop, please," and payment is made from inside the taxi through the separating panel.

2. Driver C-CCF3 takes her TAXI sign off before going home for a reason that has nothing to do with religion: she simply wants to avoid being identified as a driver with cash. "Yes—[a robber might think], 'Maybe she is coming in on a Saturday night at such a time and she will have a few pound.' So I always pull into a garage before I go home—you know the all-night garages—take my sign off, put it all away, because I then just get out of the car, *click-click,* and the car is locked again—you don't even have to stand and lock it—and then I am in. Things like that."

3. Each summer in Northern Ireland, Protestant fraternal orders—the Orange Order, the Apprentice Boys of Derry, and the Royal Black Institution—plan marches and parades to commemorate historical events of significance to the Protestant community. This schedule of processions, beginning in May and lasting through August, is commonly referred to as the "marching season." A few of the marches go through predominantly Catholic neighborhoods. Historically these marches have given rise to tensions between Protestants and Catholics, and recent years have seen an upsurge in violence between the two communities during the marching season.

4. The Royal Victoria Hospital is situated in Catholic West Belfast, the City Hospital is in a Protestant area, and the Mater Hospital is located close to an interface area in North Belfast.

Chapter 4

1. Colin Camerer and his colleagues (1997) found that yellow cab drivers in New York adjust their daily hours of work to meet a certain target income. Their finding has been challenged by Henry Farber (2005), who re-analyzed the same data and shows that the drivers' decision to stop work in any particular day is primarily related to cumulative daily hours to that point regardless of income. Several of the Belfast drivers, like P-CC12, mentioned that, like Camerer et al. contend, they work toward a target income. However, we cannot be sure that this is the general practice either in Belfast or in New York, as unfortunately we did not question drivers systematically on this point.

2. We could also speculate that wearing gloves might betray an intention not to leave fingerprints, but none of the drivers mentioned this explicitly.

Chapter 5

1. We should mention that eyes are also important for bouncers, who face some of the same problems that drivers face: "Well, you're always watching their eyes, always. They just give you an intense stare, and before anything goes off their eyes move very quickly. Normally they're looking around. They're assessing what's going on. It's an intense stare, and maybe their eyes fly left and right, and then you know they're going to lunge or something" (bouncer P-B1). In this case, however, the bouncer is observing the eyes in order to predict whether the person is about to start a fight in an already tense situation.

Chapter 6

1. The TLC, created in 1971, is the mayoral agency responsible for the taxi industry in New York. Its board has nine members, eight of whom are unsalaried commissioners, and it maintains a staff of approximately four hundred employees assigned to various divisions and bureaus. In addition to licensing and regulating taxi vehicles and drivers and seizing illegal vehicles, the TLC performs safety and emissions inspections of all yellow cabs three times a year and holds numerous hearings for violations of city and TLC rules and regulations. It considers itself the most active taxi and limousine licensing regulatory agency in the United States.

2. According to the TLC, the number of yellow taxis is set by local law and rarely changed; see TLC website, http://www.nyc.gov/html/tlc/html/about/about/shtml (accessed March 4, 2005).

3. Regulations prohibit them from prearranging service through two-way radios.

4. See TLC website, http://www.nyc.gov/html/tlc/html/home/home/shtml (accessed March 4, 2005).

5. These cars must also carry at least $500,000 to $1,000,000 in insurance coverage.

6. See TLC website, http://www.nyc.gov/html/tlc/html/about/about/shtml (accessed March 4, 2005).

7. Trained testers observed livery activity at fifty-two locations in midtown Manhattan and on the Upper East and West Sides in November 2001. Testers attempted to hail a cab and recorded the number of taxicabs and liveries that stopped (Schaller Consulting 2002).

8. Marilyn Mode, New York Police Department spokesperson, quoted in Chivers (2000a).

9. According to the 2000 census, New York's population was 8,008,278 (see United States Census 2000 website, http://www.census.gov/main/www/cen2000.html; accessed March 4, 2005).

10. Since 1990, the Dominican Republic has been the number-one source of legal immigration to New York; see New York City Department of City Planning Population Division (2004).

11. In addition, one yellow cab driver was from New Zealand.

12. By some estimates, 60 to 75 percent of New York's yellow cab drivers are of Arab, South Asian, or North African descent (Kennedy 2001b).

Chapter 7

1. In the United States as a whole, the eighteen- to twenty-four-year-old group has historically had the highest homicide offending rates of any age category, and from 1985 to 1993 its rate doubled, becoming three times as high

Table 7.3   Homicide Trends in the United States: Homicide Offending
Rates per 100,000 Population, by Age in Selected Years

Year	Under 14	14 to 17	18 to 24	25 to 34	35 to 49	50 or Older
1985	0.2%	9.8%	21.4%	16.0%	9.4%	3.0%
1993	0.3	30.2	41.3	15.9	7.4	2.4
1999	0.2	10.7	27.7	11.0	5.0	1.5

Source: FBI, Supplementary Homicide Reports, 1976 to 2002, compiled at website for U.S. Department of Justice, Bureau of Justice Statistics (2004c).

as that of the twenty-five- to thirty-four-year-old group (see table 7.3). The homicide offending rates of fourteen- to seventeen-year-olds exploded after 1985, surpassing the rates of twenty-five- to thirty-four-year-olds and thirty-five- to forty-nine-year-olds and reaching a staggering peak in 1993. Since then, offending rates for teens and young adults have declined but remain higher than levels prior to the mid-1980s. The rate for the eighteen- to twenty-four-year-old category was still nearly three times as high as for the next highest category of twenty-five- to thirty-four-year-olds in 1999.

Furthermore, Charles Rathbone's (1994/2002) study of 280 taxi drivers murdered in North America between 1980 and 1994 showed that two-thirds of the assailants were teenagers.

2. Five of them were twenty-three, twenty-one, nineteen, eighteen, and four-teen, and three were seventeen.

3. In Rathbone's (1994/2002) study, 82 percent of 280 drivers murdered between 1980 and 1994 in the United States and Canada were attacked at night.

4. We tried to find out the success rate of this operation but met with a com-plete lack of cooperation from the TLC. Although the commission never refused outright to provide the information or interviews we requested, we were continually fobbed off.

5. This appears to be a universal ploy. One respondent from a taxi Internet newsgroup who works in Melbourne, Australia, told us: "One pretty female equals possible danger. Lurking in the shadows could be a group of three or four gorillas/morons intent on having some fun at my expense" (email com-munication, November 11, 2002).

Chapter 8

1. Bullet-resistant partitions are not fully bullet-proof, but they do offer con-siderable protection to the driver.

2. Some drivers appear to prefer to rely on their screening skills rather than on partitions. For example, in San Francisco in 1994 drivers overwhelmir opposed the proposal that their cars should be fitted with ρ (Dougan and Glover 1998).

3. In April 2001, the livery driver Gurdev Lal was shot and killed by Donald Thomas, whom he had picked up in Queens. Mr. Lal's car had a partition, but it was open; he was shot in the back (Dewan 2001).

4. Early on a Saturday morning in November 1993, Suvinder Athwal was sitting in the back of his parked livery cab talking to another driver while waiting to pick up a fare from La Guardia Airport. The two men were approached by a young man with a gun who demanded their money. After collecting twenty dollars from the second driver, the robber turned his gun on Mr. Athwal, who accidentally dropped his money on the floor. When Mr. Athwal reached down to pick it up, the assailant shot once, hitting him in the chest and killing him (Tabor 1993).

Chapter 9

1. The great pressure not to waste any time is conveyed by driver YC1, who said that any hesitation displayed by a hailer is enough to dissuade him from stopping: "People, sometimes they doubt taking a taxi. They don't know, they're not sure. Those two seconds they don't know—[Should] I take a subway? [Should] I take a taxi? So you see a person in doubt, you don't stop. If he's in doubt, let him clear his mind and make his mind up and flag down the next taxi. I mean, I don't want to be a psychologist and try and say to the guy, 'What you wanna do?' We need to keep moving."

2. This story, unfortunately, has a sad conclusion. Luis Soto shot Yovanny Grullon in the legs and groin during the chase, leaving him wheelchair-bound (Chivers 2000c).

3. Initially some drivers said they never picked up street-hails, but later in the interview they admitted that they did.

4. Findings from U.S. Department of Justice (2004a) show that older teens and young adults have the highest homicide offending rates.

5. The drivers in Melbourne, Australia, were similarly suspicious. One driver wrote via an Internet taxi newsgroup: "Three males and one female are a problem as each of the males plays an 'I'm going to impress this Sheila with my loud mouth' and then proceeds to abuse me."

Chapter 10

1. Paul Ekman (2001, 106–7) notes that discrepancies between verbal and non-verbal behavior may be a sign of an intention to deceive. For example, southern Europeans use hand gestures to illustrate verbal points. A decrease in the amount of gesturing usually indicates caution about speech that may (or may not) be due to deceit.

2. In fact, there is even some evidence that having an impediment in language communication is correlated with *better* judgments of deception cues. In an experiment carried out by Mark Frank and Paul Ekman (1997), brain-damaged subjects who could process only nonverbal information outperformed

non-brain-damaged subjects. See also Decaire (2000), where these results are reviewed with other relevant literature.

Chapter 11

1. On the potential for mutually beneficial transactions that fail to occur, see Akerlof (1970).

2. It may come close to the notion of "generalized trust," which is itself rather elusive (Hardin 2002, 60ff, 176–77).

3. See Akerlof and Dickens (1982).

4. This matches a finding of a survey carried out in the Melbourne area in Australia: "Country drivers were less likely than their metro counterparts to see a solution to victimisation lying in technology (for example Global Positioning Systems, video cameras etcetera) or barriers such as screens" (Haines 1997, 64).

5. Drivers also look out for other dangers and related properties and exclude people who display signs of them. When approached by customers who are patently intoxicated, for instance, drivers still have to rely on them to have the money to pay them, to be fit enough to pay, and to be coherent enough to give them the right address, and to be resilient enough not to foul their cars. However, even though this situation involves some degree of reliance on passengers, it is not often part of a basic trust game with the potential for mimicry. Deranged, drunken, heavily drugged, or homeless people are beyond the ability to mimic being an ordinary passenger, as these are conditions that are hard to disguise. Our research therefore focuses on the more insidious perils that involve a basic trust game in which the potential for mimicry is clearly present.

6. Leung and others (2002) cites other papers on the same topic.

7. It was impossible to quantify and find any data for three of the properties— self-absorbed over inquisitive, candid over shifty, and friendly and calm over aggressive and agitated.

8. "There is no need for a trait law to be as rigid as this: k may be not a sure property but a merely probabilistic or tendential one, as in 'within each nationality, the *probabilities of various hair colors* are the same for all persons,' or 'a given individual's tendency to cheat is constant over time' " (Bacharach and Gambetta 2001, 163).

9. The major exceptions are theories of screening in economics explicitly derived from signaling theory (which also go under the name of "incentive compatibility"). However, their applications have not been linked to trust games, are unimaginative in the semiotics range that they consider, and focus more on the conditions of honest signals and the effective policies to ensure that they are honest than on mimicry and the conditions that make it possible.

10. It is the marginal cost of displaying a cue that is zero, not necessarily the historic cost of developing the capacity to display it.

11. We also found one case of diverging interpretations of the same act. In New York, sitting in the front passenger's seat is interpreted as a sign of danger, since the customer could more easily attack the driver from that position. In Belfast, however, choosing the front passenger's seat is interpreted as a friendly gesture and the driver is reassured, for the customer is making himself observable at all times. This difference may be due to local conventional beliefs: no one in New York expects passengers to be so friendly as to sit next to the driver to make conversation.

12. On October 12, 1984, the IRA exploded a bomb in the Grand Hotel in Brighton, where the Conservative Party was holding its annual conference. Five people were killed, but Margaret Thatcher was uninjured.

13. Of course, a single failure for a predator could result not only in an unsuccessful robbery but also in being caught by the police, thereby limiting future opportunities for successful attacks. However, being caught is still only a probability; it does not alter the basic asymmetry between prey and predator.

14. For an entertaining overview of Paul Ekman's research, see Gladwell (2002).

15. Paul Ekman does offer, however, an evolutionary explanation of the survival of the expression of the emotions explicitly in terms of their peculiar communicative value; see his introduction to Darwin (1999).

16. Decaire (2000) offers a most useful review of the psychological and forensic research in this field.

17. Cervantes' wicked genius, however, devises an obstacle for his characters: there are seventeen letters in Dulcinea's name, and the convention in poetry was to write stanzas of either four or five lines, which can never add up to seventeen. Thus, Don Quixote's friend could either come up one line short or write three in excess.

Glossary

Belfast

Falls Road A main road through Catholic West Belfast. The area contains a large number of Republican supporters.

Irish National Liberation Army (INLA) A Republican paramilitary group whose aims are the reunification of Ireland and the creation of a revolutionary socialist republic. The INLA is a much smaller and less active paramilitary group than the Irish Republican Army (IRA), but its members have been involved in a number of feuds after splinter groups developed, and numerous former members have died at the hands of their old associates. The INLA has killed approximately 125 people during the conflict, of whom 45 were members of the security forces. The INLA called a ceasefire on August 22, 1998.

Irish Republican Army (IRA) The main Republican paramilitary group involved in the Northern Ireland conflict. The central aim of the IRA is to end British control of Northern Ireland and to achieve the reunification of the island of Ireland. Its methods have involved violent attacks on the security forces and on the civilian population. According to Sutton (1994), the IRA was responsible for the deaths of 1,755 people between July 1969 and December 1993. The IRA has been on unbroken ceasefire since July 20, 1997, but has refused to decommission its weapons, an act it considers to be a surrender to the British government.

Loyalist or Loyalist paramilitary groups Strictly, the term "Loyalist" refers to one who is loyal to the British Crown. In Northern Ireland the term is used to imply that the person gives tacit or actual support to the use of force by Loyalist paramilitary groups who are prepared to use physical violence in an attempt to ensure the continuation of the union between Northern Ireland and Britain.

Poleglass Large working-class neighborhood in Catholic West Belfast.

Republican or Republican paramilitary groups Strictly, the term "Republican" refers to a person who supports the style of government based on a republic over a monarchy. In a Northern Ireland context, the term refers to someone who gives tacit or actual support to the use of physical force by Republican paramilitary groups, which are prepared to use physical violence in an attempt to achieve a united Ireland.

Shankill Road The main road through the Protestant area of West Belfast. The area contains many people who support the aims of Loyalist groups.

Sinn Féin (SF) A political party that represents the views of Republicans in Northern Ireland. The party is dedicated to the achievement of a united Ireland. SF supports the IRA and is viewed as the "political wing" of the IRA.

The Troubles "The Troubles" is a euphemism used by the people of Northern Ireland for the political conflict that has beset their country since 1968.

Twinbrook Large working-class neighborhood in Catholic West Belfast.

Ulster Defence Association (UDA) The largest Loyalist paramilitary group in Northern Ireland. Members of the UDA use the cover name of Ulster Freedom Fighters (UFF) to claim responsibility for the killing of Catholics. Responsible for scores of shootings and bombing attacks, the UFF stepped up its attacks on Catholics and Republicans during the 1990s with a number of multiple killings.

Ulster Volunteer Force (UVF) The second largest of the Loyalist paramilitary groups, responsible for scores of murders of innocent Catholics in Northern Ireland.

New York

New York State Federation of Taxi Drivers (NYSFTD) Founded in 1998, the NYSFTD represents eighteen thousand taxi drivers, mostly livery drivers.

New York Taxi Workers Alliance (NYTWA) Founded in 1998, the NYTWA has three thousand members who are mostly yellow cab drivers.

Taxi and Limousine Commission (TLC) The agency responsible for licensing and regulating New York City's medallion taxis (yellow cabs), for-hire vehicles (community-based liveries and black cars), commuter vans, paratransit vehicles (ambulettes), and certain luxury limousines.

References

Akerlof, George A. 1970. "The Market for 'Lemons': Quality Uncertainty and the Market Mechanism." *Quarterly Journal of Economics* 84(3): 488–500.

Akerlof, George A., and William T. Dickens. 1982. "The Economic Consequences of Economic Dissonance." *American Economic Review* 72: 307–19.

Andersonstown News. 2001. "Black Taxi Drivers Remembered." May 17.

Arrow, Kenneth J. 1998. "What Has Economics to Say About Racial Discrimination?" *Journal of Economic Perspectives* 12(2): 91–100.

Bacharach, Michael, and Diego Gambetta. 2001. "Trust in Signs." In *Trust in Society*, edited by Karen S. Cook. New York: Russell Sage Foundation.

Bennet, James. 2002. "Dread and Dreams Travel by Bus in Israel." *New York Times,* October 27, sec. 1: 1.

Bumiller, Elisabeth. 1999. "Cabbies Who Bypass Blacks Will Lose Cars, Giuliani Says." *New York Times,* November 11, sec. A: 1.

Camerer, Colin, Linda Babcock, George Loewenstein, and Richard Thaler. 1997. "Labor Supply of New York City Cabdrivers: One Day at a Time." *Quarterly Journal of Economics* 112(2): 407–41.

Chivers, C. J. 2000a. "Livery Driver Killings on the Increase, but Not Robberies, Leaving Police Puzzled." *New York Times,* April 19, sec. B: 3.

———. 2000b. "For Beleaguered Officers Now on Livery-Cab Duty, Gratitude." *New York Times,* April 22, sec. B: 1.

———. 2000c. "Cabby Is Shot When He Tries to Capture a Robbery Suspect." *New York Times,* May 1, sec. B: 7.

Ciezadlo, Annie, and Dan Janison. 1999. "Seeking Solutions, Glover Joins Discussion on Cabbie Relations with Blacks." *Newsday,* December 6: A-08.

Coleman, James. 1990. *Foundations of Social Theory.* Cambridge, Mass.: Harvard University Press.

Cooper, Michael. 1998. "Cabdriver, Shot Three Times, Captures Armed Robber, Police Say." *New York Times,* February 23, sec. B: 6.

Darwin, Charles. 1999. *The Expression of the Emotions in Man and Animals,* 3rd ed. London: HarperCollins.

Dasgupta, Partha. 1988. "Trust as a Commodity." In *Trust: Making and Breaking Cooperative Relations,* edited by Diego Gambetta. Oxford: Basil Blackwell.

Decaire, Michael W. 2000. "The Detection of Deception Via Non-verbal Deception Cues." Lakehead University Law Library (November 30). Available at: http://www.uplink.com.au/lawlibrary/Documents/Docs/Doc64.html (accessed March 3, 2005).

Dewan, Shaila. K. 2001. "Parolee Charged in Killing of Livery Driver in Queens." *New York Times,* April 28, sec. B: 6.

Doherty, Paul, and Michael Poole. 1995. *Ethnic Residential Segregation in Belfast.* Coleraine: University of Ulster, Center for the Study of Conflict.

Donath, Judith. 1998. "Identity and Deception in the Virtual Community." In *Communities in Cyberspace,* edited by Marc Smith and Peter Kollock. London: Routledge.

Dougan, Michael, and Malcolm Glover. 1998. "Cabbie Slaying Renews Drive for Protection; Items Considered Include Video Cameras, 'Panic Buttons,' Phones." *San Francisco Examiner,* October 29.

Eckel, Catherine C., and Rick K. Wilson. 2003. "The Human Face of Game Theory: Trust and Reciprocity in Sequential Games." In *Trust and Reciprocity,* edited by Elinor Ostrom and James Walker. New York: Russell Sage Foundation.

Ekman, Paul. 2001. *Telling Lies: Clues to Deceit in the Marketplace, Politics, and Marriage.* New York: W. W. Norton.

Elster, Jon. 1983. *Sour Grapes: Studies in the Subversion of Rationality.* Cambridge, U.K.: Cambridge University Press.

Farber, Henry S. 2005. "Is Tomorrow Another Day? The Labor Supply of New York City Cabdrivers." *The Journal of Political Economy* 113(1): 46–83.

Fay, Marie-Therese, Mike Morrissey, and Marie Smyth. 1999. *Northern Ireland's Troubles: The Human Costs.* London: Pluto Press in association with The Cost of the Troubles Study.

Feuer, Alan. 2000. "Two Are Accused of Trying to Murder Cabdriver." *New York Times,* April 6, sec. B: 4.

Forero, Juan. 2000. "Cabbies Ply Streets Warily on Tense Night Shift." *New York Times,* April 17, sec. B: 1.

Frank, Mark G., and Paul Ekman. 1997. "The Ability to Detect Deceit Generalizes Across Different Types of High-Stake Lies." *Journal of Personality and Social Psychology* 72(6): 1429–39.

Frankel, Tamar. Forthcoming. *Abuse of Trust: Con Artists and Ponzi Schemes.* Oxford University Press.

Fries, Jacob H. 2002. "Three Are Killed and Two Hurt in Attacks Around City." *New York Times,* March 31, sec. 1: 31.

Gambetta, Diego. 1988. "Can We Trust Trust?" In *Trust: Making and Breaking Cooperative Relations,* edited by Diego Gambetta. Oxford: Basil Blackwell.

———. 2005. "Deceptive Mimicry in Humans." In *Perspectives on Imitation: From Neuroscience to Social Science,* edited by Susan L. Hurley and Nick Chater. Cambridge, Mass.: MIT Press.

Gardiner, Sean. 2000. "U-Turn May Have Saved Cabby." *Newsday,* April 16: A-38.

General Consumer Council for Northern Ireland. 1997. *Taking Taxis.* Belfast: General Consumer Council for Northern Ireland.

———. 2000. *Submission to the Northern Ireland Affairs Committee.* Belfast: General Consumer Council for Northern Ireland.

———. 2001. *The Transport Trap: How Transport Disadvantages Poorer People.* Paper 2 in "The Price of Being Poor" series. Belfast: General Consumer Council for Northern Ireland.

Gladwell, Malcolm. 2002. "The Naked Face." *The New Yorker,* August 5.

Graham, Lawrence O. 1995. *Member of the Club: Reflections on Life in a Racially Polarized World*. New York: HarperCollins.

Graves, Neil, Rocco Parascandola, and Carl Camplinile. 1999. "Lethal Weapon Star Rips Apple's 'Racist' Cabbies." *New York Post*, November 4.

Greenfeld, Lawrence A., and Tracy L. Snell. 1999. *Women Offenders*. Bureau of Justice Statistics Special Report NCJ 175688. Washington: U.S. Department of Justice, Office of Justice Programs.

Haines, Fiona. 1997. *Taxi Driver Survey—Victoria: Understanding Victorian Taxi Drivers' Experiences of Victimisation and Their Preferred Preventative Measures*. Report prepared for the Victorian Taxi Directorate. Melbourne: University of Melbourne, Criminology Department.

Hardin, Russell. 1993. "The Street-Level Epistemology of Trust." *Politics and Society* 21(4): 505–29.

———. 2002. *Trust and Trustworthiness*. New York: Russell Sage Foundation.

Herbert, Bob. 1993. "In America; A Sea Change On Crime." *New York Times*, December 12.

Holmes, Steven A. 1999. "Correspondence/Black and Middle Class; Both a Victim of Racial Profiling—And a Practitioner." *New York Times*, April 25, sec. 4: 7.

Irish News. 1999a. "Joyriding 'Rampage' Claims over Death." January 27.

———. 1999b. "Taxis Face Weekend of Joyrider Terrorism." March 17.

———. 2000a. "Call for 'Ammunition' Supply Cut-off." June 19.

———. 2000b. "Shankill Taxis Find Safety in the Falls." September 15.

Jacobs, Andrew. 1998. "The Neediest Cases; Parents Buckle Under Crushing Grief." *New York Times*, January 20, sec. B: 3.

James, George. 1994. "A Search for Three Girls in a Slaying Is a Rarity." *New York Times*, June 3, sec. B: 3.

Jones, Richard Lezin. 2001. "Immigrant Who Didn't Understand Robber Is Killed." *New York Times*, October 6, sec. D: 1.

Kennedy, Randy. 2001a. "Yellow Taxis Battle to Keep Livery Cabs Off Their Turf." *New York Times*, May 10, sec. A: 1.

———. 2001b. "A Nation Challenged: Cabbies; Drivers Say They Risk Violence by Working, and May Even Lose Money." *New York Times*, September 24, sec. B: 8.

Kershaw, Sarah. 2000. "For a Cabby, a Night of Calculating Risks." *New York Times*, May 1, sec. A: 1.

Kugel, Seth. 2000. "After Shootings, Livery Drivers Keep a Wary Eye in the Mirror." *New York Times*, March 28, sec. B: 1.

———. 2001. "After a Grim Stretch, Killings of Livery Drivers End." *New York Times*, April 22, sec. 14: 4.

Leung, Ambrose, Frances Woolley, Richard E. Tremblay, and Frank Vitaro. 2002. "Who Gets Caught? Statistical Discrimination in Law Enforcement." Carleton Economic Papers 02–03. Northfield, Minn.: Carleton University, Department of Economics. Available at: http://ideas.repec.org/p/car/carecp/02-03.html (accessed March 3, 2005).

Lueck, Thomas J. 1999. "No Fare; New York's Cabbies Show How Multi-Colored Racism Can Be." *New York Times*, November 7, sec. 4: 3.

Martin, Douglas. 1993. "When a $75 Holdup Equals a Cabby's Life." *New York Times*, November 22.

Mayhew, Claire. 2000. "Violent Assaults on Taxi Drivers: Incidence Patterns and Risk Factors." Trends and Issues in Crime and Criminal Justice 178 (November).

Canberra: Australian Institute of Criminology. Available at: http://www.aic.gov.au/publications/tandi/ti178.pdf.

National Institute for Occupational Safety and Health. 1996. *Current Intelligence Bulletin 57: Violence in the Workplace: Risk Factors and Prevention Strategies.* DHHS (NIOSH) publication 96-100. Cincinnati, Ohio: U.S. Department of Health and Human Services, Centers for Disease Control and Prevention (July). Available at: http://www.cdc.gov/niosh/violcont.html (accessed March 3, 2005).

Newman, Andy. 1999. "Livery-Cab Driver Is Shot to Death During Robbery." *New York Times,* August 6, sec. B: 4.

New York City Department of City Planning Division. 2004. *The Newest New Yorker: Immigrant New York in the New Millennium.* New York: New York City Department of City Planning Division.

New York Times. 1998. "Cabby Hits Officer's Car to Foil a Robbery." November 29, sec. 1: 57.

New York Times. 1999. "Woman in Cab Robbery Pleads Guilty to Murder." January 9.

Northern Ireland Statistics and Research Agency. 2001. *A Commentary on Northern Ireland Crime Statistics 2001.* Belfast: Northern Ireland Office.

———. 2002. *Northern Ireland Census 2001: Key Statistics.* Belfast: Her Majesty's Stationery Office.

O'Mahoney, David, and Ronan Deazley. 2000. *Juvenile Crime and Justice.* Research report of Northern Ireland Criminal Justice Review Group 17. Belfast: Her Majesty's Stationery Office.

Phillips, Paul, and Erin Phillips. 1993. *Women and Work: Inequality in the Canadian Labour Market.* Toronto: James Lorimer & Co.

Pileggi, Nicholas. 1996. *Casino.* London: Corgi Books.

Rashbaum, William K. 2000a. "Police to Pose as Cabbies to Stop Killings of Drivers." *New York Times,* May 3, sec. B: 7.

———. 2000b. "Man Is Accused of Warning Cabby Not to Testify Against Suspect in Livery Shooting." *New York Times,* May 4, sec. B: 3.

———. 2001. "After Cabby Shooting, Council Accused of Foot-Dragging on Safety." *New York Times,* March 4, sec. 1: 31.

Rathbone, Charles. 1994/2002. *606 Taxicab Driver Homicides United States and Canada 1980–1994.* Report available at: http://c.rathbone.home.att.net/606.htm (accessed March 3, 2005). Rev. January 2002.

Sanders, Teela. 2004. *Sex Work: A Risky Business.* Cullompton, Devon, Eng.: Willan.

Schaller, Bruce. 2000. *Cab Availability and Ridership in New York City, 1990–1999.* New York: Schaller Consulting.

———. 2001. *Taxi and Livery Crashes in New York City, 1990–1999.* New York: Schaller Consulting.

Schaller Consulting. 2002. *Illegal Livery Street-Hail Study Prepared for the Taxi Policy Institute.* Available at: http://www.schallerconsult.com/taxi/liveryhail.pdf (accessed March 3, 2005).

Schelling, Thomas C. 1978. *Micromotives and Macrobehaviour.* New York, London: Norton.

Snyder, Howard A., and Melissa Sickmund. 1999. *Juvenile Offenders and Victims: 1999 National Report.* Pittsburgh: National Center for Juvenile Justice.

Strunsky, Steve. 2001. "New York: Bronx: Pleas in Cabby Killing." *New York Times,* May 1.

Sutton, Malcolm. 1994. *An Index of Deaths from the Conflict in Ireland, 1969–1993.* Belfast: Beyond the Pale Publications.

Sygnatur, Eric F., and Guy A. Toscano. 2000. "Work-Related Homicides: The Facts." *Compensation and Working Conditions* (Spring): 3–7.

Tabor, Mary B. 1993. "Limousine Driver Robbed and Slain Near Airport." *New York Times.* November 21: 45.

Thorpe, Martin. 1994. "Soccer Diary." *The Guardian,* January 29.

Times of London. 1988. "Bloodbath in Belfast: Republican Mob Shoots Two Soldiers to Death at Funeral." March 20.

U.S. Department of Justice. Bureau of Justice Statistics. 2001. *Special Report: National Crime Victimization Survey, 1999: Violence in the Workplace, 1993–1999.* NCJ 190076. Washington: U.S. Department of Justice (December).

———. 2004a. *Homicide Rates in the United States.* Washington: U.S. Department of Justice, Office of Justice Programs.

———. 2004b. *Victim Characteristics in the United States.* Washington: U.S. Department of Justice, Office of Justice Programs.

———. 2004c. Website for *Homicide Trends in the U.S.: Age Trends.* Available at http://www.ojp.usdoj.gov/bjs/homicide/tables/oagetab.htm (accessed March 3, 2005).

U.S. Department of Labor. Bureau of Labor Statistics. 1999. *National Census of Fatal Occupational Injuries, 1998.* News Bulletin USDL-99-208. Washington: U.S. Department of Labor.

Weale, Sally. 2003. "Great Night Out." *The Guardian,* March 7.

Wechsberg, Joseph. 1966. *The Merchant Bankers.* Boston: Little, Brown.

Yardley, Jim. 1997. "Two Women Arrested in Killing of Cabbie; Police See Gang Tie." *New York Times,* November 16, sec. 1: 1.

Index

Boldface numbers refer to figures and tables.

239